A Kid's Guide to Understanding Domestic Abuse

A Kid's Guide to Understanding Domestic ABUSE

Jody Cowdin

TATE PUBLISHING
AND ENTERPRISES, LLC

Published by Tate Publishing & Enterprises, LLC
127 E. Trade Center Terrace | Mustang, Oklahoma 73064 USA
1.888.361.9473 | www.tatepublishing.com

Tate Publishing is committed to excellence in the publishing industry. The company reflects the philosophy established by the founders, based on Psalm 68:11,
"The Lord gave the word and great was the company of those who published it."

Book design copyright © 2013 by Tate Publishing, LLC. All rights reserved.
Cover design by Junriel Boquecosa
Interior design by Jake Muelle

Published in the United States of America

ISBN: 978-1-62854-360-5
1. Family & Relationships / Abuse / Domestic Partner Abuse
2. Family & Relationships / General
13.07.25

Dedication

This book is dedicated to three amazing survivors,
my three kids.
You have each overcome so much and grown into
wonderful, mature adults, living free of domestic abuse.
I am so proud of you.
I love you so much.

TABLE OF CONTENTS

INTRODUCTION

A t least one in four women will be a victim of domestic abuse in her lifetime, and many if not most of those women have children who witness the violence in their homes (National Coalition Against Domestic Violence). Witnessing domestic abuse has a profound negative influence on the developing brain and impacts every area of development, including school achievement, social skills, and life outcomes. Children who witness abuse in the home are much more likely to have abusive relationships as adults.

Research indicates that there are things we can do to stop the generational cycle of domestic abuse. First, establish a peaceful and safe living environment. Second, provide a healthy, nurturing primary relationship the child or teen can trust. This is most often with the mother. And third, give children early and clear information about domestic abuse so they can make a different choice for themselves (National Center for Children Exposed to Violence).

Kids currently living with abuse in the home can also benefit from information about what domestic abuse is and why it keeps happening in their family. Understanding may not resolve the issues, but it does relieve some of the confusion and provides direction in how to handle it. When we better understand something, we are better able to cope, and we may even feel empowered to take action to get help. Kids want to make sense of what's going on (to the extent possible) and they need the empowerment that knowledge brings. If we fail to educate them, we rob them of the choice to break the generational cycle of domestic violence.

A Kid's Guide to Understanding Domestic Abuse is meant to educate and also provide a means for expression. Adults are encouraged to first read the book for their own understanding, and then decide if it is appropriate for the children or teens they know. The kids may respond with drawings, photos, or words as they feel it is safe to do so as they read through the pages.

CHAPTER 1

THE GOOD TIMES

(Feel free to draw pictures or attach photos.)
These are the people in my family:

The best time together I can remember:

Here are some other fun things we've done:

HOW FAMILIES ARE MEANT TO WORK

Families do things together. Some of those things are fun, like playing outside, and some things are hard work, like cleaning and doing laundry. It's with our family members that we learn about love and trust and respect. When we are with our family, we are meant to feel safe, protected, and cared for.

Here's a time when I felt safe and loved:

Every family has trouble and conflict. People in every family can get upset and frustrated. In healthy families, everyone works together to solve their problems and disagreements. Each person gets to talk about how they feel and why. Everyone tries hard to listen to one another and understand what the other person is saying and feeling.

Chapter 2

The Not-So-Good Times

Every family has disagreements, and they might even yell when they argue. But in some families, this can turn into abuse. *Abuse* is when one person hurts another on purpose, so they can feel powerful and in control of the other person or people in the family. The person who does the hurting is the abuser, and the person or people who get hurt are the victims. Abusers want to get their own way and be in charge and will become mean to the others to make sure nobody stands up to them. An abuser is the bully in the family.

An abuser can use lots of different ways to abuse others. Some abusers use bad words, tone of voice (sounding loud, mean, and scary), or they make threats to hurt others so that their victims will feel hurt and afraid. This is called *verbal and emotional abuse*. The words are the verbal part. The things they say cause the victims to feel bad, and that's the emotional part.

Some of the bad things I've heard are:

Emotional abuse can really hurt others deep inside. Words may not break their bones, but mean words can break their hearts. Some victims show how sad they are and that their hearts are broken by crying or looking very sad. Other victims hide their feelings deep inside so no one knows how bad they have been hurt. Some victims get angry and yell at others who don't deserve it because they are in so much pain on the inside.

This is what other people in my family do when they are hurt:

This is what I do when I feel hurt inside:

Some abusers don't stop with verbal and emotional abuse. Some use physical abuse too. *Physical abuse* is when the abuser pushes, grabs, hits, kicks, or uses any other way that hurts the victim's body. Physical abuse might leave a bruise or break a bone, and it might not.

Some physical abuse I have seen:

Abusers have other ways of making sure they stay in control of their victims. Some control all the money and won't let anyone else have any, even if they really need it. Some abusers don't work but make their victims go to work, kind of like a slave. Some won't let their victim have friends or go see other family members and make them stay home all the time.

Some other abusive things that have happened in my family are:

After awhile, victims can feel powerless and helpless. They might think the abuser has all the power and it will never change. They might believe there is nothing they can do to stop the abuse, no matter how hard they try.

Kids in the family might think the problems are their fault. Sometimes if parents fight about money or the kids, then the kids believe they caused the fight. Many kids feel this way, and some are afraid to talk about it.

Some kids try hard to help everyone get along, or they try to fix the problem so no one gets mad.

Some kids have behavior problems and get in trouble because they are upset on the inside and afraid to tell anyone what's really going on at home.

These are some things that I think about the abuse:

CHAPTER 3

THE CYCLE OF ABUSE

Abuse may not happen every day. It usually happens in a cycle. It's like a circle that keeps going around and around. In the beginning, it seems like everything is fine, and people are happy or at least okay. That's the *honeymoon stage*.

Then it starts to feel like there might be something wrong. The abuser might start to look a little mad, and the victim might try to make everything okay. Some people say this is like "walking on eggshells," trying so hard to keep the abuser from getting really angry. That's the *tension-building stage*.

Sooner or later, maybe a short time or a long time, the abuser blows up and is abusive again. Victims get hurt, and they usually get blamed by the abuser too for making it happen. That's the *battering stage*.

After that's over, the abuser might leave for a while or feel better and thinks everything should go back to normal. Some abusers say they are sorry and some don't. There can be some fun days after the abuse is done, but most of the time, there is still some pain on the inside for the victims and fear that it will happen again. And sooner or later, it does.

Everyone likes the good days and wants to believe they will last forever. But if someone is abusive, they don't do it just once. It's a pattern that happens over and over.

This is how often the abuse happens at my house:

The cycle of abuse looks like this:

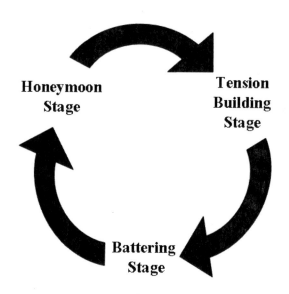

When abuse happens in a family, everyone can have lots of feelings. Sometimes it's hard to find the right words to say that tell how a person is feeling. Here are some feeling words that can help.

Circle the words you have felt.

Mad, crabby, angry, ticked off, frustrated, rage

Sad, unhappy, depressed, sullen, withdrawn

Scared, afraid, terrified, horrified

Worried, nervous

Confused, unsure, apprehensive

Disappointed, alone

Embarrassed, ashamed

Tired, exhausted, worn out

Guilty, blamed, sorry

Other:

Most of the time when the abuse is going on, I feel:

After it's over, I feel:

CHAPTER 4

QUESTIONS AND ANSWERS

M any times the abuser is a man or boy. Sometimes a woman or a girl can also be abusive. The questions can apply to either one.

WHY DOES HE ABUSE?

There are lots of reasons that someone is abusive. The reasons come from his thoughts and beliefs, and these make him very angry when he thinks about them, even if they're not true.

Here are some of them:

- ❑ Image—He thinks he has to be the tough guy, the one in control of others, and he uses power to hurt others and make them give in to him.

- ❑ Fear—He believes if he doesn't control others, they will leave him, and he will be alone. These feelings are called fear of rejection and abandonment.

- ❑ Insecurity—He thinks other people are better than him and his family might like someone else better.

- ❑ Jealousy—He thinks that his victim will find someone she likes better than him and she will leave him, so he uses abuse to make sure she doesn't find someone else.

- ❑ Rights—He believes it's his right as the boss or leader of the family to tell others what to do and even hurt them if he thinks they are challenging his authority.

- ❑ Bad habits—He grew up in an abusive family, and that's the way he learned to talk to and treat people.

Put a star by the reasons you think he's abusive.

Some abusers use drugs or alcohol, and this can make abuse worse. But drug or alcohol use does not cause someone to abuse others. It just makes it easier for abusers to think they lose control of themselves, and that's why they are abusive. The truth is they are abusive anyway, and the drugs or alcohol are the excuse they use to try and get out of being responsible for their behavior.

Some abusers also have problems with their mental health, like being depressed or having ADHD. But that's not an excuse for being abusive either. There are people with mental health problems that never hurt anyone. Someone who is abusive needs to stop making excuses and tell the truth. They need to admit they are hurting others, and there's no excuse for that.

Does the abuser you know use drugs or alcohol?

Does that make it worse?

Why Doesn't the Victim Do Something to Make It Stop?

Lots of people think the victim did something or said something to make the abuse happen and that she can do things differently so she doesn't get abused anymore. That's not true. She can't make him stop or change, and it's not her fault if he abused her. His behavior is his responsibility, not hers. He's the one who needs to make it stop. Abusers sometimes make up their own excuses to be abusive, even if she is doing everything just perfect like he told her. He shouldn't abuse her even if she yells at him first or does anything else that he says makes him mad. Nobody has the right or the excuse to hurt anyone else, even if they believe they were hurt first.

Why Doesn't She Leave Him Then?

Maybe it would be better to ask, "Why doesn't he just leave her?" He's the one who should do something about his behavior, and he should be the one to leave if he thinks he might become abusive.

But there are reasons why she doesn't leave, at least not at first.

- ❑ Fear—She thinks that he will hurt her or the kids even worse if she even tries to leave.

- ❑ Love—She still loves him and just wants the abuse to stop.

- ❑ Confusion—She doesn't know how or where to go or who could help or what to do.

- ❑ Spiritual beliefs—She promised God when they got married that she would never leave him or get a divorce.

- ❑ Hopeless—She doesn't think it will work, and he will just find her and make it worse.

- ❑ Helpless—She doesn't think she is strong enough or smart enough to get free and make it on her own.

- ❑ Money—She doesn't have the money or job to pay for her own place to live and all the bills.

It takes a lot of courage to stand up to an abuser or get away from him. It might take time and a few tries sometimes before it works.

Why do you think she stays with him?

What do you think she should do?

What Am I Supposed to Do? I'm Just a Kid.

First, you must know it is not your fault. Kids are not to blame for what adults do and say. Adults are supposed to be more mature and control themselves. It is not a kid's fault if the parent or any adult is abusive. It's the abuser's fault.

Second, you need to know it's not your problem to fix. You didn't cause it, and you can't fix it either. Only the abuser can change himself. Nobody else can make him change, not even the police or a judge.

Third, it's not your job to protect anyone or think that you have to be the one to save others in your family. In fact, if you try to stop an abuser from hurting someone, you might get hurt too.

So these are things that you should *not* do:

- ❑ blame yourself
- ❑ try to fix it
- ❑ try to stop it

There are things you *can* do.

- ❑ *Let your feelings out in good ways.* Find someone safe you can talk to, maybe someone at school or church or someone in your neighborhood or maybe someone else in your family like a grandparent or aunt. You need to let out your thoughts and feelings about the abuse. A journal can be a good idea. Some kids like to draw or write poetry to get their feelings out. All these can help you feel better.

❑ *Think about how to keep yourself safe.* Make a plan, including people you can call and places you can go to be safe. Think about what you would want to take with you for a while. Think about when you might need to call the police. Making a plan for safety can help you feel stronger and less afraid.

❑ *You can learn to be a survivor,* even if the abuse is still going on. The next chapter can help you do this.

On a separate sheet of paper, you can fill out this plan and keep it in a special place where you can find it if you need it.

Safe people I can talk to and their phone numbers are:

Safe places I can go:

Things to take with me:

CHAPTER 5

BECOMING A SURVIVOR

When kids grow up in an abusive family, they sometimes think that they will either grow up to be like the abuser or like the victim. If Mom was the victim, they see her getting hurt and feeling bad, and they don't want that to happen to them. So they might think they have to be like the abuser then, so they have the power and control instead of being the one getting hurt.

Some kids get really mad at the abuser and promise to never treat their family like that. But they don't know how to stand up to an abuser, and one day when they're older, they might realize they have become a victim too. Some boys grow up to be abusive if their dad was, and some girls grow up to be victims if their mom was. Most kids don't want to grow up to hurt others or be the one getting hurt, but they don't know what else to do.

There is another choice besides being an abuser or a victim. Kids can grow up to be survivors. Abusers and victims can learn to be survivors too. If you've never seen how a survivor talks and acts, it can be a little hard to learn how to become one. But it's the best choice, and with help, you can learn how to think and act like a survivor.

When you think of a survivor, think of someone who is mature. Adults can be grown up and still not be mature. Some kids are more mature than some adults.

A survivor is mature and doesn't try to control other people. They control themselves instead. They say what needs to be said, in a firm and confident way. They don't use mean words or tone of voice, and they don't need to yell to be heard.

They are good listeners too, even if they don't agree or like what someone is saying. They listen until it is their turn to talk. They stay calm and try to work things out without getting defensive. If it can't be worked out in a mature way right then, they take a break and try again later.

Survivors tell the truth. They don't lie to try and get out of trouble, and they don't blame other people for their own behavior. They are strong enough on the inside to be honest and say they are sorry when they make mistakes.

Survivors aren't afraid to be themselves, whether other people like them or not. They feel good about themselves and don't need to put other people down to make themselves look bigger, smarter, or stronger. In fact, survivors like to encourage other people and help them feel good about themselves.

Survivors act with respect toward others, and they don't let other people disrespect them. If someone tries to abuse them, they speak up and say stop or they leave and find a safe place with safe people who treat them right.

Survivors don't get even. They forgive and move on. A survivor might tell an abuser that they don't let people abuse them anymore and then end that friendship. But they don't find ways to get back at them or hurt them. They let it go and find other mature people to hang out with.

Survivors are smart and very strong on the inside. They don't need to abuse people to prove anything, and they don't need friends so bad that they let people walk all over them. Survivors are kind, but they are not doormats. They stand up for themselves without hurting others.

Mature people I know:

Becoming a survivor is a choice. It's a choice you have to make in every situation with every person. The more you practice being a mature survivor, the easier it gets. Abusers can end up in jail, and victims can end up in the hospital. Choose to be a survivor and have a great future.

Here's me if I decide to become an abuser:

Here's me if I decide to become a victim:

But...

Here's me as a mature survivor:

Circle the words that describe your good qualities, and add more:

I am: smart,   strong,   kind,   helpful,   loyal,

hard worker,   loving,   gentle,   funny,   creative,   friendly,

good leader,   calm,   patient,   hopeful,   honest,   focused.

_____

_____

CHAPTER 6

GOD'S PLAN FOR THE FAMILY

God's plan for the family is for a mom and dad to love each other and take good care of their children. Everyone in the family is supposed to respect one another too. Disagreements happen, but everyone knows they are still loved and no one is abused.

Real love is described in the Bible in 1 Corinthians 13:4–8:

> Love is patient, love is kind. It does not envy, it does not boast, it is not proud. It is not rude, it is not self-seeking, it is not easily angered, it keeps no record of wrongs. Love does not delight in evil but rejoices with the truth. It always protects, always trusts, always hopes, always perseveres. Love never fails.

The Bible also says that God is love. He's our father in heaven. What kind of a father is he? Since God is love, you can take the word love out of those verses and put in God to find out what kind of father he is. It would go like this:

God our Father is patient, he is kind. He does not envy, he does not boast, he is not proud. God our Father is not rude, he is not self-seeking, he is not easily angered, and he keeps no record of wrongs. God our Father does not delight in evil but rejoices with the truth. God always protects, always trusts, always hopes, always perseveres. God our Father never fails.

Underline your favorite things about God your Father in those verses.
Try replacing "God" with your own name in these verses. Are you loving others the way God loves?

In case you are not sure what all those words mean or what that would look like, here's another way to say it:

God is patient—He explains things and teaches us without getting irritated or in a hurry.

God is kind—He's gentle and gives us what is good for us because he wants to, and it makes him happy.

God does not envy—He doesn't want people's stuff because it's just stuff, and it's people he cares about. So he doesn't compare what he has with things people have and then waste money on buying expensive things he doesn't need.

God does not boast—He doesn't brag about himself to make others feel bad or to make himself feel better.

God is not proud—He's not stuck up, and he doesn't act like he's better than everyone. He's friendly and accepts people just the way they are.

God is not rude—He doesn't act mean. He wouldn't push someone out of the way so he could be first in line. And he would never hurt anyone just to try and get more power and control for himself.

God is not self-seeking—He doesn't think about himself all the time and do things that are self-centered, just for his own benefit. In fact, he's always thinking about how much he loves us. Jesus gave up everything in heaven and gave his life for us because we needed him to. That's called self-sacrifice.

God is not easily angered—God is super positive and happy most of the time. It takes a lot for him to get mad. One thing he really hates is violence and when innocent people get hurt. He gives people lots of chances to stop being violent though because he loves them too. But if they keep hurting others, he will let them suffer the consequences of their bad choices.

God keeps no record of wrongs—He doesn't write down our sins because he would much rather forgive. He does keep a record of the good things we do and writes those down in a book in heaven.

God doesn't delight in evil but rejoices with the truth—God doesn't like it when someone tries to lie their way out of trouble or blame someone else. Instead, he gets excited and celebrates when someone tells the truth about what they did.

God always protects—He guards our hearts and holds our lives in his hands so nobody can steal or destroy our relationship with him. Even when bad things happen in life, he's holding us.

God always trusts—He believes the best about people and gives them the freedom to choose to love him.

God always hopes—He has a positive expectation of good things. He believes his love will change the lives of both victims and abusers.

God always perseveres—He never gives up on anyone and keeps trying to get them to listen and receive his love.

God never fails—People can fail, but God never does. Not once.

If everyone in a family tries to love each other like God loves us, then there's no abuse in the family.

Here's my family showing love to each other:

CHAPTER 7

IT'S YOUR TURN

Most parents try to do their best in raising their kids. Even abusive parents usually still love their kids way down deep inside, even though the abuse is wrong. Both the abuser and the victim have some good qualities you may want to learn and keep for yourself as an adult. Your parents learned how to do relationships and raise kids from their parents and friends, and your grandparents learned it from the generation before them. If they grew up with abuse in their home or neighborhood, they may have passed it on to the next generation. So what are you going to do?

Now that you know more about domestic abuse, you get to make your own choices about relationships and parenting. You don't have to end up repeating the mistakes of the past generations. You get to decide to have loving and happy relationships with your own family and friends. You get to set the rules of how you are treated by others and how you will treat them. You can reject the abusive behaviors and choose real love.

If all you have seen is abuse in your family, you will need to work extra hard at learning a different way of thinking, believing, and behaving. But you can do it. You can stop the generational cycle of abuse. The adults in your life may never change, but you can. In fact, you are the only person you can control. How you turn out when you grow up is now your responsibility. You can't blame parents or teachers or friends or anyone else. You get the credit for choosing the good qualities and the blame if you make bad choices. Being responsible for your own life is tough, but that's how you grow up to be a survivor, a mature and happy adult, living your dreams. It's your turn.

Are you ready to get started? It's time to take the first step toward freedom from abuse.

CHAPTER 8

FREEDOM STARTS WITH FORGIVENESS

If you or your family have been hurt by an abuser, it's easy to be angry and refuse to forgive. After all, they're probably not sorry or even telling the truth about what they have done. You have a right to be angry. They sure don't deserve to be forgiven. But the journey to freedom from abuse starts with forgiveness.

Imagine having your abuser hanging on your shoulders, like you are giving him a piggyback ride, and he's talking in your ear all the time, saying mean things that make you feel bad and reminding you of all the pain he has caused you. The weight of carrying him around with you drags you down and drains your energy. Listening to his voice in your head over and over gives you a bad attitude and makes you angry. Unforgiveness actually gives him permission to hang onto your heart and mess with your mind. Unforgiveness is the open door that keeps letting him into your life to cause more and more pain.

Unforgiveness has a way of backfiring on us. It actually ends up hurting us, not the abuser.

- ❑ Unforgiveness is like drinking poison yourself and hoping the other person will die.

- ❑ Unforgiveness keeps the victim stuck, wanting to get revenge, and doesn't hurt the abuser at all.

- ❑ Anger, resentment, and bitterness toward one person will poison your own heart and all other relationships.

- ❏ Unforgiveness keeps you in a position of weakness as a victim, giving the other person power over you. Unforgiveness means they can still keep hurting you.

- ❏ Unforgiveness fills the heart so that there is no room for peace, joy, and freedom.

- ❏ Unforgiveness keeps you focused on the bad things of the past instead of on the good things today and in your future.

- ❏ Unforgiveness is sin. God knows unforgiveness can kill you, so he wants you to forgive for your own sake.

There is a lot of confusion about what forgiveness is. First, let's look at *what forgiveness is not*:

1. Forgiveness is not trusting. You can forgive and still not trust the person or want to be around them.

2. Forgiveness is not forgetting. You will probably always remember what happened. *Un*forgiveness means you will still hurt when you remember. Forgiveness lets you remember without the pain.

3. Forgiveness does not mean you are letting someone get away with whatever they did.

4. Forgiveness is not protecting someone, covering for them, or keeping their sin a secret. It doesn't mean you lie for them so they don't get in trouble.

5. Forgiveness is not excusing the behavior or pretending it's okay.

6. Forgiveness is not submitting to sin. It doesn't mean you have to keep letting them hurt you.

7. Forgiveness does not require ongoing relationship with the person.

8. Forgiveness is not dependent on the other person being sorry or asking for forgiveness. That may never happen.

What forgiveness is:

1. Forgiveness is a process.

2. Forgiveness starts with a conscious decision, an act of the will, determination to obey God.

3. It's best if you first receive God's love and forgiveness for yourself. It's hard to give what you don't have. God gives us more than enough forgiveness for our own sins, so we have plenty to give to others who sin against us.

4. Forgiveness is giving up your right to get even, make them pay, or teach them a lesson.

5. Forgiveness is letting them off *your* hook and leaving them on *God's* hook.

6. Forgiveness is trusting God to make things right and bring justice.

7. Forgiveness is releasing yourself from anger and fear and guilt and shame so you can be free and happy.

8. Forgiveness is separating yourself from their sin and brokenness and accepting healing for you.

9. Forgiveness is taking responsibility for *your* life and letting go of worrying about what happens to theirs.

Thinking about forgiving an abuser usually makes people angry first, and then they discover that under the anger is sadness. Abuse isn't fair. Everyone deserves to be loved unconditionally. When you realize you didn't get the dream family or two ideal parents, you may feel sad along with the anger. This is called grief. It's what people feel when someone they really love dies.

When you realize the dream for your family has died because of the abuse, it can be hard to accept. Some people believe if they hang onto their unforgiveness, it might force the abuser to get help and apologize so they can have the dream family they deserve. But it doesn't work that way. If you find yourself feeling sad about not getting the family or mom or dad you wish you could have had, it's okay to cry. Let yourself be sad for a while that you have lost this dream, for now. Feeling the sadness of letting go of this dream is a big part of forgiveness, and forgiveness is the only hope for you to leave the abuse behind and have your own happy family.

For most people, the forgiveness process starts with speaking the words "I forgive _____" out loud to God. You can also say what you forgive them for. You don't have to say it to your abuser. In fact, if you say it to someone who isn't really sorry, they might take it wrong, and it could make things worse for you. Forgiving is a decision you make in your own heart, and it's between you and God. Saying it out loud to people who are safe can be really good too.

Speaking this out loud is like planting a seed in your own heart; it takes time to grow roots and produce fruit. At first, you may not feel like you have really forgiven him. Your heart will catch up with your will, though, and you will eventually feel free. Forgiveness gives you freedom to move forward into your future instead of focusing on the past. Forgiveness gets your abuser off your back and gets his voice out of your head so you can live your own life without him dragging you down.

With unforgiveness, you are standing in the way, between God and your abuser, and telling God you want to be the one to get even and make your abuser pay for what he has done to hurt you. When you step out of the way, into forgiveness, you are actually making room for God to do what he knows is best for your abuser. With you out of the way, God can allow circumstances that could cause your abuser to change and want to make things right, which would be the best thing for your whole family. Or God will let your abuser suffer the consequences of his choices. Since God is bigger, stronger, smarter, and more creative than any of us, he can figure out what to do better than we can. Forgiveness let's you move on and live your life with joy while God deals with your abuser. That's a good deal.

If it still seems impossible to forgive, there's another idea you can try: you can write two letters to your abuser but *not* to give to him. The first letter is the angry letter. In this letter, you get to say all the reasons you are angry with your abuser, the things he has done or not done that have hurt you. You can include what he has done to hurt other people in your family too because hurting them probably hurt you. You can say all the things you've been afraid to say and say it any way you want, knowing he will not read it. When you feel like you have said everything you want to say and it's all out on paper, you will usually begin to feel better. If you don't, keep writing more about everything that has ever bothered you until there's nothing left hidden inside. This is the first step.

When you are ready, then you can write the forgiveness letter. It's like saying it out loud, but you write it to your abuser. Again, you don't give it to him. It's just for your own forgiveness process so you can be free. Do the best you can, saying, "Dear _____, I forgive you for _____." Try to include as much as you can. It's okay if you don't feel happy and free right away. You will soon.

It's a good idea to destroy the angry letter when you are done with it. It gives you the chance to show that you now have control over the bad things that were done and they no longer have control over you. If you want to, you can save the forgiveness letter and add things to it as you remember more.

One great thing about forgiveness, it gets easier the more you do it. And the more you do it, the happier you feel.

Forgiveness creates in our hearts an increased capacity to give and receive love. You will want that for sure when you start your own family.

Take some time to look up verses in the Bible about forgiveness. It helps to get this truth in your heart so you can be free to forgive.

What the Bible says:

Luke 11:4
The Lord's Prayer—"Forgive me in the same manner and to the same degree that I forgive others."

Matthew 6:14–15
Forgiving others is required for us to be forgiven.

Matthew 18:21–35
Forgive seventy times seven times; the parable of the master who forgave and the unforgiving servant.

Mark 11:25
I must forgive so God can forgive me.

Luke 23:34
Jesus on the cross forgave those who killed him.

Colossians 3:13
Forgive one another.

Ephesians 4:32
Forgive each other just as in Christ God forgave you.

APPENDIX A

UNHEALTHY RULES IN ABUSIVE FAMILIES

These rules aren't written down anywhere, and people don't usually talk about them like they're rules. They are unwritten rules that everyone just learns by growing up in a family where they are used. When you understand these rules, you realize they are bad and need to be changed.

THE DOUBLE STANDARD

This means there are two sets of rules in the family—one for the abuser and one for everyone else. And the abuser is the only one who gets to decide what the rules are for everyone. The abuser gets to do things that the rest of the family isn't allowed to do. One example is when the abuser gets to go out with friends, but the victim isn't allowed to do that. The abuser gets to spend money on stuff but doesn't let the victim spend money. The abuser gets to decide what's on TV, what everyone can wear, where they can go, and who they can be with, but nobody can tell the abuser those things. The abuser believes he doesn't have to listen to anyone else, but everyone has to listen to him. The abuser also believes he has the right to get mad, yell, and even hurt others, but no one else has the right to be angry with him.

In a healthy family, both the mom and dad talk about what the rules are and agree the rules work the same for both of them. They also listen to the kids talk about what they want the rules to be, and both parents decide what the best rules are for the kids so they can grow up to be mature adults. All the rules for everyone are decided based on love, not fear, jealousy, or power and control.

THE DOUBLE BIND

This rule is tricky to see at first, but it makes victims think they can never do the right thing to make the abuser happy. Here's an example: The abuser wants to buy more stuff, so he tells the victim to make more money. So the victim works more hours to make more money. But then the abuser gets mad and abusive because he wants her home more to take care of him, the house, and the kids. She ends up in trouble whether she works more (because she's gone from home) or she works less (because she doesn't make as much money). That's a double bind.

Or let's say she doesn't work at a job; she works at home and depends on him for the money to buy groceries. He doesn't want to give her much because he thinks all the money is his and he wants to spend it on himself. So she fixes cheap dinners like macaroni and cheese a lot. Then he gets mad and yells at her because he wants steak every week. So she buys steak for him but then can't afford to buy food for the kids' lunches at school. When he finds out, she's in trouble for not feeding the kids, but she's also in trouble if she doesn't buy him steak.

Kids can end up in a double bind too. It could be that he wants you to be in sports, so you go to practice every day after school. But then he yells when he gets home from work because you didn't get the lawn mowed. But if you skipped practice to mow the lawn, you would also be in trouble. Another double bind would be if he wants you to play a sport but then gets mad at you for needing the money to buy the equipment for it. He would be mad if you drop out of the sport, but he's also mad at you for needing money for the equipment to stay in it.

Here's another example. The abuser might tell you to get the kitchen cleaned up but then yell at you to stop making noise while he's watching TV. You can't make the dishes be silent, but you're in trouble if you stop doing the dishes. You're in trouble for making noise now or in trouble if you wait and do them later.

A double bind is also called a "no-win situation" because you end up being wrong and in trouble no matter which way you choose. It's really frustrating for everyone in the family to know someone is always going to be in trouble even if you try really hard to do everything exactly like he says.

In a healthy family, the adults understand what they expect of each other and the kids, and they don't put people in double binds. If it does happen, they can talk about it without being afraid, and the person who gives the double bind directions apologizes because they didn't realize that's what they were doing. For example, your mom tells you to clean your room, but then before you're done, she says you have to watch your two-year-old sister. You know if you bring her in your room, she will mess it up and you will get in trouble for not cleaning your room. But you could also get in trouble for not watching your sister. In a healthy family, you can say in a respectful way to your mom that you need help figuring out which one she really wants you to do the most at that minute, and she doesn't get mad. She just realizes you can't do both at the same time, and she says which one to do first.

DENY, MINIMIZE, BLAME

This rule works for the abuser and probably gets used the most of all. It basically means that he never has to take responsibility for his behavior, and he gets to use this rule to get out of trouble. Everyone is supposed to accept this and let him get away with hurting others.

So how does this work? Let's say the abuser gets mad about something and becomes abusive, and someone tries to find out what happened. Usually, the first thing the abuser tries is denial. That means he lies and says nothing happened or he didn't do anything wrong. He might act like he has no idea what happened and he wasn't even there. Or he might say something happened, but he had nothing to do with it. He will keep denying responsibility until it looks like that won't work.

Then he will probably try to minimize what happened. Minimize means to make it seem smaller than it really is. He might say they were just arguing like couples do and it was no big deal. He might admit he pushed her, but that's it, and he doesn't know how she got the bruises. When he minimizes what happened, he is admitting to a very small part and continuing to lie about the rest. If that doesn't work, he may move on to blame.

Blaming the victim is what abusers usually do. He might lie and say she's clumsy and fell or she attacked him first and he had to hold her to protect himself. He wants people to believe it's her fault, so he may blame her for doing or saying something that made him mad and she should know better. Sometimes they say they lost control and don't remember what happened. This is just another lie because abusers choose what they are going to do and who they are going to do it to. They don't lose control. They abuse to get control over their victim.

Trying to deny, minimize, or blame their way out of trouble works many times because no one was around to see what really happened. But sooner or later, people figure out who is lying and who is telling the truth. Kids in the family may see what is really going on, but they may not understand it all, and they might be afraid to tell. Some tell what really happened so everyone can be safe and get help.

In a healthy family, there's no abuse to lie about. When other mistakes are made, people tell the truth, even if it means getting in trouble. If kids are playing in the house and something gets broken, they go to the parent and tell the truth. They might get a timeout or have to pay for what they broke, but that is better than lying about it. People don't trust liars, so it's always better to tell the truth about exactly what happened. Telling the truth is part of what is needed to make sure a child doesn't grow up to be abusive. Honesty is the mature way to handle problems.

TAKE MY SIDE

With this rule, the abuser tells people he's the "real victim" and tries to get them to join his side and agree with him. He can sound really sincere so people don't know he's lying or at least not telling the whole truth. If they try to find out more information about what happened, he might increase the pressure for them to just believe him.

This happens to the kids in the family too. The abuser can try to make the kids take his side against the other parent. He might badger them until they finally give in and agree with him, or he might even threaten them if they don't take his side. This is wrong and can do a lot of damage in the relationships in the family. Kids should be able to have a healthy relationship with both parents, if that is possible, and they shouldn't have to take sides. Abusers often make it very hard for kids to feel safe with each parent, and the things they say can cause confusion, especially when they are not true. Real love is tough love, and it would stand up for the truth and not go along with the lies. Kids usually need help from an adult who can do this for them though. It's good to ask for help if this is going on because that's the only way that everyone can get the help they need to stop the cycle of abuse.

In a healthy family, no one takes sides against anyone else. Everyone tells the truth and wants to work out problems in a way that helps everyone grow and feel good about the result. They all stick together on the same side and stand up for what's right and true and good.

Appendix B

Dr. Jekyll and Mr. Hyde

An abuser is often compared to the story of Dr. Jekyll and Mr. Hyde. The story was written by Robert Louis Stevenson back in 1931, but we still hear about it today, especially when it comes to domestic abuse.

In the story, Dr. Jekyll is a well-respected doctor, very charming and friendly. He has good friends and is engaged to be married. He has a belief that every man has both a good side and an evil side. He thinks it should be okay for the evil side to come out sometimes, so he does experiments that let out the evil inside of him, and he calls that side of himself Mr. Hyde. During the day, he is Dr. Jekyll whom everyone likes, but at night, his evil side comes out as Mr. Hyde, and he is abusive and dangerously violent. Eventually, everyone figures out that Dr. Jekyll is also the Mr. Hyde they are so afraid of, and they have a hard time believing this wonderful man can also be so hurtful and destructive.

Abusers can be this way too. They can be very nice, funny, helpful, and happy one minute when others are watching and then become very mean and abusive to their victim when they are alone. Sometimes even the kids in the home don't know how bad he can be at first since he can be very good at hiding it. The abuser wants to keep his behavior a secret and might threaten the victim not to tell anyone because he knows what he's doing is wrong. It's also against the law.

Eventually, the truth comes out, and Dr. Jekyll is stopped from being Mr. Hyde and hurting people. If you hear someone say about a person, "He's a Jekyll and Hyde," you'll know he's got two sides, nice and mean. It can be confusing for kids to see their dad being nice sometimes and then mean at other times. It's hard to believe he can be both, but that's what an abuser is like. Some in the family may resent that he can be nice to everyone else but is mean to his family, and that's not fair.

You can love the good side and believe that's who he really is. But the bad side needs to be dealt with because it's just as real and does so much damage. If there is a safe way to let others know so they can help the Mr. Hyde side get help for his abusive behavior, then it's good to tell someone. Many abusers don't like that evil side of themselves and wish they could stop hurting the people they love. If there's any hope of saving the family, the Mr. Hyde side needs to go away for good.

Appendix C

Red Flags

Red flags are like the warning lights on the dashboard of a car. When a red light comes on, it tells us that there is something wrong, and we need to find out what it is so we can fix the problem or get to safety. Red flags with people are the things they say or do that make us uncomfortable or make us wonder what's wrong. Many people who ended up being victims didn't realize what the red flags were that showed a person was going to be abusive. It's important to see and understand red flags so we don't get too close to someone who would end up abusing us.

Some red flags are easy to see, like the bully at school who beats up other kids, lies, and says mean things to put other people down. Both girls and boys can be guilty of hurting others by using the computer and Internet or cell phones to tease and bully others. This is abusive behavior, and it's wrong.

Some red flags are harder to spot. At first, they can seem like they are actually good things, but later, you realize it's not good after all. When a guy likes a girl and he wants to be with her all the time, it can make her feel good at first, like she is really special. But if he wants to be the only one with her and won't let her have her own friends or do things without him, then it gets to be uncomfortable and makes her wish she could do fun things with her friends again. That's a red flag. She might like the attention he gives her, but after a while, it gets to be a way to control her.

Here's a list of red flags to think about and watch for. Some of them can sound okay, but remember it's when it's used to control someone else that it's bad and a sign of abuse.

Abusers may not use all of these ways to control, but they will use many of them:

- ❑ Starts out showing you their good side
- ❑ Wants to be with you all the time
- ❑ Checks up on where you are and who you are with if you're not together
- ❑ Tells you how you should dress and act
- ❑ Doesn't listen to you or show interest in your feelings
- ❑ Things always have to be their way
- ❑ Ignores you and gives you the silent treatment
- ❑ Hangs up on you
- ❑ Uses the Internet or phone to embarrass or hurt you
- ❑ Takes advantage of you and uses you for things
- ❑ Is physically rough with you
- ❑ Tries to isolate you and control whom you see and where you go
- ❑ Puts down people, especially your family and friends
- ❑ Always seems to be mad at someone for something
- ❑ Blames you or everyone else for problems
- ❑ Lies to you and others
- ❑ Has mood swings—happy then mad or crabby
- ❑ Accuses you of things you didn't do
- ❑ Compares you to others so you feel worse about yourself
- ❑ Tells you to shut up or calls you names
- ❑ Pressures you to do things you don't want to do
- ❑ Has a history of getting into arguments and fights
- ❑ Can be mean and hurtful to animals

❏ Threatens to hurt you, your pets, himself or people you care about if you don't go along with him

Some other signs inside you that might be red flags:

❏ You feel afraid to stop being friends with them.

❏ You feel like you always have to check in and get their permission to do what you want so they don't get mad.

❏ You feel afraid to make decisions or bring up certain subjects because you know it will make them mad.

❏ You tell yourself you just need to try harder and be nicer so they don't get mad or blame you for their anger.

❏ You find yourself worrying a lot about this friendship, afraid to get out, and afraid it might get worse if you stay in.

❏ You find yourself feeling sick and making excuses to not get together.

❏ You wish you could talk to somebody, but you're not sure how to explain it in words. You just know you feel bad.

❏ You try to avoid them or sneak around, but they keep finding you and getting angry at you for avoiding them

❏ You wish they would just go away

❏ You wish you never would have met them

Recognizing the red flags will help keep you from getting into an abusive relationship.

**The end.
Not really.
This is just the beginning of a great
life free from domestic abuse.
Enjoy!**

see what ingredients they're adding, what techniques they're using, and what other spices they're throwing in, but the exact blend of the private stash is nobody's business but their own.

Where do I stand on all of this? I think 175-ingredient blends are overkill. You can't possibly taste so many spices all at once, and at some point, they start canceling each other out. And I don't see the point of secrets in cooking, since no two batches of spice are ever alike—and besides, my blend is constantly changing.

At the restaurant, we actually make five different *ras el hanout* blends for very specific uses. But what I want to share with you here is a really great all-purpose version I've come up with over the years, and a red variation that's particularly good with poultry and fish. This version contains the essential spice pantry of Morocco, with the exception of saffron, turmeric, paprika, and white pepper, and once you stock up on the ingredients, you'll have all of those individual spices to cook with.

It'll take some sleuthing to find the whole spices and a little work to put it all together. But in the end, you'll have your own *k'meesa*—your secret stash that you can use in recipes throughout this book (and hide in a sweater between uses). This first little exercise might even get you to clean out your spice rack and start thinking about spices in a new way.

RAS EL HANOUT

GATHERING AND MEASURING: This is the part that might take a while, because you may have to order some of the ingredients. Start by weighing or measuring the ingredients. In case you don't have a scale (yet), I've also provided teaspoon and tablespoon measures.

whole spices to be toasted: Weigh or measure these and put them in a medium heavy frying pan or cast-iron skillet:

3 tablespoons (11.4 grams) coriander seeds
1½ tablespoons (11.1 grams) cumin seeds
2 teaspoons (3.2 grams) dried orange peel
1¾ teaspoons (3.2 grams) fennel seeds
1 teaspoon (2 grams) grains of paradise
14 (2 grams) allspice berries
½ teaspoon (1.7 grams) caraway seeds
One 1½-inch piece (1.7 grams) cinnamon stick, crumbled
10 (1.6 grams) green cardamom pods, shelled and seeds reserved
½ teaspoon (1.5 grams) Tellicherry peppercorns
2 (1.5 grams) black cardamom pods, shelled and seeds reserved
1½ (1.3 grams) long peppers
¾ teaspoon (1.3 grams) whole mace
1 (0.6 gram) chile de árbol
8 (0.6 gram) cloves
½ (0.5 gram) star anise

whole spices you won't toast: Weigh or measure these and put them in a bowl:

1⅛ teaspoons (4.0 grams) yellow mustard seeds
2 teaspoons (1.9 grams) dried rosebuds
½ teaspoon (1.8 grams) brown mustard seeds

ground spices: Weigh or measure these and stir them together in a separate bowl:

1¾ teaspoons (5.6 grams) granulated garlic
2¼ teaspoons (4.6 grams) grated dried ginger (use a Microplane)
½ nutmeg (2.6 grams), grated (about 2½ teaspoons)
½ teaspoon (2.6 grams) citric acid

TO TOAST THE SPICES: Put a piece of parchment paper on the work surface.

Put the frying pan with the spices in it over medium heat and stir the spices with a wooden spoon or toss them. After about a minute, you will start to smell them and you'll hear a bit of crackling. The transformation is beginning. Here's an example: carefully pick up one of the long peppers, and you'll notice how soft and pliable it has become as its oils heat up and are released.

Stay completely focused on the process, stirring, watching, and paying attention to the way the aromas are blooming. Remove the pan from the heat briefly if you think anything is starting to burn. The smell should be sweet, nutty, and appetizing, not acrid. Toast the spices for 3 to 4 minutes longer, until they have just started to smoke and darken slightly. Don't let them toast past this point, or they will burn and become bitter. Err on the side of undertoasting until you get the hang of it.

Immediately pour the spices onto the parchment paper. (Don't make the mistake of simply removing the frying pan from the heat and letting the spices cool in the pan; they'll continue to cook, and they'll burn.) Your house is beginning to smell like a Moroccan kitchen. Enjoy this intoxicating moment.

TO GRIND THE SPICES: Once the toasted spices have cooled, add them to the bowl of whole untoasted spices. (In this case, we're not toasting the mustard seeds, because they pop and fly all over the place, which means you would need to toast them separately with a lid on the pan. You can do that, of course, but here it won't make a huge flavor difference with so many other spices in the mix. And we're not toasting the dried rosebuds, because they burn easily and toasting actually kills some of their delicate flavors.)

Stir all of the spices in the bowl to combine them, then pour them back onto the piece of parchment paper, which will make it easier to transfer them to the grinder. Pick up the parchment and pour a few tablespoons of the spices into the grinder, filling it about halfway. Always grind in small batches—overfilling the grinder means that you'll have to grind for a longer time, and the heat of the blades can cook the spices and alter their flavor. Put the lid on the grinder, turn it on, and grind the spices to a fine, uniform powder, shaking the grinder and pulsing the motor occasionally. As you finish grinding each batch, add it to the bowl with the ground spices. When all of the spices have been ground, use a fork to stir the mixture until it is completely uniform in color.

Hold the bowl up to your nose and take a big, proud whiff of your own *ras el hanout*. Now, of course, you'll want to taste it. Raw, it would taste unpleasantly intense, so you'll need to cook it in some way. You can try any of the recipes in this book that call for it. It's particularly good with saffron, as in the Short Rib *Tangia* (page 278). The Rainbow Chard (page 294) would be another great place to start.

Store the mixture in an airtight container, ideally for no longer than 1 month, but it will keep for up to 3 months.

MAKES ½ CUP PLUS 2 TABLESPOONS (65.5 GRAMS)

CHEF TO CHEF: I make large batches of spice mixes, so I toast the individual spices on parchment-lined baking sheets on the center rack of a 300°F convection oven or a 325°F regular oven, stirring occasionally and watching carefully to avoid burning. If you're working in quantity, it's definitely worth toasting the mustard seeds too, but rather than using the oven, toast them in a heavy frying pan with a lid to keep them from jumping out when they pop.

SIMPLE IDEAS
WITH *RAS EL HANOUT*

In Morocco, *ras el hanout* is used exclusively as an ingredient in slow-cooked, saucy dishes, but there are lots of other ways to use it. A little goes a long way to making things "taste Moroccan." Try any of the ideas below, and you'll see what I mean.

- Dry rub for poultry and meat: Dust a whole chicken, guinea hen, poussin, or game hens with *ras el hanout* and let sit in the refrigerator for a few hours or overnight before roasting. The same technique works well with steaks or chops for grilling.

- Rice: Add a teaspoon or two of *ras el hanout* to a pot of rice at the start of cooking. Or, for more flavor, make a pilaf, sautéing onions and garlic with *ras el hanout*, then adding the rice and sautéing it before cooking it with broth or water.

- Squash and Lentil Stew (a vegetarian version of *laadiss bil khlee*, a lentil stew made with aged beef): Sauté onions in olive oil. Add some *ras el hanout* and diced tomatoes and simmer to make a thick sauce. Cook French lentils in boiling water with some garlic until tender. Roast cubes of butternut squash until tender. Add the lentils and squash to the rice and simmer briefly to blend the flavors.

- Yogurt Dip: Make a dip for flatbreads and vegetables by adding a bit of *ras el hanout* to yogurt along with salt to taste. Let the mixture sit in the refrigerator for a few hours before serving.

- Cream: Simmer heavy cream with a bit of *ras el hanout*. Strain, chill, and whip lightly. Use as a garnish for soups, or sweeten slightly before whipping and serve with desserts, especially chocolate ones.

- Pass it along. Get some little spice cans with tight-fitting lids and share your stash with your friends.

RED-STYLE *RAS EL HANOUT*

I like to think of spice mixes the way a painter thinks of paint. You start with a base and add shades of flavor and color depending on what you're cooking and the effect you're looking for. I make a red-tinged *ras el hanout* to use with fish and poultry. With a smaller proportion of rich, earthy brown spices, it's lighter in both color and flavor than the *ras el hanout* above. Aleppo pepper gives it just the right mild chile heat and a combination of paprika and pimentón (Spanish paprika) adds peppery sweetness. Aesthetically, I love the bright hit of terra-cotta red it adds to lighter-colored foods. To make it, simply take half of the *ras el hanout* from the recipe above and add the following ground spices to it.

1 tablespoon (7.2 grams) ground Aleppo pepper
2 teaspoons (5.3 grams) sweet paprika
1¾ teaspoons (4.65 grams) pimentón
    (Spanish paprika)

MAKES 7 TABLESPOONS (50 GRAMS)

My Go-To Blends and Seasonings

Now that you've gotten to know Morocco's best-known spice blend, and the spices that go into it, I want to tell you a bit about some of the other seasoning blends that I turn to again and again.

Marash Pepper and Urfa Pepper

First, let me make special mention of two dried Turkish chiles I can't live without. You'll find them throughout this book, and I hope you end up feeling the same way.

Both Marash pepper (above, left) and Urfa pepper (right) are ground when you buy them. Unlike chile flakes, they're not completely dry, but remain slightly moist because of the way they're slowly sun-dried during the day and then wrapped at night to steep in their own moisture. When you touch them, you find that they leave a little color and oily residue on your fingers.

They're fairly hot, and because they're moist, they impart flavor in a direct and immediate way. All it takes is a bit of heat or moisture (including the saliva on your tongue) to activate their full potential

and complexity. That's why most of the time I use them not in cooking, but as a finishing pepper, sprinkling them on salads or in cures for things like fish and pickled vegetables. As a garnish, they hit you with an immediate burst of excitement that makes your palate tingle from the first bite.

Urfa pepper is dark brown and looks like moist potting soil or wet coffee grounds. Of the two, it has a smokier, deeper flavor, with a molasses undertone. Marash pepper is reddish orange and has a bit more bright acidity. Both are ground with salt, which rounds out their flavor beautifully. I tend to use Marash more on lighter things, like salads, and the earthier Urfa on meats and warm cooked foods.

Get your hands on a jar of each (they're expensive, but a little goes a long way—and you don't want to buy too much at a time anyway, because you don't want them to lose their moisture) and start playing around. Try them in any recipe that calls for finishing with a sprinkling of black pepper; add them to mayo; stir them into marinades and vinaigrettes; toss them with pasta; add them to couscous with a bit of minced parsley; sprinkle them on pizza or anything grilled; or just set them out in little bowls for people to add at the table. Believe it or not, they're also great with chocolate. And your fried eggs will never be the same.

Paprika and *Pimentón*

Moroccans love to use paprika for its bright red color. What they're most fond of is sweet paprika, the mild, almost flavorless kind; it's also known as domestic paprika and is sold in the spice section of any supermarket. However, sweet paprika doesn't add much in the way of flavor. For that, I reach for Spanish *pimentón,* which tends to have a somewhat paler orange color and a more rounded, earthier sweetness.

People often think of *pimentón* as being smoked, but that isn't entirely accurate. Many varieties of *pimentón* (most famously, de la Vera) are smoke-dried. They add a distinctive oaky-smoky barbecue flavor to foods, making them especially great for indoor grilling recipes. But you can also buy non-smoked *pimentón* varieties, including *dulce* (mild), *agridulce* (bittersweet), and *picante* (spicy hot). And you can find smoked paprika that's not Spanish as well.

I often use a combination of sweet paprika, *pimentón,* and smoked paprika to get the distinctive flavor, color, and smokiness each has to offer, and I encourage you to keep a few types on hand so you can mix and match them, depending on what you're cooking.

AZIZA CURRY BLEND

Curry has nothing to do with Morocco, but a lot to do with my cooking. The blend we make at the restaurant shares many ingredients with our *ras el hanout,* but it's modeled on the flavors of a Madras or Japanese yellow curry and gets its bright golden color from turmeric. You can think of it as a kind of *ras el hanout* for lighter stuff, like vegetables, grains, and fish. Mostly I like to add curry as a flavor accent, rather than making it a main event, which, to me,

can be overkill. Check out the simple ideas here, and the recipes throughout this book, and you'll get what I'm talking about.

whole spices

2 tablespoons plus 1 teaspoon (8.9 grams) coriander seeds

2½ teaspoons (6.2 grams) cumin seeds

½ teaspoon (1.5 grams) Tellicherry peppercorns

1 (0.7 gram) black cardamom pod, shelled and seeds reserved

8 (0.6 gram) cloves

¼ teaspoon (0.6 gram) fennel seeds

½ (0.2 gram) chile de árbol, seeds removed

¼ (0.3 gram) star anise

ground spices

5 tablespoons (40.5 grams) ground turmeric

⅛ teaspoon (0.9 gram) grated nutmeg

Put a piece of parchment paper on the work surface.

Put the whole spices in a medium heavy frying pan, set it over medium heat, and swirl the pan, flipping or stirring the spices occasionally so they toast evenly, until fragrant, 2 to 3 minutes. Pour the spices onto the parchment paper and let cool.

Pour the spices into a spice grinder and finely grind them, then combine them with the ground spices.

Store the mixture in an airtight container, ideally for no longer than 1 month, but it will keep for up to 3 months.

MAKES ½ CUP (58 GRAMS)

SIMPLE IDEAS
WITH AZIZA CURRY BLEND

◆ Curry Oil: Simmer 2 cups of neutral oil (such as grapeseed or canola) with 2 teaspoons curry blend for about 30 minutes. Strain through cheesecloth,

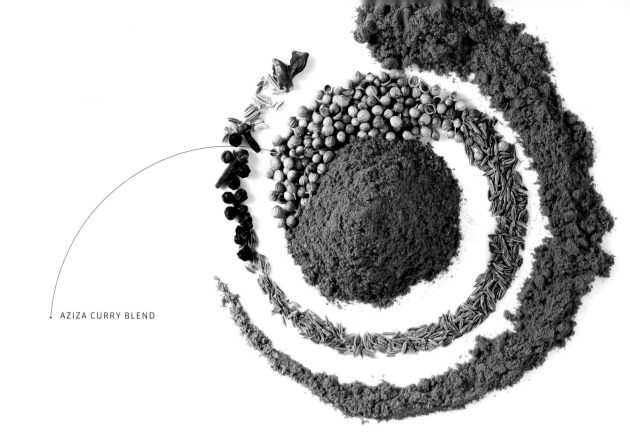

let cool, and use the infused oil to drizzle on sliced raw fish, grilled steak or chicken, soups, and stews. Or use the oil to make a mayonnaise or aioli.

- ◆ Curry Vinaigrette: Sauté shallots in oil with some curry blend for about 10 minutes. Cool, then whisk with lemon juice or vinegar and oil to make an emulsion. Excellent on broccoli, cauliflower, bok choy, grilled fish, steamed mussels, and boiled potatoes.
- ◆ Add to grains like barley or farro (see page 302) at the start of cooking.
- ◆ Dust on Grilled Flatbreads (page 192) instead of *za'atar* before grilling.

VADOUVAN

I can't think about curry without going straight to *vadouvan,* one of my all-time favorite seasoning ingredients. I discovered it several years ago, when a young chef from France, Ludo Lefebvre, was doing a guest stint at my friend David Kinch's restaurant,

Manresa. At one point, he pulled out a canister of *vadouvan* and sprinkled it on something as a finishing accent. No one in the kitchen had ever tasted or even heard of the stuff, and everyone went nuts.

Basically, *vadouvan* is a seasoning made from minced shallots and onions sautéed with curry spices and then dried to make a chunky blend. It lets you add the rich flavor of sautéed curry (as opposed to the unpleasant raw flavor of curry powder) to foods without having to cook that flavor into the dish. (Imagine wanting to add a bit of curry flavor to a poached egg—with *vadouvan,* you just sprinkle it on top.)

Lefebvre didn't leave behind a detailed recipe for his *vadouvan,* but he did leave some with David, who took it to Le Sanctuaire, an amazing specialty ingredients shop in San Francisco, and eventually they created their own version. For a while, I was buying it from them, for nearly a hundred dollars a pound, but I started using so much I had to figure out how to make it myself. Here's where I ended up.

I've had the best results drying *vadouvan* slowly in a dehydrator, but if you don't have one, you can make it in the oven. If you're going that route, just sweat the onions, shallots, garlic, and ginger until the mixture is barely brown, then add the rest of the ingredients, spread the mixture on parchment-lined baking sheets, and toast in the oven on its lowest setting for 3 to 4 hours, stirring every hour.

½ cup (106 grams) grapeseed or canola oil

6½ cups (775 grams) finely chopped shallots

1 cup (128 grams) thinly sliced garlic

5 tablespoons (56 grams) finely chopped onion

½ cup plus 2 tablespoons (115.4 grams) finely chopped fresh ginger

13 (3.9 grams) small fresh curry leaves

Six 1- to 1½-inch pieces (20.4 grams) fresh turmeric, grated on a Microplane grater, or 1½ teaspoons (4.1 grams) ground turmeric

1 tablespoon plus 2¼ teaspoons (13.4 grams) Aziza Curry Blend (page 33) or Madras curry powder

2¾ teaspoons (8.3 grams) kosher salt

2⅛ teaspoons (7.6 grams) yellow mustard seeds

2⅛ teaspoons (7.6 grams) brown mustard seeds

2¾ teaspoons (7 grams) ground cumin

1 tablespoon plus ¾ teaspoon (6.9 grams) ground coriander

1½ teaspoons (5.2 grams) ground fenugreek or 2 teaspoons (9.2 grams) fenugreek seeds, crushed

1¼ teaspoons (3 grams) Marash pepper

1¾ teaspoons (2.2 grams) coriander seeds

¾ teaspoon (2 grams) ground green cardamom

½ teaspoon (0.7 gram) grated nutmeg

¼ teaspoon (0.6 gram) ground cloves

¼ teaspoon (0.6 gram) cayenne

2 tablespoons (26.5 grams) extra virgin olive oil

Set a large pot over medium-low heat and pour in the grapeseed oil. Add the shallots, garlic, onion, and ginger and cook for about 20 minutes, or until the liquid has come out of the onions. Increase the heat to medium and cook for about 1¼ hours, stirring often and adjusting the heat to keep the mixture from burning, until all of the moisture has evaporated.

Meanwhile, stack the curry leaves and cut them crosswise into thin slivers. Reserve them with the fresh turmeric.

Combine all the dry spices.

Increase the heat under the onion mixture to medium-high and cook, stirring often, for about 7 minutes, until the mixture is richly caramelized. You'll see the oil begin bubbling around the edges of the pot as you fry the mixture. Add the olive oil, fresh turmeric, and curry leaves and stir to combine. Stir in the dry spices and cook for about 2 minutes to toast the spices, until they are fragrant. Spread the mixture in thin layers on dehydrator racks. You will probably need two racks.

Heat the dehydrator to 125°F. Place the racks in the dehydrator and check the *vadouvan* every 1½ hours, turning the mixture with a spatula and rotating the trays so that it dries evenly. Depending on your dehydrator, the drying process can take from 4 to 7 hours. The finished *vadouvan* will be a dark caramel brown and although it is dried, there will still be some moisture remaining from the fat.

Store the mixture in an airtight container in the refrigerator for up to 1 month, or in the freezer for up to 3 months.

MAKES 3½ CUPS (383 GRAMS)

SIMPLE IDEAS
WITH *VADOUVAN*

- *Vadouvan* is insanely good with eggs—it's kind of like a vegetarian version of bacon bits. Sprinkle it on fried, poached, or scrambled eggs; or add it to omelets. deviled eggs, or egg salad.
- Sprinkle on salads made with hearty greens, such as chicory or treviso, and with duck confit.

- *Vadouvan* Compound Butter: Stir *vadouvan* into softened butter, form into a log, wrap in plastic wrap, and refrigerate. Use for cooking eggs, on toast, or as a garnish for steak or chicken.
- Add to rice when you fluff it, just before serving.
- *Vadouvan* Scallop Quenelles: Make a mousse by pureeing scallops, a bit of cream, and a little *vadouvan* in a food processor. Shape into quenelles and poach them in water or fish stock.

VADOUVAN BROWN BUTTER

Once you've made *vadouvan*, you can use it to create a rich brown butter sauce.

½ pound (227 grams) unsalted butter
2 tablespoons (15 grams) *Vadouvan* (page 34)

Melt the butter in a large saucepan with high sides (when you add the *vadouvan,* the butter will foam up) over medium heat, swirling the pan to melt the butter evenly. Once the butter is melted, simmer it for 5 to 10 minutes, or until it is golden brown and the solids at the bottom of the pan are a caramel color (not dark brown like coffee grounds).

Carefully stir in the *vadouvan.* Remove from the heat and let sit for 1 hour.

Pour the butter and *vadouvan* into a container and refrigerate. (It is not necessary to strain the butter.) It will keep refrigerated for several months.

MAKES ¾ CUP PLUS 2 TABLESPOONS (185 GRAMS)

SIMPLE IDEAS
WITH *VADOUVAN* BROWN BUTTER

- Toss with warm popcorn.
- Drizzle over roast guinea hen, squab, or chicken.
- Drizzle on grilled lamb chops.
- Spoon over grilled or poached halibut.
- Serve as a drawn butter with crab, prawns, or lobster.

- Drizzle over steamed couscous or other grains.
- Fold into mashed potatoes or stir into sautéed or steamed vegetables just before serving.

CHEF TO CHEF: You can make a large quantity of vadouvan *brown butter without the dehydration step. Follow the* vadouvan *recipe, but do not dry the spice mixture. Make brown butter with 4 pounds (1.81 kilograms) butter and add the* vadouvan *mixture to it. Simmer for 5 minutes, then set in a warm spot to infuse (but not solidify) for about 4 hours. Stir well, transfer to jars, and refrigerate; or put the butter in bags or plastic tubs and freeze it.*

BERBERE

Berbere is to Ethiopia what *ras el hanout* is to Morocco. I reach for it when I want a nutty, smoky, tobacco-y flavor, especially when I'm making crusts and coatings for seared foods (as in *Berbere*-Crusted Scallops, page 212). One of its key ingredients is *ajwain,* a seed that looks like aniseed with a flavor somewhere between cumin and thyme.

whole spices

3½ tablespoons (13.3 grams) coriander seeds
2½ teaspoons (6.2 grams) cumin seeds
2 teaspoons (3.6 grams) fennel seeds
½ teaspoon (2.3 grams) fenugreek seeds
¾ teaspoon (1.6 grams) *ajwain* seeds
½ teaspoon (1.5 grams) Tellicherry peppercorns
¾ teaspoon (1.3 grams) whole mace
7 (1.2 grams) green cardamom pods, shelled and seeds reserved
One 1-inch piece (1.1 grams) cinnamon stick, crumbled
4 (0.6 gram) allspice berries
3 (0.2 gram) cloves

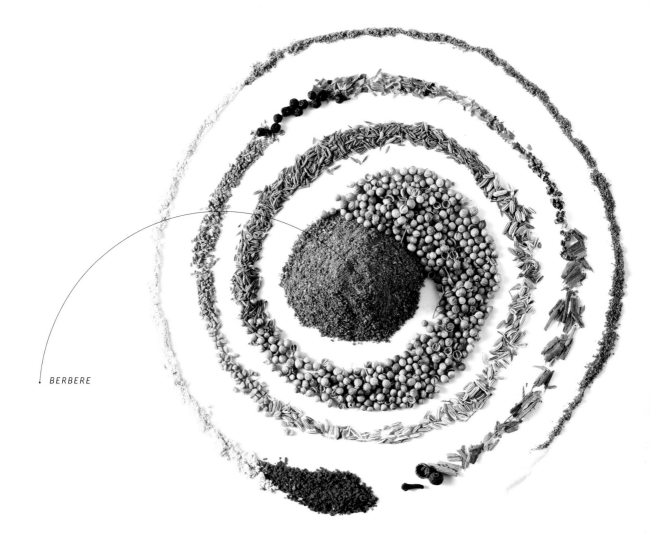

BERBERE

ground spices

1½ teaspoons (3.6 grams) Aleppo pepper

¾ teaspoon (1.5 grams) ground ginger

¾ teaspoon (1.1 grams) grated nutmeg

¼ teaspoon (1.3 grams) citric acid

Put a piece of parchment paper on the work surface.

Put the whole spices in a medium heavy frying pan, set it over medium heat, and swirl the pan, flipping or stirring the spices occasionally so they toast evenly, until fragrant, 2 to 3 minutes. Pour the spices onto the parchment paper and let cool.

Pour the spices into a spice grinder and finely grind them, then combine them with the dry spices.

Store the mixture in an airtight container, ideally for no longer than 1 month, but it will keep for up to 3 months.

MAKES ½ CUP (60 GRAMS)

SIMPLE IDEAS
WITH *BERBERE*

- Add ½ teaspoon *berbere* per cup of raw rice at the start of cooking; or sauté the same amount with the onions and butter or oil when making a rice pilaf. It's great with other grains too, like barley and farro.
- Add to meat and/or vegetable stews early in the cooking process. (*Berbere* is not great as a seasoning for sautéing, because its flavors will remain too harsh.)
- Lightly dust steak, chicken, or fatty fish, like black cod, with *berbere* before grilling.
- Sprinkle on vegetables such as squash, carrots, parsnips, or sweet potatoes before roasting them.
- Add a pinch to honey cake, spice cake, fruit cake, or gingerbread batter.

ZA'ATAR

In Morocco, if you say *"za'atar,"* you'll be referring not to this blend but to a particular herb that looks like thyme and tastes like a blend of oregano and marjoram. (The herb is not easy to find in the United States; I have it grown for me by Annabelle Lenderink at La Tercera Farms in west Marin County.) But in the rest of the Middle East, *za'atar* is a spice blend made from herbs, sesame seeds, and sumac (a reddish sour seasoning made from ground dried sumac berries).

Sumac and, by association, *za'atar* are great for adding complex acidity to a dish when you don't want to introduce a liquid like lemon juice or vinegar. Look for high-quality, preferably Turkish, sumac. Cheaper sumac has sometimes been dyed red and will bleed into other ingredients. If it stains your fingers red when you touch it, it's probably the dyed stuff.

You can buy *za'atar* (the blend) in specialty foods stores, but it's easy to make your own, and it will have much more flavor, especially if you use fresh ingredients to make it.

2 tablespoons (18.6 grams) white sesame seeds
2 tablespoons (17.4 grams) sumac
1½ teaspoons (1.1 grams) dried oregano,
    preferably Mexican

Toast the sesame seeds in a large heavy frying pan, set it over medium heat, and swirl the pan, flipping or stirring frequently, for about 2 minutes, until golden and fragrant. Allow the sesame seeds to cool, then lightly grind them in small batches in a spice grinder. You don't want to completely pulverize them—just grind them enough to break them down a bit.

Rub the oregano between your fingers to crumble it slightly. Put the sesame seeds, oregano, and sumac in a bowl and stir well to combine.

Store the mixture in an airtight container, ideally for no longer than 1 month, but it will keep for up to 3 months.

MAKES ABOUT ¼ CUP (37 GRAMS)

SIMPLE IDEAS
WITH *ZA'ATAR*

- Sprinkle on flatbreads (see page 192) before grilling or baking.
- Drizzle goat cheese or feta with olive oil and sprinkle *za'atar* on top.
- Make a vinaigrette with olive oil, vinegar, and *za'atar;* allow to infuse for at least 30 minutes. Use on salads or vegetables.
- Marinate chicken in yogurt with *za'atar.* Scrape off most of the marinade before grilling or roasting.
- Grind *za'atar* in a spice grinder and fold it into aioli.
- Sprinkle over sliced ripe tomatoes and cucumbers; garnish with lemon basil.
- Add to dips, especially those made with yogurt.
- Sprinkle on fried eggs or deviled eggs.

CHEF TO CHEF: To make ultratender poached chicken, Cryovac boneless chicken with buttermilk and za'atar *and cook* sous-vide.

Z'HUG

Z'hug ("z'hoog") is a Yemeni seasoning with a spicy kick. It's usually a paste made with moist ingredients, including fresh chiles, garlic, cilantro, parsley, and oil, but I like to make this dry version, which can be sprinkled onto foods as a seasoning. I use Marash pepper, which has a nice bite and adds a reddish color, but if you don't have it, you can use a smaller amount of cayenne, as directed. You'll have a greener blend that's a bit less spicy.

2 tablespoons (14.4 grams) Marash pepper or
   1 teaspoon (2.26 grams) cayenne

2 tablespoons (11 grams) ground coriander

2 tablespoons (2.7 grams) dried cilantro

2 tablespoons (2.7 grams) dried parsley

1 tablespoon (12 grams) kosher salt

1 tablespoon (9.6 grams) roasted garlic granules or
   1 tablespoon (10.2 grams) granulated garlic

1 tablespoon (7.7 grams) ground cumin

1 tablespoon (5.4 grams) ground caraway

1 teaspoon (2.6 grams) ground cardamom

½ teaspoon (2.3 grams) citric acid

½ teaspoon (0.9 gram) ground black pepper

Combine all the ingredients and grind, in batches, to a uniform texture in a spice grinder.

Store the mixture in an airtight container, ideally for no longer than 1 month, but it will keep for up to 3 months.

MAKES ABOUT ¾ CUP (70 GRAMS MARASH VERSION; 58 GRAMS CAYENNE VERSION)

SIMPLE IDEAS
WITH *Z'HUG*

◆ Rub on chicken or steak and let marinate before grilling.

◆ Use as a dry rub when roasting red meat.

◆ Add to cooked fava beans or chickpeas toward the end of cooking.

◆ Toss root vegetables in clarified butter, dust with *z'hug,* wrap in aluminum foil, and set the packet on the grill to steam.

◆ Toast mixed nuts in a light coating of olive oil, and sprinkle with *z'hug* while still warm. Or add a bit of *z'hug* to the coating mixture for Spiced Almonds (page 106).

◆ Try the *Z'hug*–Pumpkin Seed Granola (page 377) on soups, salads, or vegetables.

Spice Consciously

So, yes, getting a sense of Moroccan flavor is, in large part, about the spices you buy and what you do with them. But as you explore the nuances of that very Moroccan verb, "to spice," the best advice I can give you comes down to a single word: *restraint*. If the spices are what makes a dish taste Moroccan, it's the amount and the balance of those spices that make all the difference.

Like so many chefs living in California with access to great raw materials all year long, I often find myself wanting to do less rather than more, to use spice simply as an accent that brings focus to a perfect ingredient. But I come from the tradition of Moroccan cooking, in which spices and seasonings have been used for centuries not only to enhance, but also, often, to transform (and sometimes in the past even to mask) a main ingredient. I often struggle with these two quite different ways of looking at flavor. But it's the kind of struggle that keeps me excited about cooking. So, even though you'll find more than seventy spices used in this book, you'll discover that they are usually not used heavily, but moderately and in balanced combinations. I hope that you'll be inspired by these combinations to try new spices and new ways of using them.

In the end, especially when it comes to spicing and seasoning, I think the sweet spot between the big, lush, assertive, aromatic flavors I love in Moroccan food and the fresh, direct "ingredient celebration" of California cooking is that simple idea of restraint. Start with less, take it slow, taste as you go, and, most of all, season for a reason.

dude.
preserved
lemons.

2

I'm going to go out on a limb here—the limb of a lemon tree—and say that preserved lemons are Morocco's greatest culinary contribution to the world. No, wait, I'm going all the way with this: they're Morocco's greatest contribution to the world, period.

Lots of cultures, from North Africa to Italy to Asia, came up with the idea of salting lemons as a way to keep them throughout the year. But in Morocco, that necessity really turned into the mother of invention, ultimately creating a culinary phenomenon that had a huge effect on the cuisine, to the extent that the preserved lemon completely displaced the fresh article. Moroccans don't even think of fresh lemons in connection with food beyond garnishing drinks and making lemonade. Preserved lemons, on the other hand, can turn up in practically any savory dish on the table. If *ras el hanout* is the country's national spice blend, preserved lemons are its national anthem of flavor.

Sure, a preserved lemon is a piece of brined fruit. Like an olive, a pickle, or a plate of *kimchee,* it's cured and fermented in heavy salt. But unlike those foods, which are nibbles that sometimes get used as ingredients in cooking, a preserved lemon is never a nibble and always a seasoning, with an unmistakable, irreplaceable flavor—not to mention flavor-enhancing qualities that have a mysterious effect on other ingredients in a dish as well.

What soy sauce and fish sauce are to Asian cooking, preserved lemons are to Moroccan food. They bring saltiness, acidity, and a perfumy citrus quality to everything from stews and tagines to salads. They're the bright "ping" that balances the earthy flavors of cooked greens, soups, marinades, and sauces for lamb, beef, chicken, vegetables, and fish. And wherever they're used, they add a particular kind of almost intoxicating intensity that's unlike any other ingredient I know. The best word I can think of for this effect is *mouthwateringness,* and believe me, once you experience it, you'll instantly get what I mean.

That's why we're about to make a batch. It's incredibly easy, and the payoff is huge. All you need are lemons, salt, and a little patience. If you start today, you'll have preserved lemons in about a month.

Making Preserved Lemons

In my restaurant kitchen, we use a ton of preserved lemons. Literally. One guy is in charge of making a 200-pound mega-batch every month. In a year, that adds up to 1.2 tons of lemons! But in your kitchen, I suggest you start by making a single quart jar of them.

I'm going to share with you what I think is the best all-purpose method for making them: packing them in salt and then immersing them in lemon juice. In Morocco, people sometimes go the less-expensive route of using vinegar instead of lemon juice, which results in a more intensely acidic taste that overpowers the delicate perfume of the citrus. There's also a Jewish tradition of preserving lemons in olive oil. They cure much more slowly and have a taste and texture that's more like fresh lemons. I sometimes use those in salads, or add their oil to vinaigrettes.

But for now, I want you to experience the quintessential salt-and-lemon-juice-cured version. Once you have that as a point of reference, you can experiment with some other curing options I'll also tell you about. You'll realize, when you try these, that they bear almost no resemblance to store-bought preserved lemons—or at least any brand I've ever tried. I recommend avoiding those at all costs (and the cost can be ridiculously high, especially considering all you're buying is lemons and salt).

The Jar

You're going to be preserving your lemons whole. Cramming them into an ordinary jar can be tricky, so I recommend a wide-mouthed 1-quart canning jar with a two-piece screw-on lid or a clamp-on glass lid and rubber gasket, either of which will give you a nice tight seal. The kind with the neck that's slightly narrower than the sides is ideal, because your lemons will have less exposed surface area, meaning the ones on top won't oxidize as much. You can sterilize the jar in boiling water, or just run it through the hottest wash-and-dry cycle of your dishwasher right before you start. Either way, make sure it's bone-dry. I've found that tap water is the enemy of preserved lemons, causing them to mildew.

The Lemons

For any recipe with just a few ingredients, it's important to use good ones. Look for fresh, juicy Eureka or Lisbon lemons (the kinds sold in most supermarkets), organic and pesticide-free if possible. For your first batch, I'd avoid Meyer lemons, which are softer than Eureka and Lisbon and have much lower acidity. For a better way to preserve those, see page 47.

You'll need about twice as many lemons as you're going to preserve, because you'll use half of them for their juice. Just to be safe, buy a few extras to ensure that your jar is packed very tightly and completely filled with juice.

Before you start juicing, you might want to do what we do at the restaurant: use a zester to strip off the zest (from only the lemons you're juicing, not the ones you're preserving). Spread the zest on a parchment-lined baking sheet, cover it tightly with plastic wrap, and put it in the freezer. Once it's frozen, transfer it to a resealable freezer bag, and you'll have a ready supply of lemon zest to use in cooking.

The Salt

I use kosher salt because it has a clean, iodine-free flavor. You can also use coarse sea salt, which is more intensely salty; it has the advantage of extracting more juice immediately, speeding up the process and often requiring less added lemon juice, but in the end, your preserved lemons will be a bit saltier.

The Process

For a 1-quart batch, you will need:

About 6 (141-gram) lemons for preserving
About 6 more lemons for juicing, or enough to make
  ½ to 1 cup (120 to 240 grams) lemon juice
About ¾ cup (108 grams) kosher salt

Scrub the 6 lemons you will be preserving with a vegetable brush under cold running water, then dry them very thoroughly. If you plan to zest the other 6 lemons, scrub them too.

Pour the salt into a large bowl. Stand a lemon stem end down on a cutting board and use a sharp knife to cut down into it as though you were going to cut it in half, stopping about ½ inch above the stem. Now make a perpendicular cut, again stopping short of the stem, so the lemon is quartered but still intact.

Holding the lemon over the bowl, spread the four quarters open and pack in as much salt as you can, allowing the excess to fall back into the bowl. Don't be shy—you're not just salting here, you're really jamming in a solid pack of salt, up to 2 tablespoons (18 grams) per lemon. Put the lemon cut side up (to keep the salt from spilling out) in the jar and repeat with as many lemons as the jar will hold, pushing them down hard so they're squeezed in tightly. (If you can't fit the 6th lemon into the jar, you can add it the next day, when the lemons are softer.) Put the lid on the jar and leave it on the counter overnight.

The lemons will have softened and released some liquid. Use a clean spoon to push them down, and add another salted lemon or two if they fit. If there's only a little extra room, it's fine to add a salted half or quarter lemon.

Juice the remaining lemons a few at a time, pouring the juice into the jar until it is filled to the brim and the salted lemons are completely submerged.

Put the lid on the jar, turning it until it's just finger-tight (overtightening can keep air from escaping and cause the lid to buckle), or clamp it closed if that's the kind of jar you're using. Put the jar in a dark spot, like a cupboard or pantry, not in the refrigerator. For the next week, turn and shake the jar once a day to redistribute the salt that has settled to the bottom. Add more lemon juice if you notice that the lemons are no longer submerged.

That's all there is to it. Just let the jar sit in that dark cupboard for a month. If you notice a little bubbling around the edge of the jar lid, don't worry. That's a normal part of the fermentation process.

The Moment of Truth

After you've waited patiently for a month, it's time for the big reveal: open the jar. If the lemons on top have floated above the surface of the liquid, they will have oxidized a bit, which will have caused them to turn brown, but they're fine. Take out a lemon, cut off a little slice of the peel, and pop it in your mouth. This is what I'm talking about. Your whole mouth will be filled with a powerful flavor that goes from salty to citrusy to piney to almost tingly, and you'll discover that the rind has lost its bitterness and softened to a creamy texture like a slice of gravlax.

In Morocco, it's usually only the yellow rind of the preserved lemon, stripped of most of its white pith, that's used in cooking. In some long-cooked dishes like Short Rib *Tangia* (page 278), a whole preserved lemon is sometimes simply thrown into the mix, and it eventually just melts away, but most of the time, the rind is used, and the rest of the fruit is discarded. That said, you may want to use the entire thing—and even the syrupy brining liquid—in various ways, as I often do. It all depends on the lemons you start with and your personal tolerance for flavor intensity.

Start by cutting a lemon into quarters. Put one

3

couscous.
here's
how I roll.

If you want to understand couscous, start by sitting down. No, not in a chair, on the floor. All across North Africa, from Morocco to Algeria, Tunisia, and Libya, that's where couscous starts, with a woman (and it's pretty much always a woman, and usually more than one) sitting on the floor of a kitchen or a courtyard, cradling a huge terra-cotta tray in her lap, the perfect position for hand-rolling. That's right—couscous is rolled. Since most people here are used to buying it in a little box and serving it as an alternative to rice, they tend to assume it's a grain, like cracked wheat or polenta. But couscous is actually more like a kind of tiny pasta—one that gets steamed, not boiled—made by rolling coarsely ground semolina (milled from durum wheat, the kind of hard wheat used to make dried pasta, like spaghetti) with salted water and a bit of flour until it forms little spheres.

What transforms those three ingredients into a rich, fluffy delicacy and not a ball of Play-Doh is the rolling technique and the slow steaming, and that's why I want you to give real made-from-scratch couscous a shot. It might take you one or two attempts to get the hang of it, but you'll have fun, and you'll be amazed at the process of making something incredible from almost nothing at all.

As for the stuff you buy in the little boxes in the rice aisle, that's instant couscous. It has been steamed until it's fully cooked and then dehydrated, so you just pour boiling water over it and let it soak to rehydrate the dried granules. It's convenient, but I've got to say, talking about it in the same breath as real couscous is kind of like comparing a noodle cup you make with boiling water from the office coffee machine to a nice bowl of pasta. I'm not saying you shouldn't buy it, but what we're going to get into right now is a world-class delicacy it barely resembles.

One way to experience real couscous is by getting your hands on some *non*instant store-bought dry couscous and slowly steaming it. We'll get to that a bit later. But making homemade, hand-rolled couscous from scratch is the project I have in mind for you right now. It's what I grew up with, and sadly, even in Morocco it's becoming a vanishing art, because most people, at least in the cities, now buy their couscous at a market and do only the steaming at home.

Couscous Culture

Even if Moroccans are hand-rolling their couscous less frequently these days, it's still prepared and served in the same way as it always has been. Which is to say, it's absolutely not a side dish or a starch. It's never served alongside a tagine, or, for that matter, alongside anything. It's served in one way, and one way only: steamed over a broth with meat and/or vegetables, mounded on a huge platter, and topped with the ingredients over which it was steamed. Always.

First the couscous is poured out onto the platter. Then a skimmer is used to push it out to the edges of the plate, creating a well. Any pieces of meat from the broth are pulled out and placed in the center of that well, the vegetables are piled over the meat, and a bit of the broth is ladled on top to moisten everything. Everyone eats directly from that single platter. It would be sacrilegious to serve individual plates of couscous with stuff piled on top. And so important is the notion of sharing that the meal absolutely can't begin until everyone in the family is assembled around the table.

Why? Because in Islam, Friday is the holiest day of the week, and on that day the midday meal is always couscous. It's almost never served on any other day. On weekdays, the midday prayer ritual can be done anywhere, but on Fridays, it has to be performed at the mosque. People come home hungry, and couscous is their reward—a dish lovingly prepared earlier by the women of the house as a once-a-week treat.

It's believed that each granule of couscous is a blessing from God, and families share that blessing by making enough for themselves and another big platter to take to the mosque, where poor people will gather and eat after the prayers.

In our house, making the couscous was my great-grandmother's job every Friday for decades. Occasionally some of us young people would get tired of it and ask her to make something different for Friday lunch, just once. Her response was always a sad little tilt of the head followed by something like, "Ah. I see. You don't want my couscous. That's fine. Really. It just means I might as well be dead, that's all." And then we'd have couscous. And we'd eat even more than usual to soothe her bruised ego.

The soft granules and the even-softer boiled ingredients served on top are made that way for a reason. Couscous is about inclusiveness and sharing. Old people in Morocco, when I was growing up, would generally have lost most or all of their teeth. So this was a dish they could enjoy with great gusto—and very little chewing.

The couscous I knew as a kid was finger food. You'd take a handful of it and squeeze it into a ball with some of the toppings (it's a whole technique that's trickier than it sounds), and pop the whole thing into your mouth. These days in Moroccan homes, couscous is still served family-style, but eating it with a spoon rather than your fingers (still right off the central platter) is more the norm.

The classic preparation goes something like this: You sauté onions with saffron, ginger, turmeric, cumin, pepper, and herbs. Then you add chunks of lamb, sauté them quickly, and add a lot of water. The couscous steams over that, and root vegetables are added to the liquid during the second or third steaming. Everyone gets a small bowl of extra broth, sometimes with a bit of *harissa* stirred into it, to drizzle over the part of the big central couscous mountain they're eating from. And on very hot days, couscous is often accompanied by a glass of cold buttermilk to sip between bites.

To be perfectly honest, I have mixed feelings about that traditional couscous. On the one hand, it tastes soulfully wonderful and takes me back to where I started out in the world. On the other hand, it's a dish that's philosophically very much at odds with how I think about food. The object, in the traditional

version, is to extract as much flavor from whatever ingredients you're using to make the sauce as flavorful as you can, because the real bulk of the meal is the couscous and sauce. That means that the meat and vegetables give it up for the team, losing most of their individual flavor and texture and becoming mushy.

But when I very untraditionally steam the couscous over water or broth and cook the vegetables and/or meat separately, I can serve a dish with the best of everything: fluffy, flavorful couscous and sauce, and perfectly cooked vegetables and meat that keep their taste and integrity.

We'll get to that, but first, I want you to experience making hand-rolled couscous from scratch, not because I think you're going to take the time to do it very often, but because I know that if you do it just once (or even just read about how to do it), you'll really get what couscous is and what it isn't.

Couscous: A Buyer's Guide

What is sold as couscous varies enormously from store to store and city to city. If you have a good specialty foods store, health foods grocery, or upscale supermarket in your area, you can probably find most or all of these couscous varieties.

- INSTANT COUSCOUS: By far the most common kind sold in America, this is the precooked and dried stuff in small boxes that you rehydrate with boiling water or broth. If it says something like "cooks in 5 minutes" on the box, it's instant. It can't be used to make real steamed couscous in a couscoussier.
- COUSCOUS: Sometimes called "French couscous" (because the French were the first to commercially produce and mass-market couscous after being exposed to it in Morocco), this is the machine-made equivalent of hand-rolled couscous. It's ready to be moistened and then steamed in a couscoussier in the traditional way. Look for it in bulk bins of good supermarkets or other stores that sell grain products in bulk, and steam it following the directions on page 62.
- HAND-ROLLED COUSCOUS: The kind of couscous you can make at home using the directions on page

56 is also commercially available (see Sources, page 380). Steam it as directed on page 62.
- ISRAELI COUSCOUS: I've always thought this should really be called Israeli "couscous" (in quotes), because it's an extruded pasta that simply looks like giant couscous, about the size of BBs. However you think of it, don't mistake it for traditional couscous. It needs to be simmered in water or broth, not steamed. (By the way, fregola—see page 282—is the Italian/Sardinian toasted version of this kind of pasta.)
- *M'HAMSA* COUSCOUS: This is the generic name for a Moroccan pasta that resembles Israeli couscous and is boiled, not steamed. But note that it's also the name of a precooked and dried hand-rolled couscous product from Tunisia, which you rehydrate with boiling water, like instant couscous.
- COUSCOUS MADE FROM OTHER GRAINS: In Morocco, *balboula* is couscous made from milled barley, which is steamed and has a stickier, starchier texture than traditional semolina couscous. Whole wheat couscous is also now readily available in both instant and traditional forms.

of your fully extended fingers to gently roll the grains in a circular motion so that they absorb the water evenly. Don't use your palms at all—that would put too much pressure on the grains. The idea is to pull some of the couscous upward toward you as you roll and let it fall back down to the lower part of the tray so that you're constantly working through all the particles. The traditional, most efficient way to do this is to move both hands in a circular motion, one clockwise, the other counterclockwise, coordinating them so they don't crash into each other. This is why a larger terra-cotta tray is better than a smaller one: it gives you plenty of room to move.

The grains will look and feel damp, and initially not much will happen. Spray another 15 sprays over them, and continue to roll with your extended fingers. It's a good idea to start slowly, with just a little water, to get a feel for rolling with your fingers. You can always get more liberal with the water later. It's helpful to think about how your rolling is creating very tiny balls of moistened grain, because that is, in fact, what you are doing. If the dampened semolina starts to stick to the bottom of the tray, you're pressing too hard. Likewise, if it starts sticking to your hands, you're applying too much pressure there. But don't get hung up on trying to peel it off, just continue to work your fingers over the semolina so that it can continue to absorb the water. Try to keep this whole process just between your fingers and the grains.

Keep rolling for a few minutes, and you'll see that the semolina particles will start to get a little bigger. If you've angled the tray, as the particles roll downward, you'll get a sense of how rounded they're becoming. Continue to roll until the particles stop feeling at all wet, then spray with another 15 sprays. Roll again, and evaluate: you want the semolina to have absorbed as much water as it can, so that it feels moist and slightly sticky and no longer gets dry as you continue to roll it. If that's not how things are looking, spray on more water and roll some more until it is.

At this point, you're ready to sprinkle about a tablespoon (8 grams) of the all-purpose flour over the wet grains. Roll with your fingers in the same way you did before to incorporate all the flour. If your fingers leave behind light lines that continually change with your movement, you're doing great. What's happening here is that you're applying a final "smooth coat" of flour to the tiny spheres you've created. Depending on how much water you added, you may need to add more flour. Add about ½ tablespoon (4 grams) at a time.

You should now have granules about the size of that familiar dry instant couscous, with a fairly

spherical shape. And that's one of the best rules of thumb (or, in this case, finger) I can give you: throughout the process of rolling couscous from this early stage all the way until the end, keep that image of instant couscous in mind as a size gauge. Here's what I can't really tell you definitively: exactly how much water, how much flour, and how much rolling—all this depends on how coarse your semolina is, whether it had any fine semolina mixed in, and even the humidity of both your house and the place where the semolina was stored before you bought it.

The finer your semolina was ground, the more fine semolina it includes, and/or the drier it is, the more quickly it will drink up water, release starch, and turn into the small balls that are grains of couscous. So, experiment with rolling, spraying, and sprinkling on flour in small amounts until you get a feel for the process. Patience and a light touch are golden here. Don't rush. Don't squash. Just gently roll with the flow. And don't sweat it if all of the particles aren't exactly the same size. That's part of the beauty of hand-rolled couscous. Just know that the more you practice (and really, it'll take less practice than you might think), the closer you can get to uniformity, and the more consistent the texture will be. If, however, at any point the granules start to clump up and form noticeably larger balls, roll them under your fingertips to break them up.

When the granules feel dry and most of them look couscous-sized, put them in the *tamis* and shake it gently over a bowl. This will remove any excess flour, which would cause the couscous to stick together when cooked. You can pour the excess flour that falls into the bowl right back into the rest of the coarse semolina you'll be using for the remaining batches.

Spread a clean tablecloth or sheet (or several flour-sack towels) over your work surface. Hold the colander (or the steamer basket of your couscoussier) over the cloth, and pour the couscous from the

tamis into the colander. Then swirl the colander with one hand and use the other hand to gently toss and stir the couscous so that it falls through the holes. (Now you can see why that 3⁄32-inch measurement is so important.) After a minute or so, most of the couscous will have sprinkled down onto the cloth. What's left in the colander are particles that are too big. Pour them back into the terra-cotta tray, roll them again to break them up, and pour them through the colander onto the cloth. Eventually everything should make it through the colander onto the cloth.

Repeat the entire process with the rest of the semolina, working in batches, until you've rolled all of the semolina into couscous.

The First Steaming

Now it's time to "parsteam" and dry the couscous. This will essentially turn it from tiny pellets of raw dough into a dried product that you can store almost indefinitely. My mom says that if you just dry it without first steaming it, it will mildew, and I believe her.

Fill the couscoussier pot about one-third full with water and bring it to a rolling boil (or, if using the clay steamer insert, fill the pot to about 4 inches below the bottom of the steamer). Put the couscous in the steamer basket, gently spreading it in an even layer without packing it down, and set the basket on top of the pot. Some recipes and some cooks will advise you to seal the place where the rim of the lower pot meets the bottom of the steamer with plastic wrap or cheesecloth soaked in a flour-and-water slurry. This is done in Morocco, where couscoussiers are often quite old and battered, or have terra-cotta steamer baskets, and a lot of steam can escape from the crack between the top and the bottom. But with a relatively new, not banged-up couscoussier, I find that this sealing step is unnecessary.

Steam the couscous, uncovered, over the boiling

water for 5 to 8 minutes, or until the couscous no longer feels hard when touched. Let me just say right here that couscous is *always* steamed uncovered. The lid that came with your couscoussier is for other purposes (like steaming vegetables or lamb, or if you're just using the pot part to make a stew and you want to cover it).

Pour the couscous out into the terra-cotta tray. It will look stuck together. Don't be alarmed. When it's cool enough to handle, rub it gently between your fingers and upper palms and you'll see that it separates easily. Break up any large lumps, then roll it with your fingers as you did before. Pour the couscous in a few batches through the colander (or the couscoussier's steamer basket) onto the cloth. If any particles are too large to fall through the holes, put them back in the terra-cotta tray and re-roll them to break them up. When you've finished straining all of the couscous, use your fingers to spread it out in a thin layer over the surface of the cloth. You should see plenty of cloth showing through.

Congratulations! You are now looking at your first batch of hand-rolled couscous. Take a moment to admire the uniform shape and size of the particles. You did that. You started with grain, and you turned it into couscous, just like millions of North Africans before you. And you didn't even have to sit on the floor. But, now that you've done it, doesn't the whole floor thing make sense? Can you see how cradling the tray between your legs with the far side on the ground and the near side tilted slightly upward toward you would give you the perfect angle for the two-handed rolling technique? And can't you picture a bedsheet or two, spread across a tiled kitchen floor, covered with an enormous batch of couscous left out to dry?

Good, because that's your next step. Let the couscous rest undisturbed overnight (in a dry area, with the windows closed if it's foggy, rainy, or humid) and get some well-deserved rest yourself.

And Now, the Cooking

So, you now have about 4½ cups of dried couscous. Three cups will be plenty to serve 6 people—the simple rule is, the dry amount you start with will double in volume when you steam it. Keep the additional for another smaller gathering. It can be stored in an airtight container at room temperature almost indefinitely.

And now we can proceed with the basic cooking method. (Note that if you buy couscous [not the instant kind], you should follow these same directions.)

If you're not having 6 people for dinner, I encourage you to make the 3-cup batch anyway, because any leftover steamed couscous can be refrigerated for up to 4 days. Reheat it by steaming it over water in the couscoussier or, even easier, by drizzling it with a few tablespoons of water or stock and zapping it in the microwave in a covered dish for 30-second intervals, stirring after each one, until the couscous is steamy and fluffy.

I pay a lot of attention to the steaming liquid that goes in the bottom of the couscoussier, always using onions, carrots, and celery at a minimum, as in this recipe. I often add meat or bones along with the vegetables, flavoring both the couscous and the broth that develops. If I'm serving the couscous with chicken or lamb (both of which I always cook separately), I add chicken or lamb bones. And if I want a vegetarian dish, I substitute water for the chicken stock called for in this recipe.

The key to great couscous is cooking it gradually, so that all the starch doesn't come out of the grains at once. That's why it's steamed and cooled repeatedly. It's important that it cool down very quickly between steamings, because if it sits around too long under its own weight and steam, it will clump up—so be sure to use your terra-cotta tray or a really big bowl to spread out the grains between steamings.

CLASSIC STEAMED COUSCOUS

2½ cups (586 grams) Chicken Stock (page 365)

2 tablespoons (27 grams) extra virgin olive oil

⅛ teaspoon (0.1 gram) saffron threads

2 teaspoons (6 grams) kosher salt

1 medium onion, cut into large pieces

2 large carrots, peeled and cut into large pieces

1 celery rib, cut into large pieces

12 flat-leaf parsley sprigs

3 cups (490 grams) couscous, hand-rolled
  (see page 56) or store-bought (not instant)

Combine 2 cups (469 grams) of the chicken stock, the olive oil, saffron, and salt in a medium pot. Bring to a simmer over medium heat for 5 minutes, stirring to dissolve the salt. Remove from the heat and let sit at room temperature for 30 minutes to infuse with the flavor of the saffron.

Fill the bottom of a couscoussier half-full with water. Add the onion, carrots, celery, and parsley and bring to a simmer.

Put the couscous in the terra-cotta tray or a very large bowl, pour the infused stock over it (if you like, strain the liquid so you won't have pieces of saffron in your couscous), and let the couscous absorb the liquid, stirring occasionally, for about 15 minutes.

Scoop up some of the couscous and rub it with your fingers to separate any lumps, letting it pour back onto the tray. Keep scooping and rubbing in this way until there are no lumps. Repeatedly separating the couscous into individual grains is an important part of the process, so be diligent and unhurried about this.

Meanwhile, increase the heat under the couscoussier to bring the water to a gentle boil; add more water if needed to maintain the level.

TO STEAM THE COUSCOUS: Put the couscous in the steamer basket set over a plate, to catch any grains that might come through (put them back in the basket). Run your fingers lightly over the top to make sure the couscous is evenly distributed, and set it over the gently boiling water. If necessary, carefully wrap a large piece of plastic wrap around the rim of the bottom pot to keep the steam from escaping. Once you see steam coming from the top of the couscous, steam for 30 minutes. (Remember, no lid or covering of any kind goes over the couscous, and don't be tempted to stir it.)

Carefully remove the plastic wrap, if you used it, and then the steamer basket. When you do this, always pull the basket toward you so you don't get burned by the escaping steam. Spread the couscous in the terra-cotta tray or bowl and let it sit until cool enough to handle.

Meanwhile, add enough water to the bottom of the couscoussier to bring its level back to the halfway point. Return to a boil. Clean and dry the steamer basket, discarding any couscous that stuck to it.

Run the couscous through your fingers as you did before to separate all the grains. If you come across any lumps that refuse to separate, discard them. When the couscous is at room temperature, you can begin the second steaming. Return the couscous to the steamer basket, add the plastic wrap if needed, and steam for 15 to 30 minutes. The time will depend on how evenly the couscous is steaming. The couscous will take on a sweaty appearance and will feel tender.

Spread the couscous out in the tray or bowl as you did before and let cool. The couscous can be held at room temperature for several hours before the final steaming.

Put the remaining ½ cup (117 grams) chicken stock in a spray bottle or in a bowl.

If you have let the couscous sit for a few hours and it is no longer warm, add water to the couscoussier to return it to the original level and bring the liquid to a gentle boil. Put the couscous into the

steamer and steam it until it is warm. Then transfer to the terra-cotta tray or bowl and run it through your fingers to separate the grains.

TO FINISH THE COUSCOUS: You now have warm, almost finished couscous that still needs one last round of steaming. Return the couscous to the basket, set it over the bottom pot, and bring the liquid to a gentle boil. Immediately begin to add the remaining stock, spraying the couscous with 15 to 20 sprays from the spray bottle or drizzling about 2 tablespoons (29 grams) of it over the grains. Continue to add the stock in the same way and stir occasionally for 15 minutes. (By now, the couscous has released most of its starch, and so, for this steaming, and this one only, stirring is not only okay, it's necessary to fluff the couscous.)

Pour the couscous into the tray or bowl. It should have doubled in size to about 6 cups (870 grams) during the steaming process. (Discard the steaming liquid and vegetables.)

SERVES 6

THREE SIMPLE FINISHES

If you want to serve some or all of the couscous right away as a side dish, here are three simple ways to finish it. For all three versions, have ½ cup (117 grams) Chicken Stock (page 365) in a spray bottle or warmed in a small saucepan to add as needed when fluffing the steamed couscous.

BUTTER AND PARSLEY

Fluff the steamed couscous, adding stock as needed. Stir in 2 tablespoons (1 ounce/28 grams) room-temperature unsalted butter. (A teaspoon of butter per cup of couscous is my standard proportion.) Season to taste with kosher salt, and fold in 6 tablespoons (25 grams) chopped flat-leaf parsley.

GARLIC BUTTER

3 tablespoons (72 grams) Clarified Butter (page 375)
3 garlic cloves, crushed
3 tablespoons (13 grams) finely chopped flat-leaf
    parsley
Kosher salt

Combine the clarified butter and garlic in a small saucepan and heat the butter to just below a simmer, swirling the pan as the butter melts. Remove from the heat and set the pan in a warm spot for at least 30 minutes to allow the garlic to infuse the butter.

Fluff the couscous, adding stock as needed. Put them in a large frying pan. Remove the garlic cloves from the butter (discard them) and heat the butter until warm. Drizzle about half of the butter over the couscous, then add more to taste, and heat over medium heat until hot. Stir in the parsley and season to taste with salt.

BROWN BUTTER

This version calls for a lot more butter than the previous two, because it's really about the rich brown butter flavor, and I love it. But feel free to use less if you like.

Fluff the steamed couscous, adding stock as needed. Melt 6 tablespoons (85 grams) unsalted butter in a small frying pan over medium heat. Continue to heat until it is a rich nutty brown color. Add the butter to taste to the couscous and season with kosher salt.

ONE SIMPLE GARNISH
FRIED CHICKPEAS

Spicy fried chickpeas or small beans (like navy beans, cranberry beans, or cannellini) are a nice garnish for topping couscous. Use the method for making the fried beans coated with *harissa* powder in the Vegetable Stew on page 286.

E Pluribus Couscous

What couscous is really about is, in a weird way, individuality. That mound of fluffy perfection is very much the sum of its particles—and of all the techniques that go into keeping each individual grain uniform and separate. I love that idea, because it appeals to me to think of couscous not as an "it," but as a galaxy of many planets. All the rolling, sizing, steaming, and drying followed by the steaming, cooling, steaming, cooling, and steaming might sound a little crazy, but the method is one of those universal truths you just can't mess with—and that's coming from a guy who loves to mess with stuff like this.

Of course, what you put on it or mix into it after it's cooked is a whole different story. If you're looking for inspiration, try the Couscous with Prunes and Toasted Almonds (page 305) and Couscous with Meyer Lemons and Parsley (page 305). Or steam a batch and top it with the Vegetable Tagine (page 98) or the Lamb Shank (page 257), the Beef Cheeks (page 274), the Short Rib *Tangia* (page 278), or the Braised Oxtail (page 282). But, most of all, treat it the way you would treat a cornerstone of any great cuisine. First learn to make it, and then you can make it your own.

the way to warqa

4

I had been building up this moment all week, and now, here we were, a couple of American friends and I, in my Aunt Samira's house in Marrakesh for an afternoon of cooking and shooting photos for this book. We were eager to start, but before we got down to work, there was a good hour of socializing over minted lemonade and pineapple parfaits.

As we were having tea and making a small dent in a large platter of almond cookies, a woman wearing a black overcoat, several sweaters (although it was a warm spring day), and a long black skirt, her hair wrapped in a white scarf, came in carrying a battered nonstick frying pan. She had a regal way about her, and the young girl who followed close behind her and looked like her handmaiden, weighed down as she was with several shopping bags, added to the effect.

She removed her overcoat and a few of her sweaters and gave them to the girl, who turned out to be her daughter, Fatima. She put on a chef's coat, tied a checked apron around her waist, and lowered herself with dignity onto a crate in the middle of the kitchen floor, her legs straddling a propane tank with a burner, which she lit.

A few days before, I had told Samira and her best friend, Souad, that we wanted to get some shots of them making *warqa,* the paper-thin sheets of dough used to make *Basteeya* (page 237), stuffed *brik* turnovers, fried *briwat* triangles filled with almonds, and other pastries. They stared at me incredulously.

"I can make any Moroccan specialty you like," said Souad with breezy confidence. "Anything," she said, raising an index finger, "except *warqa.*" Samira nodded gravely. "It's better to buy it."

That's pretty much the answer I always get when I ask Moroccan cooks about how they make *warqa.* It's kind of like asking a Chinese cook how they prepare their hand-pulled noodles, or a Mexican how they make their masa. They don't. They buy it.

But they don't buy it in a package. They get it freshly made. Which was why, the day before, we had made a pilgrimage to my personal mecca of *warqa,* a tiny stall in the medina of Marrakesh, to see how the pros do it. There, at the end of a narrow hallway, lit by a single bare lightbulb, the rock stars of *warqa,* two skinny young guys in scruffy T-shirts, turn out hundreds of sheets of the stuff every hour.

Now, here's the thing about *warqa*. Unlike phyllo or strudel dough, which is rolled and stretched, *warqa* is made by holding a blob of sticky flour-and-water dough in your hand and dabbing it onto a hot pan to leave a little film of dough on the surface. You slap, slap, slap the dough in a circular pattern until you've got a solid layer of overlapping dabs that covers the surface of the pan, and then you peel the whole thing off as a single translucent sheet.

The *warqa* rock stars are so good at this they don't even look at the griddle as they slap down the dough and then snap it back. And the whole time they're working, they're dancing and singing along to Berber music and eighties heavy metal blaring from a boom box, laughing, and shouting to friends and customers a stream of greetings along the lines of the Moroccan equivalent of, "Who's your daddy?" Watching them, you think, "This *has* to be easy. And fun."

I sat down on a second crate next to the woman in the chef's coat and introduced myself. She was Naima Raihane, the master chef of one of the city's leading culinary schools, and Samira had summoned her for our *warqa* demo. Fatima brought her some flour, water, oil, and salt, which she mixed in a small plastic bowl, using the fingers of her right hand to whisk everything together.

Soon it was a gummy mass, which she tested by stretching and snapping it in and out of the bowl. She heated her frying pan over the propane burner and, after a moment, began to dab on the dough in a circular pattern. I gave my travel companions, who were busy videotaping and shooting stills, a smile and knowing wink of satisfaction. This was what it took. No fancy equipment, no measuring, just the hands of a master craftswoman.

And then it all went south. By the time Naima got to the outer circle of dabs, the ones in the center had cooked through and started to detach. She lifted the edge of the sheet and it tore. She peeled it off and threw it into a bucket behind her, but the edge stayed stuck in the pan, so she patiently scrubbed the shards off with a rag, set the pan back on the burner, lowered the heat, and tried again. This time it looked better. But it wasn't. The sheet fell apart and now the center was stuck to the pan. She tried three more times, adding a bit of water to the dough, which only made it less cooperative.

"It's not *'warqin,'*" whispered my friend from behind his video camera.

Naima finger-whisked some flour into the dough and started dabbing again. Even worse. Now the pan had a ring of baked-on dough all around the edges that couldn't really be wiped off. Fatima took it to the sink and scrubbed it clean.

I told Naima that I liked to heat the pan over steaming water. She frowned. "I know about that," she said, "but that makes it soft. I do it over an open flame so it's crisper when it's cooked."

"That is," I thought, "if you can get it out of the pan." But I bit my tongue.

Another round of dough slapping. Souad, watching from the sidelines, couldn't resist poking a finger into the pan, spreading a bit of dough to fill a hole. But nothing helped. The ripping and scraping continued for well over an hour, and we ended up with two small, somewhat misshapen sheets.

"It happens," Naima said, nodding without the slightest hint of embarrassment or frustration. "The weather. The burner."

She shrugged, smiled wearily, called for Fatima to get her coat, and left the building.

The next day, when I told my Uncle Latif about this, he clapped his hands and headed back to the kitchen of his house, where several cooks, including one from a well-known local restaurant, whose name also turned out to be Fatima, were preparing food for a big party that night. *Basteeya* was on the menu, and Latif thought we might get our *warqa* demo after all. But the *warqa* had already been bought for the occasion, so he asked Fatima if she could make some just to show us.

"Of course!" she said, smiling sweetly. Then her smile faded, and she added, "But I need my special pan."

Four hours later, having taken two buses to her town twenty kilometers from Marrakesh to get her well-worn *tobsil*—a round, low-sided *basteeya* pan, which is inverted to make *warqa* on the underside—Fatima (whom we were now referring to as Fatima 2.0) was back at Latif's house.

Just like Naima had done, she whipped up a sticky dough with her right hand, stretching and snapping it in and out of the bowl until it looked just right. She inverted her pan over a propane burner, and we gathered around.

The gentle slapping began. And then, so did the failing. Shards and flakes fluttering in the air; sheets of torn, ragged *warqa;* plenty of scrubbing and scraping; and, in the end, just a few usable pieces. And, once again, not the slightest sign of frustration or self-consciousness—just a serious, patient focus on the pan, the task, and the present moment, as if each new attempt was sure to turn out perfectly.

And this is what we're about to make in your kitchen!

But first, let me say that I didn't tell you that story to scare you or, in any way, to belittle the talents of Moroccan cooks. I didn't even tell it to you to make a point about *warqa* and how mysteriously temperamental it can be, though that's certainly true. I told it to you because it's an example of something bigger—a very Moroccan kind of culinary and, I think, also cultural fatalism.

There's a resigned quality about the place and the people that says, "This is how it is here. This is how we do things, how we have always done things. If, sometimes, my friend, it doesn't work, it's not for us to question."

I admire that quality. Really, I do. It allows you to let go of so much fear and second-guessing and simply release into an unending tradition that lifts you up and carries you right along. I admire it, but I've come to realize I don't share it. I've lived outside Morocco too long. I'm restless. I want to question everything, to understand it, to make it better, or at least to make it work consistently, even if where I end up is not "the way it's done." I want to get to the spirit of the thing, not just preserve the letter of it.

So, *warqa*.

When I opened my first restaurant, I tried making my own *warqa* and had pretty much the same results as those Moroccan women. Sometimes it *"warqed,"* but most of the time, it didn't. I was always curious about finding a way to make it more foolproof, but I just didn't have the time. We made our *basteeya* with commercial phyllo, as we still do.

Years later, after we'd opened Aziza, Jacques Pépin came in one night for dinner. Eventually we got to talking about *warqa,* and Jacques told me he had come upon a new way to make it, which involved thinning the dough to the consistency of a soupy batter and brushing it onto the pan. He wouldn't say where he'd gotten the idea. He just grinned and told me to try it, which, naturally, I did the following morning.

I was stunned the first time I used this technique, and I think you will be too. The batter seems to form too thin a layer in the pan to actually cohere into a sheet, but it does. Wanting the strongest, most elastic batter, I tried high-gluten flour, which helped. And for a few years, I made *warqa* using this method for special sweet and savory pastries we'd have on the menu from time to time.

But there was still one problem. We'd always have to keep a spoon in the batter, because it was so watery, it would separate quickly. So you'd stir, brush, make a sheet, and have to stir again before starting the next one. Then I hit on the idea of adding a stabilizer, and since I had some xanthan gum in the kitchen, I tried that. It worked perfectly, creating a light, creamy batter that never separates and has a smooth consistency that's more like paint than soup.

Now, don't be scared. Xanthan gum isn't as strange as it sounds. It's easy to find in natural foods groceries and online, and it's really not so different from using other kinds of thickeners you might be more familiar with, like cornstarch. And I've found that it also has the advantage of eliminating the need for high-gluten flour, allowing you to use everyday all-purpose flour, which is a nice trade-off.

HANDMADE *WARQA*

The Gear

- A 12-inch nonstick frying pan that is new or in very good condition. A pan with even a few dings or scratches in the surface will cause the paper-thin *warqa* to stick and tear.
- A large stockpot, ideally just big enough that your frying pan will sit snugly inside its rim.
- A 2- to 2½-inch-wide natural-bristle paintbrush (not silicone), ideally the kind with bristles cut at an angle. These are not cheap, but the better the quality, the more easily and evenly the batter will spread. Don't even think about using one of those two-dollar disposable brushes. It will tear the dough.
- Three clean kitchen towels: two for stacking the *warqa* and a third for cleaning the pan.
- A laser thermometer (the kind that works like a gun, reading the temperature of whatever you're pointing it at). This is not absolutely necessary, but it's helpful for regulating the heat of the pan.
- A can of neutral nonstick cooking spray. This keeps the stacked *warqa* sheets from sticking together and also softens them to the perfect degree of pliability.

The Batter

I've tweaked this recipe for years, and I'm now very happy with it. The vinegar improves the elasticity of the batter and gives it a little extra flavor, and the sugar balances that flavor while also helping with browning. You'll have about 3 cups (750 grams) batter.

2 cups (262 grams) all-purpose flour
1½ teaspoons (4.5 grams) kosher salt
1 teaspoon (4.2 grams) granulated sugar
2 cups (465 grams) hot water
2 tablespoons (26.5 grams) extra virgin olive oil
2 teaspoons (9.6 grams) champagne vinegar
¼ teaspoon (0.9 grams) xanthan gum

Put the flour, salt, and sugar in a blender and blend on the lowest speed to combine and "sift" the mixture. With the blender running on low, add half of the water. Once it's incorporated, increase the speed to medium and add the rest of the water. Increase the speed to medium-high, add the oil and vinegar, and blend until you have a smooth batter.

If you're the curious experimenter type like me, you'll love what happens next. Add the xanthan gum and blend on high for a few seconds to thoroughly combine. You'll be amazed at how that tiny amount immediately alters the look and texture of the batter.

(If you don't have a blender, you can whisk the flour, salt, and sugar together in a large bowl. Then, while whisking constantly, add half of the water. Once it's incorporated, whisk in the remaining water, and then the oil and vinegar. Once the batter is smooth, whisk in the xanthan gum.)

I strain the batter through a fine-mesh strainer at this point to remove any lumps, but that's not absolutely necessary. You can use the batter right away, but it's better to let it rest in the refrigerator for 4 to 8 hours. That will make it more elastic, giving you *warqa* with softer, less brittle edges.

THE SETUP: Fill your large pot about one-third full with water, and bring it to a simmer. Set the frying pan firmly on top of the pot. Have your can of the nonstick spray close at hand, and lay one of the towels on your work surface. Have a second towel ready to cover the *warqa*. Set the third towel near the stove.

If you have a laser thermometer, check the temperature of the surface of the frying pan. You're looking for 200° to 210°F; adjust the heat as necessary. If you don't have a thermometer, start with the water

at a low simmer, and then adjust if necessary once you've made a few sheets.

Give the batter a stir, and transfer it to a tall container that will be easy to dip the brush into. Dip in the brush, just as if you were going to paint a wall, and then, holding the handle of the frying pan with your other hand, paint a sweep of batter about one-third of the way around the outer edge of the frying pan (without going up the sides). It helps to keep the brush at a low angle, almost parallel to the frying pan, as you do this. If the brush is curved from use, brush with the curve rather than against it, which could tear the very delicate batter as it cooks. You're going for as even a thickness as you can get. If the part of your sweep where you started painting looks a bit thicker, go back over it with the brush to smooth it out. Immediately paint on two more sweeps in the

same way, overlapping them slightly, to cover the entire perimeter of the frying pan, and then brush a sweep of batter over the center. Repeat with another round of sweeps, starting in a different place, to create a second layer of even thickness in the same way. If you see any holes in the first layer, fill them in with this second round of brushstrokes. The entire process should take only about 30 seconds.

If the temperature is right, the batter will begin to cook on contact with the frying pan, going quickly from translucent to white. If the pan is too hot, it will start to flake off right away. To lower the temperature, lift the frying pan off the pot for a few seconds to release some of the steam from the pot (do this carefully, tilting the pan toward you to avoid getting burned by the steam), then replace the pan. If that doesn't work, lower the heat of the burner.

harissa.
seasoned
heat.

You know Sriracha, right? That thick, brick-red Thai hot pepper sauce that comes in a clear plastic squeeze bottle with a rooster on it. I always have it in my fridge at home, and I squeeze it onto just about everything. And I suppose in a way, that's a habit that comes from growing up in Morocco, where *harissa* is our version of the same kind of condiment. It hits you with a similar combination of heat, garlic, and acid, plus a little extra herb-and-spice action in the background.

Actually, *harissa* isn't originally Moroccan. It's from Tunisia, where the food tends to be much hotter, in the chile-heat sense of the word. In Morocco, we're more interested in spices than spicy heat, and we love the interplay of those spices with sweet elements. It's a delicate balance, and too much heat would risk throwing it off. So chiles are used in moderation, sauces are never blazingly hot, and people prefer to add heat to taste at the table, which is where *harissa* comes in.

Like *warqa,* it's one of those things almost no one makes at home, except maybe in the kitchens of very wealthy people who have a staff of cooks—less because it's hard to make than because most people simply think of it as the iconic store-bought version, the way Americans think of a condiment like ketchup.

Harissa is typically sold in shops that specialize in olives and preserved lemons, where you'll find it mounded on huge platters, to be scooped up and plopped into a plastic bag for you to take home. And even those vendors don't make it. If you buy or eat *harissa* in Morocco, 99 percent of the time, it's mass-produced, and I've often imagined a single giant factory churning out all the *harissa* for the entire country, because everywhere I've had it, it tastes the same.

In homes, *harissa* gets set out in a little bowl, sometimes flavored with a bit of cumin or coriander, as a condiment for couscous, soups, and stews. It's also a fixture on the countertops of market stalls that sell snack foods like brochettes and sandwiches. But no matter where you find it, it's seldom used in cooking, and most likely to be a finishing touch.

I'm going to tell you about two ways to make your own. Both

will end up with the same result: a fiery but very flavorful paste that you can keep in a jar in the refrigerator to spice up just about anything you can think of. I encourage you to try making both. And after that, I also want to turn you on to my powdered version, which is a lot of fun to have around.

I have yet to taste a commercial *harissa* that I like. The stuff in squeeze tubes is particularly disappointing. I really recommend that you make your own, but if you want a store-bought alternative that comes reasonably close, buy Chinese chile-garlic paste and stir in some finely chopped preserved lemon rind.

SIMPLE IDEAS
WITH *HARISSA*

- Like Tabasco, *harissa* is a natural with eggs. Spoon it over fried or poached eggs, mix it into scrambled eggs, or use it in an omelet filling.
- Use as a sandwich spread, or, for a more mellow effect, mix *harissa* with a bit of homemade or prepared mayonnaise.
- Add a little *harissa* to couscous or rice during cooking, or serve it as a condiment with couscous or rice.
- Rub on meat, poultry, or seafood and marinate for 30 minutes, or up to overnight, before grilling, broiling, or roasting.
- Add to soups as a finishing dollop, straight or blended with crème fraîche or yogurt.
- Add to any pasta sauce that might welcome chile flakes.
- Toss olives with a bit of *harissa* and some chopped cilantro just before serving.

D'JEMAA EL F'NA POTATO SANDWICH

Watching the guys make this sandwich at the night market in D'jemaa el F'na, the vast main plaza of Marrakesh, is almost as much fun as eating it. The process is a steamy blur of potato and egg peeling, bread splitting, mashing, and splashing that takes three men just a few seconds to complete. And the result is a soulful snack on a par with any of the world's great sandwiches.

Split, hollow out, and butter a soft roll (ideally, White Bread with Sesame Seeds [page 197], which is exactly what the D'jemaa el F'na vendors use). Peel 2 or 3 small (28 grams each) just-boiled Yukon Gold potatoes and a hard-boiled egg, preferably still warm. Smear a wedge (30 grams) of Laughing Cow cheese or Philadelphia-style cream cheese inside the roll,

then stuff it with the potatoes and egg. Sprinkle with a bit of white vinegar and add a generous dollop of *harissa*. Hold the roll in one hand and, with the other hand, use a table knife or sandwich spreader to mash and chop the potato and egg into chunks and mix everything together.

HARISSA BLOODY MARY

Here's another easy way to experience how *harissa* can take something familiar to a whole new place. It's one of the most popular cocktails at our restaurant.

½ cup (75 grams) halved cherry tomatoes, plus 3 for garnish
2 ounces (56 grams) vodka, preferably Hangar One
1 tablespoon (15 grams) fresh lime juice
½ cup (138 grams) spicy organic tomato juice (we use R. W. Knudsen)
1 teaspoon (4.6 grams) Quick *Harissa* (page 82)
1 teaspoon (5 grams) balsamic vinegar
Crunchy sea salt and ground black pepper

Put the tomatoes in a cocktail shaker and crush them with a muddler or the bottom of a wooden spoon. Add the vodka, lime juice, tomato juice, and *harissa*.

Fill a 10-ounce rocks glass with ice, then add the ice to the shaker; add a few more ice cubes to the rocks glass. Cover the shaker with the lid and shake until the Bloody Mary is chilled. Pour through a strainer into the rocks glass, drizzle the vinegar on top, and season with a pinch each of salt and pepper. Garnish with the cherry tomatoes.

MAKES 1 COCKTAIL

HARISSA POWDER

I came up with this dry spice blend to use whenever I want the flavor of *harissa* without its moisture. The Fried Chickpeas on page 64 are a perfect example—*harissa* would make them gloppy, but *harissa* powder and a squeeze of lemon juice coats them perfectly.

Harissa powder has the added advantage that you can store it for up to 6 months, while *harissa* lasts only about half as long. And it's as simple as stirring together a bunch of dry ingredients in a bowl. The citric acid is a stand-in for lemon juice and/or vinegar, and it's important in the overall flavor balance. Look for it in specialty grocery and natural foods stores, or order it online.

½ cup plus 1 tablespoon (64.8 grams) Aleppo pepper
1½ tablespoons (15.4 grams) granulated garlic
1½ teaspoons (7 grams) citric acid
2¼ teaspoons (5.9 grams) pimentón (Spanish paprika)
2¼ teaspoons (5.7 grams) ground cumin
1½ teaspoons (4.8 grams) roasted garlic powder
1½ teaspoons (4.5 grams) kosher salt
1½ teaspoons (4 grams) sweet paprika
1½ teaspoons (2.7 grams) ground caraway
⅛ teaspoon (0.3 gram) cayenne

Combine all the ingredients in a bowl. Transfer to a tightly sealed glass jar and store at room temperature for up to 6 months.

MAKES ABOUT 1 CUP (110 GRAMS)

SIMPLE IDEAS
WITH *HARISSA* POWDER

- Add a pinch to vinaigrettes, dressings, and sauces.
- Use to season steaks, chops, burgers, chicken, prawns or shrimp, fish, or vegetables before grilling.
- *Harissa Beurre Blanc:* Sweat minced shallots in butter, add wine or sherry, reduce it, and then, off the heat, whisk in butter and harissa powder.
- Toss whole blanched almonds with olive oil, salt, and *harissa* powder and toast in the oven. (And check out the Chile and Lime Almonds on page 104.)
- Add to vegetables at the start of sautéing.
- Whip softened butter with *harissa* powder and chopped cilantro to make a compound butter for steak, fish, or vegetables. Form into a log, wrap in plastic, and keep refrigerated.
- Toss with lightly buttered popcorn.
- Add to the filling for deviled eggs and sprinkle a bit on top as a garnish.
- Add a pinch to lightly sweetened whipped cream or crème fraîche to make a great garnish for chocolate cake.

Heat That's Complete

I bet you've got at least one bottle of hot sauce in your fridge right now. Maybe, like me, you keep a bottle of Sriracha on the top shelf of the door, where you always know just where to find it. Or maybe it's a jar of *sambal oelek* or Chinese chile-garlic paste. If you love those spicy condiments, you've got to try *harissa*. And once you have, every time you want a little heat, you'll be tempted to reach for it, because it's got so much more going on than just Scoville units. It's seasoned heat with serious possibilities.

the *charmoula* effect

6

Is it me, or is *charmoula* suddenly everywhere? I see it discussed on blogs and in magazines, I come across it in cookbooks, and it seems to be showing up on more and more restaurant menus all the time. Good. To me, it all points to one simple idea. People are discovering—and craving—North African flavor combinations. And *charmoula* is exactly that, a seriously craveable flavor combination. It's variously referred to as a sauce, a marinade, a dip, or a condiment. But I encourage you to look past those labels and see it, like *ras el hanout* and preserved lemons, as a defining Moroccan flavor that's more than the sum of its parts.

One key to understanding this is the derivation of the word. It comes from the Latin term for brine, *sal muria* (*sal* meaning salt, and *muria* meaning pickle or brine—as in muriatic acid), which shows up in Spanish as *salmuera* and French as *saumure*. This points to the origins of *charmoula* as a way not only to flavor foods, but also to preserve them. *Charmoula* gets its pickley-spicy qualities from a combination of lemon, garlic, cumin, paprika, oil, and plenty of salt. Depending on the preparation, tomato, hot peppers, and vinegar might also find their way into the mix. The result may be raw, slightly cooked, or simmered for hours. But no matter how you put those flavors together, a Moroccan will take one bite—even one whiff—and say, "*Charmoula*."

There's a famous type of stew called *twejeen m'charml*— literally, a "charmoulized" tagine. I think that "verbalization" of *charmoula* says a lot about what *charmoula* means to Moroccan cooks. It's less something you make, and more something you do. If you combine those elemental ingredients, whether fresh or simmered down, spicy or mild, you've "charmoulized" a dish.

Take the example of a classic Moroccan relish that's served as a snack in the night markets and as one of the seven salads that start a meal. It's tomato and roasted red peppers briefly simmered with cumin, garlic, preserved lemon, cilantro, parsley, and oil— essentially *charmoula* in salad form. Cook it longer, and it becomes a stewing sauce for vegetables or meat. Add more water, and it's the simmering liquid for slow-cooked beans. You're getting the idea. *Charmoula* is more about the end than the means.

Red or Green

Now, in Morocco, when you say *charmoula,* people do tend to first think of a red sauce for fish, like Roasted Whole Black Bass (page 219). But look at the Vegetable Stew on page 286. Its seasoning includes cumin, paprika, onion, tomato, cilantro, parsley, and preserved lemons—and that makes it a melody composed in the key of *charmoula.*

Less common, but no less tasty, is green *charmoula,* which generally omits the paprika and tomatoes, ups some of the herbal elements, and adds brinier ingredients like capers and anchovies. Think of it like an Italian *salsa verde* with an overlay of Moroccan spice.

Since in my cooking I'm less concerned with traditional precedents and more interested in what makes sense on the plate, when I think about taking a dish down a *charmoula* path, I start with the main ingredient and work my way out from there. For a lighter, less-cooked dish, like grilled fish, or a salad, I'll lean toward green *charmoula.* For a heartier, slow-cooked preparation, I'll go with the darker colors and flavors of red. But I also love green *charmoula,* thinned to the consistency of a vinaigrette, as a very "contrasty" finishing sauce for slowly braised short ribs, and I often use a paste-thick red *charmoula* as a rub for quickly grilled meats, like lamb chops.

Rather than burdening you with rules, I want you to get your head around a basic principle about ingredients, flavor, and time that applies here, as it does throughout Moroccan cooking. The more substantial your main ingredient, and the longer you plan to cook it, the more assertively you can spice and season it with ingredients that need cooking, like onions, garlic, and tomatoes. The more delicate the main ingredient, and the more the preparation tends toward fresh and raw, the lighter your hand should be, and the more you can draw on ingredients that don't need cooking, like capers, fresh herbs, and anchovies.

In that spirit, here are two very simple recipes for red and green *charmoula.* Neither takes very long to make, and that's the beauty of any kind of *charmoula:* it comes from a rustic way of cooking that doesn't draw on stocks, bases, or reductions to achieve its complex flavor. So, make up a batch of each, and then check out the ideas following the recipes that will let you taste how they work with different foods and cooking techniques.

RED *CHARMOULA*

1 tablespoon (9 grams) kosher salt

1 tablespoon (8 grams) sweet paprika

1 teaspoon (2.6 grams) smoked paprika

1 teaspoon (2.6 grams) ground cumin

⅛ teaspoon (0.2 gram) ground black pepper

1 tablespoon (9.2 grams) finely chopped garlic

2 tablespoons (8.4 grams) coarsely chopped flat-leaf parsley

2 tablespooons (8.4 grams) coarsely chopped cilantro

1 tablespoon (12 grams) chopped preserved lemon rind (see page 45)

1 tablespoon (15 grams) fresh lemon juice

1 cup (212 grams) extra virgin olive oil

1 cup (234 grams) water

½ cup (142 grams) tomato puree, preferably San Marzano

Put the salt and all of the spices in a medium bowl and whisk together to combine. Add the garlic, parsley, cilantro, lemon rind, and lemon juice, then whisk in the oil, water, and tomato puree.

Store in an airtight container in the refrigerator for up to 2 weeks.

MAKES ABOUT 2¾ CUPS (643 GRAMS)

Red *Charmoula* at Work

If you want to experience *charmoula* at its most traditionally Moroccan, go directly to page 219 and use your red *charmoula* to make the whole fish recipe you'll find there.

If you'd like to try something a little less involved, here's my recipe for unbelievably good chicken wings with a sweet red *charmoula* sauce—kind of a Moroccan take on the whole Buffalo wings thing.

RED *CHARMOULA* CHICKEN WINGS

Cut the tips from 6 chicken wings (1¼ pounds/566 grams) and discard. Cut through the wing joint to separate each wing into two sections. Season with kosher salt and let sit at room temperature while you prepare the sauce.

Combine 1 cup (270 grams) *charmoula* with 2 tablespoons (42 grams) honey or (40 grams) agave nectar in a medium saucepan, bring to a simmer over medium heat, and cook, stirring often and adjusting the heat as needed so it doesn't scorch, for about 20 minutes, until reduced to ⅔ cup (155 grams). Set aside in a warm spot.

Fill a small stockpot fitted with a thermometer about one-third full with grapeseed or canola oil; you will need about 4 cups (848 grams) oil. Heat to 360°F, and fry the wings in batches, so as not to overcrowd the pot, turning occasionally, for 4 to 5 minutes, or until golden on all sides and cooked through. Drain the wings briefly on paper towels. Put the wings in a large bowl, add the *charmoula,* and toss to coat. Sprinkle with minced fresh parsley.

Green *Charmoula* Trout Sandwich

SIMPLE IDEAS
WITH RED *CHARMOULA*

- Rub a frenched rack of lamb or lamb chops with red *charmoula* and marinate in the refrigerator overnight. Grill, broil, or pansear.
- Rub the inside of a butterflied leg of lamb with red *charmoula,* roll and tie the leg, rub more *charmoula* on the outside, and refrigerate overnight. Roast in the oven or on a covered grill over indirect heat.
- Sauté prawns or shrimp in olive oil, adding some red *charmoula* during the last few minutes. Serve over creamy mashed potatoes. You can also add or substitute chunks of firm-fleshed fish and/or scallops or squid.
- Marinate chicken in red *charmoula* before grilling, then brush additional *charmoula* on the chicken during the last 5 minutes of grilling, as you would a barbecue sauce.
- Brush red *charmoula* on vegetables, such as corn on the cob or sliced eggplant or squash, before grilling.
- Brown chicken legs or lamb shanks in a Dutch oven, then braise them in red *charmoula,* preserved lemons, and chicken stock. Stir in butter just before serving.
- Rub a chicken inside and out with red (or green) *charmoula* and let it sit for 30 minutes, or up to 8 hours in the refrigerator, before roasting it.

GREEN *CHARMOULA*

If you own a mortar and pestle, this is the time to bust it out. Like muddling a cocktail, the pestle will bruise the ingredients, giving you more flavor and a chunky texture that just feels right when you eat it. If not, you can use a food processor, but be sure to pulse the motor. You're going for a texture that's more ground than pureed here.

12 (48 grams) anchovy fillets, preferably salt-packed, rinsed and patted dry
5 (12.5 grams) garlic cloves
2 tablespoons (35 grams) capers, drained
Kosher salt
1 tablespoon (12 grams) diced preserved lemon rind (see page 45)
½ teaspoon (1.3 grams) ground cumin
½ teaspoon (0.9 gram) ground black pepper
¼ teaspoon (0.6 gram) cayenne
1 teaspoon (5 grams) fresh lemon juice
½ cup (33.6 grams) chopped cilantro
½ cup (33.6 grams) chopped flat-leaf parsley
1½ cups (318 grams) extra virgin olive oil

Put the anchovies, garlic, capers, and a pinch of salt (which will act as an abrasive to break down the other ingredients) in a mortar or food processor and mash or pulse to form a paste. Add the lemon rind (if you are using a food processor, reserve the rind to stir in later), cumin, pepper, cayenne, and lemon juice and mash or pulse to form a paste. Scrape down the sides of the bowl as needed. Add the cilantro and parsley and mash or pulse until well combined. Transfer to a bowl and stir in the olive oil (fold in the lemon rind if you used a food processor).

Store in an airtight container in the refrigerator for up to 2 weeks. The oil will separate; before using the *charmoula,* bring it to room temperature and stir.

MAKES ABOUT 2 CUPS (455 GRAMS)

The Charms of Green *Charmoula*

When I taste the green stuff, the first thing that comes to mind is fish, or, more precisely, fresh sardines. Since those aren't always easy to come by, here's what I would do with them, but modified to work with trout fillets.

GREEN *CHARMOULA* TROUT "SANDWICHES"

You'll need 2 fresh trout fillets, any bones removed but skin left on. Lay 1 fillet on a work surface, flesh side up, and spoon green *charmoula* generously on the flesh. Top with the second fillet, flesh side down. Heat a generous film of grapeseed or canola oil in a small frying pan over medium-high heat. Place the "sandwich" in the frying pan and cook, basting frequently with the pan juices, until the skin of the first side is crisp and golden brown, about 1½ minutes. Flip to the second side and cook, basting the fish, for about 3 minutes, until the trout is just cooked through. Drain briefly on paper towels. Serve with a lemon half (grilled, if you like) and extra green *charmoula* on the side.

SIMPLE IDEAS
WITH GREEN *CHARMOULA*

- Spoon green *charmoula* over grilled chicken or fish fillets, such as black cod or salmon.
- Sauté prawns or shrimp in olive oil with chunks of young zucchini or other summer squash. Add toasted blanched almonds and green *charmoula* during the last minute or two of cooking.
- Stir a bit of green *charmoula* into good olive-oil-packed tuna. Spread on a slice of baguette and top with sliced hard-boiled eggs and olives. Or serve over greens as a salad.

- Grill double-cut lamb chops, split the chops, and arrange on a platter, grilled side down. Drizzle green *charmoula* over the chops. Or grill a lamb loin or a steak (such as rib eye or strip), slice it, and drizzle green *charmoula* over the slices, as you would *chimichurri*.

- Make a *charmoula* pesto by pulverizing toasted pine nuts or walnuts in a mortar or food processor and then folding them into the *charmoula*. Use as a pasta sauce or a drizzle for grilled or sautéed fish, chicken, or steak.

- Whisk together softened unsalted butter with green *charmoula* to make a compound butter for steak, lamb, or vegetables. Shape into a log, wrap in plastic wrap, and chill.

- Add more oil to green *charmoula* and use it as a vinaigrette; you may want to add a bit of white wine vinegar, to taste. This is particularly good with more flavorful greens like arugula or radicchio.

- Stir some green *charmoula* into store-bought or homemade mayo to make a sauce for seafood, or add a bit to mayonnaise-based dishes like egg salad and potato salad.

- Toss cracked green olives with green *charmoula*—a classic Moroccan way to flavor them.

- Mix equal parts green *charmoula* and finely chopped kalamata olives to make a *tapenade*. Serve with grilled fish or chicken, or spread on crostini.

The Flavor Factor

The red *charmoula* is rich and earthy, with an explosive flavor somewhere between an Italian *ragù* and a down-home barbecue sauce. The green, which shares many of the same base ingredients, is something else altogether—splashy and garlicky, with rich anchovy *umami* and that irresistible preserved lemon "mouthwateringness." And then that little bit of cayenne hits you with just enough heat to make it interesting without overpowering the other flavors.

Both *charmoulas* are raw, but the green one tastes finished, while the red one really does taste somewhat raw. You wouldn't want to eat a lot of it in this state.

Once you've made your first batches of red and green *charmoula,* you'll find all kinds of ways to use them. But, more important, making them will get you thinking about the way their ingredients come together to create something perfect and irresistibly direct. That's the *charmoula* effect, and once you get a feel for it, you'll be one giant step closer to understanding and appreciating the Moroccan flavor palette.

the ingenious tagine

A tagine is, of course, that famous Moroccan conical-lidded pot used to make braised dishes. But the word has come to mean any braised dish of the kind typically made in a tagine, whether it was actually cooked in one or not. Tagines are traditionally made of terra-cotta and were designed to be a kind of stovetop (or brazier-top) oven.

Their ingenuity is twofold. First, they're designed to circulate heat in a way that's not unlike what a convection oven does. The tapering lid forces hot air back down onto the food, so that when everything is mounded in the right way—the meat on the bottom, the vegetables over it, with the softest ones on top—everything cooks in the same amount of time. The meat gets the direct heat of the fire, while the vegetables above get cooked by indirect radiant heat.

Second, like any clay pot, a traditional unglazed terra-cotta tagine is porous, absorbing moisture, fat, and flavorings, all of which season it over time. If you heat water in a tagine that has been cooked in regularly for ten years, you'll get a lightly flavored consommé before you add any seasoning at all!

That's why my mom has always had six or seven tagines in her kitchen. She uses some for chicken, others for fish, lamb, or vegetables, knowing that each will give the right flavor to whatever she's designated it for. The newer ones are her backups, and the very old ones her prized possessions. One of my aunts might ask to borrow the twenty-year-old chicken tagine for a special occasion, but before my mom lets it out of her sight, she'll make her promise not to "ruin" it with supermarket chicken. In Morocco, when a woman gets married and the family really wants to show the love, they'll send her off with a set of seasoned tagines, not brand-new ones.

Terra-cotta tagines are as beautiful as they are functional. In Morocco, you can tell where they come from by their color. The redder ones are made of dark clay from the Ourika Valley, near Marrakesh. The lighter, more golden ones tend to be from up north.

Seasoning a Tagine

If you have an unglazed terra-cotta tagine, you'll need to season it to seal the cooking surface and keep the tagine from shattering when you cook in it. First, submerge the base and lid in room-temperature water and leave it to soak overnight. You'll see and hear bubbling as the clay drinks up the water.

Dry the tagine well with a towel and rub it inside and out with a neutral oil, like canola. Put the tagine in a 375°F oven for half an hour, then turn off the heat and leave the tagine in the oven overnight without opening the door. It's now seasoned, and using it at least every few months will keep it that way. If you don't cook in it for several months, you should reseason it in the same way. You can use it on the stovetop, with a heat diffuser over the burner, or in the oven at 250° to 325°F.

Tagine Alternatives

A good tagine made from anything other than unglazed terra-cotta will work well for braising. If you don't have one, you can use a small stockpot or Dutch oven. To approximate the effect of the cone-shaped lid, make a cone using a few layers of heavy-duty aluminum foil. Shape it so that it will fit inside the pot with its lid on, set it over the ingredients, and then cover the pot with the lid.

If your tagine is made of metal, enameled cast-iron, or glazed ceramic, there's no need to season it. But regardless of what it's made from, a heat diffuser is always a good idea when you're using it on the stovetop for slow braising.

Now that you're ready for a trial run, here are a few ideas to start with.

CURRIED POTATOES

Toss 3 pounds (1.36 kilograms) waxy potatoes, peeled if you like, cut into 1-inch chunks, with 1 tablespoon (7.8 grams) Aziza Curry Blend (page 33) and 1 teaspoon (3 grams) kosher salt in the base of a tagine. Set the tagine on a heat diffuser, mound the potatoes to make a pyramid, and pour 1 cup (235 grams) water or Vegetable Stock (page 364) around the potatoes. Bring to a simmer over medium heat, cover the tagine with its lid, and bake in a 325°F oven for about 1 hour. Add salt to taste, drizzle with extra virgin olive oil, and sprinkle some chopped cilantro on top.

VEGETABLE TAGINE

This is as much a technique as it is a recipe—a simple method for cooking vegetables in red *charmoula* in a tagine. As long as you use a quantity that makes a cone-shaped pile that fills the tagine about halfway and doesn't touch the inner walls of the lid (so there's plenty of space for air to circulate), you can't really go wrong. This recipe, for 3½ pounds (1.58 kilograms) of vegetables, was tested in a tagine with a diameter of 11 inches.

You can make a combination as simple as carrots and peas, or as varied as the mixture suggested here. It's a great way to use a lot of vegetables—like the stuff in that weekly organic farm delivery box in your pantry, or the produce you purchased with a little too much enthusiasm at the farmers' market. I like to save a few of the more tender vegetables and add them raw, whole, sliced, or thinly shaved, on top of the finished tagine as a garnish.

2 recipes Red *Charmoula* (page 89), made using only
    1 cup (234 grams) water and ½ cup (106 grams) olive
    oil and adding ¼ teaspoon (0.2 gram) saffron
    threads and ⅛ teaspoon (0.3 gram) cayenne

vegetables

3½ pounds (1.58 kilograms; about 12 cups) trimmed
    vegetables, which may include:
Cipollini onions, about 1 inch in diameter
Yukon Gold potatoes, small potatoes (1½ inches) peeled
    and halved, larger potatoes cut into 1½-inch pieces
Thumbelina carrots, peeled and cut lengthwise in half
Baby carrots (4 inches long), unpeeled, or large
    carrots, peeled and cut into 1½-inch pieces
Cauliflower, cut into 1-inch florets
Baby turnips (about 1 inch in diameter), cut in half
    lengthwise, or larger turnips cut into wedges
Baby fennel (about 3 inches long), tough outer layer
    removed, or larger fennel bulbs, tough outer
    layers removed and cut into wedges
½ cup (90 grams) cooked chickpeas
    (see Cooking Beans, page 378; optional)
¼ cup (40 grams) raisins (optional)

Paper-thin slices (raw) of some of the vegetables used
    in the tagine, for garnish
Flat-leaf parsley leaves
4 quarters (154 grams) preserved lemon rind
    (see page 45), cut into 8 petals
Crunchy sea salt

Put the *charmoula* in a saucepan, bring to a simmer, and cook for 25 to 30 minutes, stirring and scraping the bottom often to prevent scorching, until it has reduced by one-quarter. Remove from the heat.

Place an oven rack in the bottom of the oven and remove the others. Preheat the oven to 325°F.

Layer the vegetables in the tagine, placing the larger ones toward the bottom, where there is more heat. Start with the larger cipollini onions and continue to layer the vegetables, adding the chickpeas and raisins toward the middle; as you layer, shape the vegetables into a mound, checking to be sure the lid fits securely without touching the vegetables. End with the smallest pieces of vegetables.

Pour the warm *charmoula* over the vegetables. Put the tagine on a heat diffuser over medium-high heat and bring it to a simmer. Place the tagine on a baking sheet, cover it with the lid, and put it in the oven for 1 hour, or until the vegetables are tender.

Garnish the tagine with the raw vegetable slices, parsley leaves, and preserved lemon, and return the lid to the tagine so you can unveil it at the table. Serve with crunchy sea salt.

SERVES 6

Fun Meets Function

The ingenuity of the tagine goes beyond the way it cooks food. It's a pretty amazing bit of theater too. Set it on the table with its dramatic lid in place. Give everyone a minute to admire its beauty, and then lift the lid. As the steam and the scent of spices billow up, you'll know just what I'm talking about.

bites to begin

Show up in a Moroccan home, whether you're invited or just dropping by, and someone's going to greet you with a big bowl of dates, figs, and raw almonds. That's just the way it is. I like to welcome people to my restaurant in the same spirit, so we've always got a few items like seasoned nuts or olives to nibble on while you're sipping cocktails, reading the menu, and waiting for that one chronically late friend to show up.

Along these lines, we also serve a little sampler of three or four contrasting spreads. They vary according to the season, and we put a lot of thought into making them unexpected and interesting. After all, they set the tone for the meal ahead. So I want them to be very different small tastes, little dabs of complexity to get people talking and gently draw them into our way of thinking.

I've included a few of our most popular spreads here. You can make your own sampler—great with the Grilled Flatbreads (page 192)—or just serve one as a starter or a coffee-table dip. I also encourage you to try thinning them with a little water or vegetable stock (adjusting the seasoning accordingly) to use them as room-temperature sauces that will add a little creamy extra to whatever you're serving.

TOMATO JAM

The balance of sweet, sour, savory, and spice is the master key to Moroccan cooking. This little tomato relish hits that balance right between the eyes, and I have yet to meet someone who doesn't love it. At Aziza, it's the star of a wildly popular appetizer: we drizzle a square of tangy Andante goat cheese from Petaluma with a bit of argan oil, top it with the jam, and garnish it with finely shaved hazelnuts and a scattering of nasturtium flowers and leaves. That presentation is my invention, the goat cheese providing exactly the right creamy-tangy accent to the sweet, spiced tomatoes. But the jam itself is classically Moroccan.

Starting in June, my grandpa would bring home more tomatoes from his farm outside Marrakesh than we knew what to do with. The women of the house would use some in cooking, pickle some, and make what was left into jam. I call it jam, but in Morocco, it's got nothing to do with breakfast. It's served as part of the traditional seven salads spread. In our house, tomato jam was the only sweet item among those salads, and we all knew it would be around for just a short while—so it was the dish everyone reached for first all summer long, especially us kids.

I make it with whole cherry tomatoes because I like the resulting chunky texture—a bit like whole-berry cranberry sauce—and I've found that Sweet 100 tomatoes have the best ratio of skin and seeds to sweet, juicy flesh. If you want a smoother sauce for spreading on a plate or drizzling, you can use any kind of ripe, flavorful tomato, puree the jam with an immersion blender while it's still in the saucepan, and then strain it through a wide-mesh sieve. But do try the chunky style first.

You'll want to use it on everything. Some great places to start: with grilled or roasted lamb; on crostini toasted with olive oil and spread with Fresh Cheese (page 113) and a garnish of grated almonds, as shown on page 111; or (another Aziza favorite) on brioche toasts with cured sardines. Stored in a jar in the refrigerator with a slick of olive oil on top, it will keep for 1 month. You can also can it in the usual way, and keep it refrigerated for up to 6 months.

2 (270 grams) lemons, washed
1 (19 grams) medium red jalapeño
1 tablespoon (7.4 grams) whole cumin seeds, toasted
Three (9.9 grams) 3-inch cinnamon sticks
1 tablespoon (2.8 grams) dried rosebuds (optional)
20 (2 grams) juniper berries
10 (0.7 gram) whole cloves
½ teaspoon (1.5 grams) Telicherry peppercorns
4 (0.7 gram) green cardamom pods, cracked
5 (0.6 gram) allspice berries
2 pounds (907 grams) Sweet 100 tomatoes, stems removed
2 cups (400 grams) granulated sugar
2 tablespoons (1 ounce/28.3 grams) unsalted butter
1 cup (233 grams) champagne vinegar
3 tablespoons (45 grams) freshly squeezed lime juice
1 tablespoon (21 grams) molasses
One 3-inch piece (52 grams) ginger, peeled and cut into ¼-inch slices
1 teaspoon (3 grams) kosher salt

Cut off the ends of the lemons and discard. Cut the lemons in half lengthwise, lay them on a cutting surface flat side down, and cut crosswise into very thin half moon slices. Set aside.

Cut the jalapeño in half lengthwise and remove the stem and seeds. If making a chunky jam, cut the

jalapeño into 1/8-inch dice. If making a smooth jam, finely chop. Set aside.

Put the cumin, cinnamon sticks, rosebuds (if using), juniper berries, cloves, peppercorns, cardamom pods, and allspice berries in a piece of cheesecloth and tie to make a large sachet.

Heat a large saucepan over medium-high heat. Add the tomatoes, sugar, and butter to the pan and stir to combine. Bring to a boil, stirring constantly with a flat-bottomed wooden spoon, scraping the bottom and corners of the pan to prevent the sugar from burning.

After about 7 minutes, the tomatoes will begin to split and release their juice, causing the sugar to melt very quickly. Once the sugar has melted, stir in the lemons and continue to boil the mixture for another 3 minutes.

Stir in the vinegar, lime juice, molasses, and ginger. Add the sachet. Return to a boil, then reduce the heat and cook at a gentle simmer for about 30 to 40 minutes or until the jam has reduced by about half. Stir in the salt. Continue to cook until the jam is thick and has reduced to about 4 cups (1.1 kilograms). For a smooth jam, one that can be spread on a plate, use a handheld immersion blender. If the puree is not completely smooth, strain through a fine-mesh strainer.

Spread the jam in a nonreactive 9-by-13-inch pan, preferably stainless steel, to cool. Once cool, place in a jar or other covered container. Pour a film of olive oil over the top, cover, and refrigerate for up to 1 month.

MAKES ABOUT 4 CUPS (1.1 KILOGRAMS)

Crostini, Grated Almonds, Fresh Cheese, Tomato Jam

FRESH CHEESE

We Moroccans are not a cheese-eating people. Let's just say we buy a lot of Laughing Cow. And sometimes we'll serve a kind of cream cheese called *jaban*. But we're big on butter, and that's how this homemade fresh cheese came about. I like to serve homemade butter with our breads, so every day, we whip out the heavy cream and whip it into butter (that recipe is on page 373).

If you've ever made butter, you know that once it comes together and solidifies, you're left with a lot of liquid, which is buttermilk. For years, we were throwing all of that beautiful home-churned buttermilk away. Then one day I asked one of my cooks to help me figure out something to do with it. We tried poaching and *sous-vide*-ing things in buttermilk, and that was good. But there was still a lot left. So we set our sights on cheese.

It took a fair amount of trial and error, especially because we really got into the challenge of figuring it out without a lot of help from the Internet. After six months, we came up with this method, which uses milk, buttermilk, heavy cream, and lemon juice. And eventually we hit on the idea of brining the fresh cheese in its own salted whey, which heightens its flavor and gives it a texture somewhere between ricotta and feta. For a milder, softer fresh cheese, you can just skip the brining step.

If you've never made cheese, this is a good recipe to start with, because it's easy and you'll get instant gratification. You can use either uncultured buttermilk —store-bought or homemade—or the cultured buttermilk you find in every supermarket.

Either way, what you'll get are rounds of cheese you can cut into wedges to serve with flatbreads or crackers. If you like, you can roll the edges in Marash pepper, black pepper, or sumac, as directed; I also like minced fresh arugula or fresh herbs like chervil, parsley, or lemon thyme. For an even smoother, creamier texture and richer flavor, try marinating the rounds overnight (or up to a few days) in olive oil with a little cracked black pepper. This cheese is ideal for crumbling and sprinkling on salads, soups, and stews. And it's nice with Tomato Jam (page 108) or a slice of honeycomb and a few chopped toasted almonds as part of a cheese course.

4 cups (1 kilogram) whole milk
1 cup (245 grams) buttermilk
Kosher salt
½ cup (117 grams) heavy cream
Up to ½ cup (120 grams) fresh lemon juice

Extra virgin olive oil or honey for finishing (optional)
Marash pepper, sumac, or coarsely ground black pepper (optional)

Line a large fine-mesh strainer or chinois with cheesecloth and put over a large deep bowl or pot. Wrap a small cooling rack in a double layer of cheesecloth and put it on a baking sheet. Cut four 1½-by-12-inch-long strips of parchment paper and use them to line four 3-by-¾-inch-high ring molds. Arrange them on the rack. Cut four rounds of parchment paper the size of the rings and set aside.

Combine 2 cups (500 grams) of the milk and ½ cup (122.5 grams) of the buttermilk in a medium saucepan fitted with a thermometer and heat over medium heat, stirring occasionally to prevent scorching, until it reaches 178°F. Stir in ½ teaspoon (1.5 grams) salt, remove from the heat, and let sit for 20 minutes.

Meanwhile, combine the remaining 2 cups (500 grams) milk and the cream in a large saucepan fitted with a thermometer and heat over medium heat, stirring occasionally to prevent scorching, until it

reaches 185°F. Remove from the heat and stir in the remaining ½ cup (122.5 grams) buttermilk, ½ teaspoon (1.5 grams) salt, and 3 tablespoons (45 grams) of the lemon juice. To form the largest curds, the temperature should be between 175° and 180°F. If it is too low, heat it to the correct temperature and then remove from the heat.

Insert the tip of a spatula into the cream mixture. You want to see two separate areas: the top section (curds) should look white, with a clear liquid (the whey) underneath. If it is not clear, stir in more lemon juice, ½ tablespoon (7.5 grams) at a time, until it is clear. Let sit for 20 minutes.

Add the milk mixture from the first pan to the cream mixture. Pour a ladleful of the mixture into the cheesecloth-lined strainer. Gently lift the cheesecloth on one side, easing the curds toward the center and releasing more whey into the bowl. Continue adding ladlefuls and lifting new areas of the cheesecloth until all the liquid has been drained. The curds will still have some moisture, which will continue to drain in the molds.

Divide the curds among the rings and press gently on the tops to make the surface even. Reserve the whey. Top the cheeses with the rounds of parchment and let them sit at room temperature for 1 hour, then refrigerate the cheese and the whey (if brining the cheese) overnight.

The cheese can be eaten now as fresh cheese, or you can brine the cheese in the whey.

TO BRINE THE CHEESE: Taste the whey, adding more salt as needed to give it the intensity of heavily salted pasta water. Lay a triple layer of cheesecloth on the work surface and wrap one portion of the cheese in it, tucking the ends of the cheesecloth underneath (the cheese is too fragile to tie it). Repeat with the remaining cheeses. Place the packets in a deep storage container and pour in enough whey, about 3 cups (715 grams), to cover the cheese. Refrigerate for 2 hours.

Line a small cooling rack with cheesecloth and place on a baking sheet. Unwrap the cheeses, place on the rack, and refrigerate overnight, or for up to 1 week.

TO SERVE: The cheese can be served as is or with a drizzle of olive oil or honey. If you would like to roll the cheese in a spice, spread the spice on a plate and roll the sides of the cheese in it. For each round, you'll need about ¾ teaspoon (1.8 grams) Marash, (1.4 grams) black pepper, or (2.2 grams) sumac.

I like to serve fresh cheese cold, but you can let it sit at room temperature for 15 minutes before serving.

MAKES FOUR 3-BY-½-INCH ROUNDS
(60 GRAMS EACH)

CHARRED EGGPLANT PUREE

You know *baba ganoush?* This is not that. Flavorwise, it's got more to do with *zaalouk,* one of the many Moroccan "seven salads" options: strips or chunks of boiled eggplant seasoned with garlic, *harissa,* cumin, and preserved lemons. I wanted to whip that idea into a puree for our popular spreads-and-flatbread sampler. But I'm not a big fan of boiled eggplant, so I came up with this method of charring—not the skin, as people often do, but the flesh. Bingo. It cooks the eggplant, making the pieces easy to peel, and adds smoky flavor, as well as drawing out some of the bitter moisture, the way salting would.

And I do mean charring. As in burning. Don't be put off by this—just give it a try. You'll find that the burnt part ends up being only a small portion of the mix, because a lot of it remains in the strainer. Use firm eggplants with small seeds. If you want to use the slender Asian kind, just cut them in half the long way before charring. You can also do your charring on the grill or under the broiler instead of in a skillet, brushing the pieces with a light coating of oil first.

Lamb with eggplant is a major Moroccan combination, and this spread suggests all kinds of lamb-enhancing possibilities. Smear it on the plate with grilled lamb chops, dollop it onto slices of roasted leg of lamb, or spread it on a lamb sandwich with some fresh spinach or arugula.

eggplant puree

2 pounds (907 grams) eggplant, preferably
   Rosa Bianca or globe
6 tablespoons (79.5 grams) extra virgin olive oil
¼ cup (71 grams) Garlic Puree (page 360)
3 tablespoons (45 grams) fresh lemon juice, or to taste
2 teaspoons (6 grams) kosher salt, or to taste
1 teaspoon (2.6 grams) ground cumin
¼ teaspoon (0.7 gram) sweet paprika
⅛ teaspoon (0.4 gram) ground white pepper, or to taste
Pinch of cayenne
Pinch of smoked paprika

Extra virgin olive oil for finishing
Marash pepper
Grilled Flatbreads (page 192) or pita chips (optional)

FOR THE EGGPLANT PUREE: Cut off and discard the ends of the eggplants. Cut the eggplant crosswise into ¾-inch slices.

The eggplant is best if charred in a large dry cast-iron skillet. Turn the fan over the stove to high and set the pan over medium-high heat. Let it heat for about 5 minutes. Add as many eggplant slices as you can fit without crowding the pan. Char for about 10 minutes, using a spatula to press down on the slices and rotate them in the pan as necessary until the bottoms are blackened and burnt. Turn each piece over once it is charred and repeat on the second side. As the pieces are charred, move them to a large bowl. Repeat with the remaining slices. Cover the bowl tightly with plastic wrap and allow the eggplant to steam for about 10 minutes. Pull away and discard the peel from each slice of eggplant. Chop the eggplant and put in a colander in the sink to drain for 20 minutes.

CONTINUED

Put the eggplant in a food processor and add all the remaining ingredients. Process to a smooth puree. Pass the puree through a fine-mesh strainer to strain out the charred bits (there will still be small dark flecks in the puree). Taste it and adjust the seasoning, adding more lemon juice, salt, and/or pepper if you think it's needed.

The spread is wonderful when just made, but it can be stored in the refrigerator for about a week. Bring to room temperature before serving.

TO SERVE: Put the puree in a serving bowl, drizzle the top with olive oil, and sprinkle with Marash pepper. Serve with warm flatbread or pita chips, if desired.

MAKES 2 CUPS (492 GRAMS)

CHICKPEA SPREAD

We all love hummus, but I'm thinking we may be nearing a saturation point. So I came up with this version that replaces the usual tahini with a ton of sweet, creamy melted onions and a mix of spices I borrowed from a classic Moroccan chickpea and tomato stew (losing the tomatoes in the process, to focus more on the nutty richness of the chickpeas). I serve it as a spread, sometimes garnished with *harissa*-fried chickpeas (made like the fried butter beans with the Vegetable Stew on page 286), but I also like to warm it and use it as a sauce to smear on the plate with grilled lamb chops or roasted lamb.

While we're on the subject of hummus alternatives, let me encourage you to try making a puree of bright green fresh chickpeas when they're in season during the spring and summer. Just shuck them, blanch them, and chill them in a large bowl of ice water (as directed in the Fresh Chickpea Relish recipe on page 126), then drain and puree them with a bit of water and extra virgin olive oil. Strain the puree through a *tamis* or fine-mesh sieve, and stir in a bit of cumin, salt, and white pepper.

chickpea spread

Grapeseed or canola oil

4 cups (424 grams) thinly sliced yellow onions

1½ teaspoons (3.8 grams) ground cumin

1¼ teaspoons (3.6 grams) smoked paprika

¾ teaspoon (2.1 grams) mixed pure chile powder

¼ teaspoon (0.7 gram) ground white pepper

¼ teaspoon (0.6 gram) Marash pepper, plus extra for sprinkling

Kosher salt

1 cup (235 grams) Chicken Stock (page 365)

7 tablespoons (125 grams) Garlic Puree (page 360)

3 cups (495 grams) cooked chickpeas (see Cooking Beans, page 378), liquid reserved

⅓ cup (70 grams) plus ¼ cup (53 grams) extra virgin olive oil

A small pinch (about 10 pistils) of saffron threads

2 tablespoons (30 grams) fresh lemon juice

Extra virgin olive oil for finishing

Grilled Flatbreads (page 192) or pita chips (optional)

FOR THE SPREAD: Pour a light film of grapeseed oil into a large frying pan set over medium-high heat. Add the onions and cook, stirring often, for about 15 minutes, or until tender; lower the heat as necessary to keep the onions from browning.

Stir in the spices and 1½ teaspoons (4.5 grams) salt and stir and toast the spices for 1½ minutes. Add the chicken stock, garlic puree, chickpeas (not their liquid), the ⅓ cup (70 grams) extra virgin olive oil, and the saffron. Bring to a simmer and cook for about 25 minutes, stirring often, until the liquid has evaporated (there will still be some oil remaining in the pan) and the onions are soft enough to puree.

Put the onion mixture in a food processor, pulse the mixture a few times to release some steam, and then puree it, scraping down the sides of the bowl as necessary. Add enough of the reserved chickpea cooking liquid (¼ to ½ cup/57 to 114 grams) to make the mixture light and creamy. With the processor running, add the lemon juice and the remaining ¼ cup (53 grams) olive oil. To check the consistency of the spread, lift a spoonful and tip the spoon; the spread should fall from the spoon. If it is too thick, add small amounts of additional cooking liquid. (It will thicken as it cools.)

Pass the puree through a fine-mesh strainer and season to taste with salt. You can refrigerate the spread for up to a week in a covered container, but the consistency will change from light and airy to more dense.

TO SERVE: Put the spread in a serving bowl, drizzle with olive oil, and sprinkle with Marash. Serve, if desired, with warm flatbread or pita chips.

MAKES 2½ CUPS (633 GRAMS)

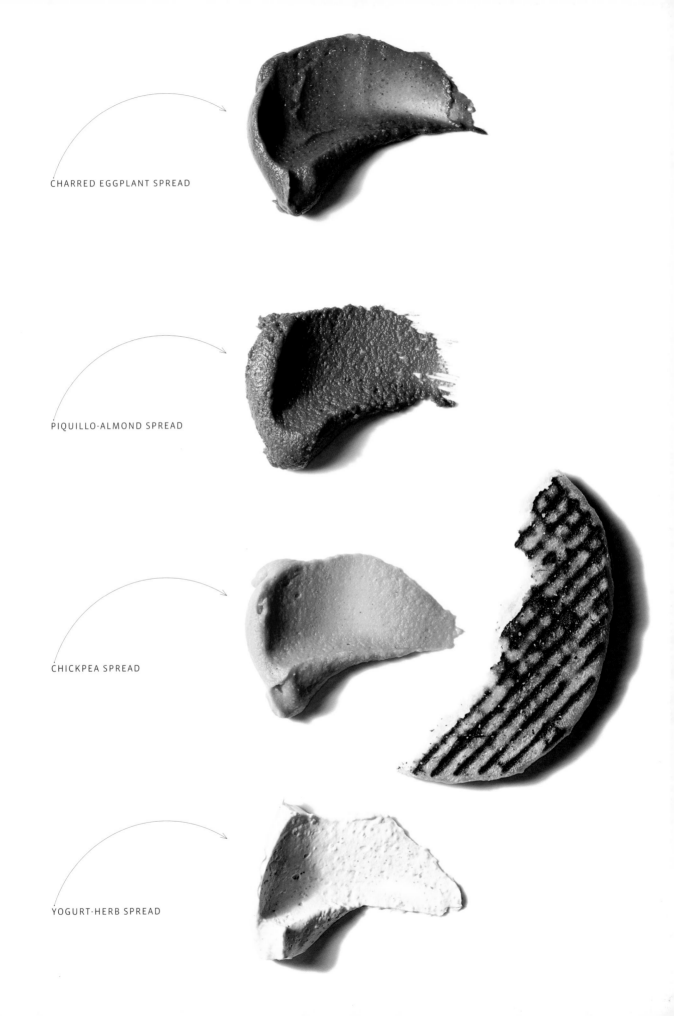

CHARRED EGGPLANT SPREAD

PIQUILLO-ALMOND SPREAD

CHICKPEA SPREAD

YOGURT-HERB SPREAD

PIQUILLO-ALMOND SPREAD

This is my take on *muhammara,* a brick-red dip made from chiles, ground walnuts, and bread crumbs. I took a page from *romesco* sauce, which is thickened with almonds, and came up with this buttery, sweet spread. (Ultimately, I went with almond meal, rather than home-ground almonds, because it melds seamlessly with the puree.) I use small, meaty piquillo peppers, which have more sweet pepper flavor and bright red color than your typical red bell. And, for an extra layer of musky sweetness that really reminds me of Morocco, I add molasses.

Beyond dipping and spreading, this is perfect in sandwiches or dolloped onto grilled or roast chicken or fish. For grilled vegetables, I like to thin it with a little water and drizzle it on top. Anywhere a roasted red pepper would be welcome, this creamy stuff will be right at home.

piquillo-almond spread

¼ cup (43 grams) cooked white navy beans
  (see Cooking Beans, page 378), liquid reserved
5 tablespoons (73 grams) champagne vinegar
½ cup (106 grams) drained piquillo peppers
1¼ cups (125 grams) almond meal/flour
½ cup (106 grams) extra virgin olive oil
¼ cup (87 grams) unsulfured blackstrap molasses
⅓ cup (79 grams) tahini

¼ cup (72 grams) Garlic Puree (page 360)
2½ teaspoons (6.4 grams) ground cumin
2 teaspoons (5.3 grams) sweet paprika
1½ teaspoons (4.5 grams) kosher salt
1 teaspoon (2.7 grams) ground white pepper
¾ teaspoon (2 grams) smoked paprika
¼ teaspoon (0.7 gram) mixed pure chile powder or
  ¼ teaspoon (1.8 grams) *Harissa* Powder (page 85)

Grilled Flatbreads (page 192) or pita chips (optional)

Put the beans (not their liquid) and vinegar in a blender. Begin to puree the beans on low speed, adding enough of the reserved cooking liquid to keep things moving. Gradually increase the speed, stopping to scrape down the sides of the blender as necessary. Add the peppers and puree until the mixture is completely smooth.

Transfer the mixture to a food processor, add all the remaining ingredients, and blend until the spread is smooth. The spread can be kept in the refrigerator for about a week; bring to room temperature before serving.

I like this best served with warm grilled flatbread or pita chips.

MAKES 2½ CUPS (645 GRAMS)

YOGURT-HERB SPREAD

On paralyzingly hot summer days in Marrakesh, my mom's best friend, a Jewish lady with the unlikely name of Marie, used to bring over the only thing anybody wanted to eat: a cool salad that was a popular summertime favorite of Moroccan Jews, made with big cubes of cucumber, sweet red pepper strips, red onions, and olives, tossed with yogurt, cumin, and cayenne. My *tzadziki*-style spread is refreshing in the same way that salad was, and great in hot weather or as a balancing element to hot or spicy food.

It's quite thick—firm enough to shape into quenelles, if you'd like to serve it that way (see page 379). The secret to its texture is cheesecloth. You use it both to hang and drain the yogurt (I like Fage Greek yogurt or Byblos "Lebni" yogurt) overnight and to squeeze most of the liquid out of the grated cucumber (I'm partial to Armenian cucumbers for this recipe, but English cukes work well too). You can keep the spread for up to 3 days, after which it will start to oxidize. If it thins out a bit as it sits, just strain it again in cheesecloth.

yogurt-herb spread

2 cups (476 grams) whole-milk Greek yogurt
1 small or ½ large cucumber, preferably Armenian
1 tablespoon (15 grams) fresh lemon juice
1½ teaspoons (4.5 grams) kosher salt
1½ teaspoons (2.2 grams) grated nutmeg
½ teaspoon (1.5 grams) ground white pepper
1 garlic clove, grated on a Microplane
2 teaspoons (2 grams) chopped dill

Grilled Flatbreads (page 192) or pita chips (optional)

TO DRAIN THE YOGURT: You'll need a deep bowl or other container and a wooden spoon or dowel. Line the bowl with a double thickness of cheesecloth. Spoon the yogurt into the center of the cloth and pull up the edges to form a pouch. Tie the ends around the spoon or dowel, adjusting the length so that the pouch is at least 2 inches above the bottom of the bowl. Refrigerate overnight to drain the excess liquid.

FOR THE SPREAD: The next day, remove the yogurt from the cheesecloth and put it in a large bowl; discard the liquid.

Peel and seed the cucumber. Grate it on the medium-fine holes of a box grater to produce a pulpy mush. Put the cucumber pulp on a piece of cheesecloth, pick up the edges, and twist the cloth over the sink to remove as much liquid as you can.

Stir the cucumber into the yogurt, along with the remaining ingredients. Refrigerate for at least 1 hour, or up to 3 days before serving.

I like this best with warm grilled flatbread or pita chips.

MAKES 2 CUPS (458 GRAMS)

CHEF TO CHEF: At the restaurant, I do a spin on the classic combination of salmon, cucumbers, and yogurt or crème fraîche. I compress cucumbers with a little fresh dill and cucumber water, then slice them into "noodles" on a Japanese mandoline. I pile the noodles on a plate, top them with a quenelle of the yogurt spread, and garnish with salmon eggs and dill sprigs— it's a salad that looks like a pasta dish.

BERBERE-CURED
CHICKEN LIVER MOUSSE

In Morocco, chicken livers are generally encountered in the company of onions—sautéed with them, or marinated in *charmoula* and skewered with them to make brochettes. Here I'm going for a subtle reference to that culinary tradition in the form of an intensely flavored yet stunningly fluffy and light liver mousse. When I make it, I cure the livers overnight with *berbere* and then soak them in three changes of milk, but for you, I've combined all of that into a single milk-*berbere* cure mixture and just two soakings. The idea is to add flavor while gradually drawing out the blood, and with it, some of that typical livery taste. And the result is a delicate, pale pinkish-tan mousse that comes closer to the look and texture of foie gras than your average gray-brown liver pâté.

For better color, I use a small amount of pink salt (also known as curing salt), which doesn't *add* pink color but actually brings it out in the curing process. But if you don't have any, it's fine to omit it. The chicken sauce, a fortified and reduced stock that goes into the mix, does make an enormous difference in terms of complexity and smoothness, so I encourage you to make it, even though it's a fairly involved process, and add it. You can also use chicken jus.

To serve the mousse, I like to toast our house-baked dark rye and pulverize some of it, to make "soil" in which I plant baby turnips and pickled green strawberries. But you can also spread the mousse on crostini made from that same bread or a good hearth-style loaf, like *levain* (see photograph, page 125), and then top it with a scattering of turnips and green strawberries and a drizzle of aged balsamic.

cure

1 cup (250 grams) whole milk
1 tablespoon (9 grams) kosher salt
1½ teaspoons (6.3 grams) granulated sugar
1¼ teaspoons (3.3 grams) *Berbere* (page 36)
¼ teaspoon (1.2 grams) pink salt (optional)

mousse

1 pound (453 grams) chicken livers
½ cup (117 grams) heavy cream, cold
¼ cup (48 grams) Clarified Butter (page 375)
¾ cup (90 grams) thinly sliced onion
2 tablespoons (26 grams) aged sherry vinegar, preferably from Jerez
1 tablespoon (7 grams) crème fraîche
½ cup (120 grams) Chicken Sauce or Chicken Jus (page 367 or 366)
About ¼ cup (50 grams) duck fat or ¼ cup (48 grams) Clarified Butter (page 375), melted and cooled

garnish

½ loaf (735 grams) unsliced Rye Bread (page 204)
¼ cup (48 grams) Clarified Butter (page 375), melted
Kosher salt
40 baby turnips
Extra virgin olive oil
Fresh lemon juice
Pickled Green Strawberries (page 361)
Aged balsamic vinegar, preferably 30 to 40 years old

FOR THE CURE: Combine the ingredients in a small saucepan over medium heat and whisk to dissolve the salt and sugar. Chill over ice or refrigerate until cold.

MEANWHILE, FOR THE MOUSSE: Put the chicken livers in a strainer set over a bowl and let drain for 30 minutes.

Fill two large bowls with ice water and put a smaller bowl in each one. Put the livers in one bowl. Clean the livers, removing any fat, veins, blood, or discolorations, and put in the second bowl. Cover the livers with half the cure mixture and refrigerate for 12 hours (refrigerate the remaining cure). Drain the livers in a fine-mesh strainer; discard the milk. Put the livers in a clean bowl and cover with the remaining cure mixture. Refrigerate for another 12 hours.

Line a baking sheet with clean kitchen towels. Drain the livers and rinse them under cold water. Then pick up each one and remove any spices. Some blood clots may have risen to the surface of the livers. Removing them lightens the final color and the flavor of the mousse. To remove them, push them off the livers with your fingertip. There may also be clots in any holes you see. Flush them out by running cold water into the holes and then pressing on the liver to squeeze out the water and clots. Put the livers on the baking sheet, cover with more kitchen towels to dry the livers, and refrigerate for 1 hour.

Whip the cream to soft peaks and refrigerate.

Drain the livers one last time by squeezing gently to remove any water trapped inside that you may have missed (any remaining water moisture would cause the livers to pop when added to the hot oil). Place a fine-mesh strainer over a bowl.

Heat a large cast-iron skillet over high heat. Melt 2 tablespoons (24 grams) of the clarified butter, then add half the livers, without allowing them to touch each other (which would cause them to steam rather than brown). Reduce the heat to medium-high and cook for 30 seconds to 1 minute on each side, or until lightly browned. As the livers are done, transfer to the strainer to drain, and then brown the remaining livers.

Wipe out the pan with paper towels and lower the heat to medium. Add the remaining 2 tablespoons (24 grams) clarified butter and the onion and cook for about 7 minutes, stirring often, until the onion is golden brown. Add the sherry vinegar, stirring to evaporate the vinegar and glaze the onions.

Transfer the livers and onions to a food processor and process until smooth. Touch the mixture: if it is hot, let it cool until it is barely warm. Then add the crème fraîche and process briefly.

Set a fine-mesh strainer over a bowl and drain the liver mixture. Discard the liquid.

If you have a *tamis,* this is the time to use it. Put the *tamis* on a piece of parchment paper and spoon the liver mixture into a mound to one side. Using a rubber scraper, grab a small amount at a time and pass it through the *tamis*. Put the mixture in a bowl. Or pass the mixture through a fine-mesh strainer into a bowl.

If the chicken sauce (or jus) has solidified, warm it gently to melt about half of it, then remove from the heat and stir until it has all liquified. Let cool to room temperature.

Stir the sauce into the liver, then fold in the whipped cream. Spoon the mousse into a crock or other airtight container(s). Spoon the duck fat (or clarified butter) over the top to keep the liver from discoloring, and refrigerate for at least 2 hours, or up to 3 days.

FOR THE GARNISH: Preheat the oven to 325°F.

Cut the crusts from the bread and reserve. Cut the bread lengthwise in half and then cut across into eighteen ⅛-inch-thick slices. Lightly brush on both sides with the clarified butter and sprinkle with salt. Place on a Silpat- or parchment-lined baking sheet. Top with a second Silpat or piece of parchment and a second baking sheet.

Bake the toasts for 20 minutes. Be careful not to overcook them—the best indication will be the smell of toasted bread. They may still be pliable but will crisp as they cool. Transfer the toasts to a cooling rack.

Meanwhile, pulse the bread trimmings in the food processor to uniform coarse crumbs.

Spread the crumbs on the same lined baking sheet and toast for 10 minutes, just until dry. Remove from the oven and let cool.

Put the crumbs in the food processor and pulse just until they are finely ground, not powdered.

TO SERVE: Toss the turnips lightly with olive oil, lemon juice, and salt.

Remove the fat covering the mousse: spoon off the duck fat, which will be soft (or if you used clarified butter, run a knife around the edge and lift if off in one piece).

Sprinkle some rye crumbs onto each serving plate to form a base under the mousse. Form the mousse into quenelles (see page 379) and place it on the crumbs. Arrange the toasts, the remaining additional crumbs, the turnips, and strawberries around the plates. With a very small spoon or dropper, dot small drops of balsamic vinegar around each plate.

MAKES 2 CUPS (565 GRAMS)

FRESH CHICKPEA RELISH

I grew up eating chickpeas, but I was barely aware of the fresh version until I came to the United States. In Morocco, fresh chickpeas are hard to find, and people almost always buy them dry and soak them. But in northern California, when fresh green chickpeas are at the market, I snap them up and serve them in simple ways, like this relish, which seems to make everything taste better.

You can set it out as a dip with flatbreads, or use it as a finishing condiment for just about anything grilled. I like to spoon it over grilled or roasted vegetables. I'm fond of seasoning meat with a hint of fish to add saltiness with unexpected depth, and the anchovies here do just that. Try the relish on steak or lamb chops, and you'll see what I'm talking about. That anchovy note makes the relish great with fish too, especially if you add a squeeze of lemon or lime juice to it.

Before you make this, taste your olive oil. If it's very strong, its flavor will overpower the delicate fresh beans, so substitute grapeseed or "pure" olive oil for up to two-thirds of the extra virgin olive oil called for.

Fresh chickpeas come one or two to a pod, and, if they're young and tender, once you shell them, they don't need to be peeled. Start by shelling, blanching, and icing them, then taste a few. If you're getting more chewy peel than creamy meat, you should peel the blanched beans. This is easily done by spreading them on a dish towel, folding it over, and gently rubbing to loosen the skins. Many will come right off this way, and it shouldn't take you long to peel off the rest individually.

For favas, you can run a vegetable peeler down the string side of the pod to open it, and then run your finger inside the pod to pop out the beans. Blanch the beans and taste them. Unfortunately, if they need peeling, you'll have to peel them individually. Just pinch the skin open at one end and squeeze the bean out. You'll need about 1½ pounds (680 grams) chickpeas, 3 pounds (1.36 kilograms) fava beans, or 3 pounds (1.36 kilograms) peas in the pod to get 3 cups (425 grams).

3 cups (about 425 grams) shelled chickpeas, fava beans, or peas
5 tablespoons (41 grams) slivered almonds
3 (12 grams) anchovy fillets, salt- or oil-packed, finely minced (see Note)
3 tablespoons (10 grams) finely diced Parmigiano-Reggiano or Grana
2 tablespoons (6 grams) finely chopped mint
½ teaspoon (1.3 grams) ground cumin
1¼ cups (265 grams) mild extra virgin olive oil
1 teaspoon (3 grams) kosher salt, or to taste

Bring a large pot of salted water to a boil. Fill a large bowl with ice water.

Add the chickpeas (or favas or peas) to the boiling water and blanch for 1 to 2 minutes, until they are almost tender. Drain them in a strainer and plunge the strainer into the ice water to chill. Remove the strainer from the water, set it over a bowl, and let the chickpeas drain for about 30 minutes.

Toast the almonds in a dry frying pan over medium heat for about 2 minutes, or until golden brown. Let cool, then coarsely chop them.

Don't be tempted to chop the chickpeas in a food processor; if you do, you'll lose the texture of relish and turn it into a spread. Instead, coarsely chop them on a cutting board, and put them in a medium bowl. Stir in the remaining ingredients. The relish can be refrigerated for up to 3 days; bring to room temperature before serving.

MAKES 2¾ CUPS (635 GRAMS)

NOTE: If you're using salt-packed anchovies, rinse them in cold water, soak them in milk for 20 to 30 minutes, and then drain; repeat two more times with fresh milk. You'll get really creamy, delicate-tasting anchovies.

RGHAIF
WITH THREE FILLINGS

When I was growing up, whenever a wedding, a big celebration, or Eid S'ghir, the end of Ramadan, rolled around, no matter how young you were, you'd stay up all night dancing and singing with a few hundred people. And then in the morning, before you crashed, this (along with *Beghrir,* page 195) is what you'd stuff yourself with for breakfast: soft, warm yeasted dough rolled around a sweet filling of almonds, rose water, and cinnamon, drizzled with melted butter, honey, and maybe a bit of argan oil.

These crêpe-like pastries are called *rghaif* (which is pronounced kind of like clearing your throat and then saying "ife"), and besides being a favorite holiday breakfast, they're a ubiquitous teatime snack and street food, often with savory fillings like preserved beef or a kind of ratatouille.

When someone's making *rghaif,* chances are they'll also turn out some *m'lwee* (literally, "folded"), a kind of Moroccan version of Danish pastry for which the same dough is rolled out, rolled up, flattened, and rerolled to make a flaky layered pastry that is then fried. I remember watching my mom and the other women in our house make *rghaif* and *m'lwee,* their butter-coated hands making squishy sounds as they worked the rich yeasted dough.

It's nice to serve an assortment of *rghaif* with two or three different fillings as an appetizer, and I also like to slice them into bite-sized pieces to serve as a finger food. I've given you three options for what to put inside: a lemony cheese mixture that will remind you a bit of blintzes; a completely traditional sweet spiced onion and raisin filling (which is equally traditional and wonderful as a topping for couscous with toasted almonds); and shredded braised oxtail.

yeast mixture
2½ teaspoons (7.5 grams) active dry yeast (not quick-rising)
½ teaspoon (2.18 grams) granulated sugar
¼ cup (58.5 grams) warm water (about 110°F)

dough
3¾ cups (491 grams) all-purpose flour, plus additional as needed
2 tablespoons (25 grams) granulated sugar
2 teaspoons (6 grams) kosher salt
12 tablespoons (145 grams) Clarified Butter (page 375), melted and cooled
2 tablespoons (27 grams) extra virgin olive oil, plus additional for brushing
3 tablespoons (45 grams) evaporated milk
2 large eggs
6 tablespoons (88 grams) warm water (about 110°F)

Goat Cheese, Pine Nut, and Meyer Lemon Zest Filling (recipe follows), Caramelized Onion with Spice and Currant Filling (recipe follows), or 2½ cups (330 grams) shredded oxtail from Braised Oxtail (page 282)
Grapeseed or canola oil

FOR THE YEAST MIXTURE: Combine the yeast and sugar in a small bowl. Stir in the warm water and let sit to proof in a warm spot for about 10 minutes, or until the mixture is foamy and bubbling.

CONTINUED

MEANWHILE, FOR THE DOUGH: Put the flour, sugar, and salt in the bowl of a stand mixer. Spray the hook attachment with nonstick spray to keep the dough from sticking to it, and fit the hook on the mixer. Turn the machine to low and add the yeast mixture. Once it is combined, drizzle in the butter, the 2 tablespoons olive oil, and evaporated milk. As a dough begins to form around the hook, turn the speed to medium-low. (I mix bread doughs at lower speeds than you might expect. Mixing at high speeds can heat up the machine and adversely affect the bread. Don't rush the process!) Add the eggs one at a time, mixing to combine, and drizzle in the water. Knead the dough until completely smooth, about 10 minutes, stopping the mixer occasionally to release any dough sticking to the hook. The finished dough will wrap around the hook and should feel smooth and silky. It will feel somewhat tacky, but it shouldn't stick to your fingers when you touch it. If it does, add a bit more flour.

Dust a board with flour, turn the dough out, and knead with the heels of your hands for about 2 minutes. Then, lift the dough and tuck the edges under to form a round ball.

Spray a large bowl with nonstick spray and dust with flour. Add the dough and lightly press a piece of plastic wrap against it. Let it rise in a warm spot for about 1½ hours, or until it has doubled in size.

TO SHAPE THE DOUGH: Lightly dust the cleaned board with flour. Return the dough to the board and knead it to work out any air bubbles. Form the dough into a ball.

Line two baking sheets with parchment paper and spray with the nonstick cooking spray. Cut the dough into 10 equal portions (about 100 grams each). Using the palm of your hand, roll each portion against the board to form a ball. (When you become good at this, you'll be able to use both hands and roll 2 balls at a time.)

Space the balls evenly on the sheets and brush the tops with the olive oil. Cover tightly with plastic wrap and place in a warm spot to rise for 1 hour, or until doubled in size.

Brush a work surface with olive oil and place 1 ball of dough on it. Generously oil your hands and pat the dough into a circle 10 to 12 inches in diameter.

Put ¼ cup of the filling in the center of the dough and form the filling into a rectangle, leaving a border of 2 to 3 inches on the sides of the filling and about 1 inch at the bottom. Fold the bottom of the dough over the filling. Fold one side over to cover the filling, then fold over the opposite side, stretching it to reach the far edge of the dough. Fold the bottom over, then fold over again to form a packet. Repeat with the remaining dough and filling, placing the finished packets on the baking sheets.

Cover the baking sheets with plastic wrap and let the packets rise for 30 minutes.

Place 1 packet on an oiled work surface and gently press it down to flatten into a rectangle about 5 by 3 inches, working carefully to avoid tearing the dough and exposing the filling. Repeat with the remaining packets. Let rest uncovered for 20 minutes.

TO COOK THE PASTRIES: Preheat the oven to 200°F. Place a cooling rack on a baking sheet in the oven.

Heat a generous film of grapeseed oil in a large nonstick frying pan over medium heat. Add a few of the packets, without crowding, and cook until browned and crisp, about 3 minutes per side. Put the *rghaif* on the rack on the baking sheet and keep warm in the oven while you cook the remaining packets, adding additional oil to the pan as needed.

Cut the *rghaif* into whatever size pieces you'd like.

MAKES 10 PASTRIES

GOAT CHEESE, PINE NUT, AND MEYER LEMON ZEST FILLING

1 cup (144 grams) pine nuts
Kosher salt
15 ounces (425 grams) soft goat cheese, at room temperature
2¼ teaspoons (4.2 grams) grated Meyer lemon zest
½ cup plus 2 tablespoons (132.5 grams) extra virgin olive oil

Spread the nuts in a medium frying pan, sprinkle with a generous pinch of salt, and toast over medium heat for 3 to 5 minutes, or until a rich golden brown. Transfer the nuts to a plate and let cool completely.

Combine the goat cheese, lemon zest, pine nuts, and olive oil in a medium bowl, mixing until smooth. Season to taste with salt.

MAKES ABOUT 2½ CUPS (705 GRAMS)

CARAMELIZED ONION WITH SPICE AND CURRANT FILLING

¾ cup (159 grams) grapeseed or canola oil
14 cups (1175 grams) thinly sliced red onions (about 4 large onions)
2½ teaspoons (7.5 grams) kosher salt
⅜ teaspoon (1 gram) ground cinnamon
⅜ teaspoon (0.6 gram) grated nutmeg
⅛ teaspoon (0.3 gram) ground cloves
¾ teaspoon (1.8 grams) Marash or Urfa pepper
⅜ teaspoon (0.7 gram) freshly ground black pepper
¾ teaspoon (0.7 gram) saffron threads
½ cup (70 grams) dried currants
1½ tablespoons (32 grams) orange blossom honey, preferably from Marshall Farms
½ teaspoon (3 grams) sherry vinegar, or to taste

Heat the oil in a large sauté pan over medium heat. Add the onions and salt and cook, stirring occasionally, for 25 minutes, or until tender; reduce the heat as necessary to keep the onions from browning.

Add the spices and saffron and continue to cook, stirring often, for another 45 minutes, or until the onions are very tender and golden brown.

Meanwhile, put the currants in a small bowl. Bring enough water to cover the currants to a simmer and pour it over them. Let sit for about 10 minutes, or until softened and plump. Drain.

Add the currants, honey, and vinegar to the onions and simmer gently for 20 minutes. Remove from the heat and let cool to room temperature.

Add more sherry vinegar to taste if necessary.

MAKES 2¾ CUPS (624 GRAMS)

SPINACH ROLLS
CAPER–PINE NUT SAUCE

Briwat, pastry triangles with a sweet or savory filling wrapped in *warqa* dough and deep-fried, are the star finger food of Morocco. The sweet version, filled with cinnamony almonds, dipped in honey, and rolled in sesame seeds, was the milk-and-cookies snack of my childhood.

On the savory side, *briwat* are often filled with greens like purslane, chard, and beet tops cooked down with spices to make a dense herb jam. I make my spring-roll-shaped version with Bloomsdale spinach, a thick, sturdy variety that's much less watery and more flavorful than the supermarket stuff. And, borrowing from Greek *spanakotyropita,* I add a bit of feta.

You can use either *warqa* or phyllo dough to make these. Frying *warqa* makes it light and crispy, which is why it's my preferred approach. You can also bake rolls made with *warqa,* but they'll be chewier. Rolls made with phyllo, on the other hand, won't stand up to the heat of deep-frying and should only be baked. When you're working with either kind of dough, if it tears, open the roll back up, reposition the filling so it's not where the tear is, and reroll. Or start over with a new piece of dough if you have to—but don't use a second sheet to cover the tear; you'll end up with too many layers and a chewy texture.

I often finish food with a sprinkling of salt, but since salt wouldn't stick here, I came up with a decidedly salty dipping sauce. Serve these as a first course, or cut them in half on the diagonal and pass them around on a platter with the sauce in a little bowl.

Once you've got the hang of making these, try some other fillings, like the cooked *kefta* mixture on page 139 or the chicken and almond mixtures from the *Basteeya* (page 237; leave out the eggs). Or, for a very simple variation that's great with the caper sauce, roll a sheet of *warqa* around a small thin piece of raw tuna seasoned with coarse salt and fry it. You may need to experiment a bit with the size of the piece of tuna so that when the wrapper is golden and crisp, the tuna is still rare at the center.

spinach filling
¼ cup (53 grams) grapeseed or canola oil
2½ cups (240 grams) thinly sliced leeks
    (white and light green parts only), rinsed
Kosher salt
½ cup (64 grams) thinly sliced garlic
1 pound (453 grams) spinach, stems removed
1 tablespoon (12 grams) finely chopped preserved
    lemon rind (see page 45)
1 teaspoon (2.4 grams) Marash pepper
½ teaspoon (1 gram) ground black pepper
⅛ teaspoon (0.2 gram) grated nutmeg
1 large egg yolk
One 5-ounce (141-gram) piece dry-packed feta cheese,
    such as Mt. Vikos or Redwood Hill, crumbled
                    (MAKES 3 CUPS/575 GRAMS)

caper–pine nut sauce
½ cup (66 grams) pine nuts
6 tablespoons (93 grams) half-and-half
2 tablespoons (35 grams) capers, with their liquid
¼ teaspoon (0.5 gram) ground black pepper

Grapeseed or canola oil for deep-frying (optional)
18 pieces Handmade *Warqa* (page 74), or 9 sheets
    phyllo, cut crosswise in half
About ⅓ cup (61 grams) Clarified Butter (page 375),
    melted
1 large egg white, lightly beaten
                    (MAKES ¾ CUP/160 GRAMS)

FOR THE SPINACH FILLING: Heat the oil in a large sauté pan over medium-high heat. Add the leeks, reduce the heat to medium, add 2 pinches of salt, and cook for 5 minutes, or until the leeks begin to soften. Add the garlic and continue to sauté for 10 to 12 minutes, lowering the heat as necessary to soften the vegetables without browning them.

Add half the spinach, sprinkle lightly with salt, and turn the spinach as it wilts; gradually add the remaining spinach, salting it lightly, as there is room in the pan. Cook for about 8 minutes, until the spinach is tender. Remove from the heat.

Place a strainer over a bowl and line it with two layers of dampened cheesecloth, leaving a generous overhang. Add the spinach and let drain for several minutes.

Lift the edges of the cheesecloth and twist it to wring out as much moisture as possible, then transfer the spinach to a bowl. Stir in the lemon rind, Marash pepper, black pepper, nutmeg, and egg yolk, and let cool completely.

Stir in the feta cheese.

FOR THE SAUCE: Preheat the oven to 350°F.

Spread the pine nuts on a small baking sheet and toast in the oven for about 10 minutes, or until golden brown. Let cool.

Transfer the pine nuts to a blender, add the remaining ingredients, and puree at high speed. Pour into individual dipping bowls and set aside.

TO SHAPE AND COOK THE ROLLS: *If deep-frying the rolls,* fill a deep-fryer or a high-sided small pot, fitted with a thermometer, one-third full with canola oil and heat to 360°F. Set a cooling rack on a baking sheet.

Preheat the oven to 200°F. Place the baking sheet in the oven.

If baking, preheat the oven to 400°F. Line two baking sheets with parchment paper.

When working with *warqa* or phyllo, it is important to keep the sheets covered to keep them from drying out. Place a damp towel on the counter and cover it with a piece of parchment or half the sheet of paper from the phyllo. Lay the *warqa* on top, or open up the phyllo sheets and lay them on top. Cover with another piece of parchment or the other half of the phyllo paper and then another slightly damp towel.

Lay a piece of *warqa* or sheet of phyllo (short end facing you) on the work surface. Trim any ragged edges. Brush the *warqa* or phyllo generously with butter. Shape 2 tablespoons (24 grams) of the spinach into a ball, then form it into a 4-inch-long log and place it on the pastry, about ½ inch up from the bottom edge and 1 inch in from each side. Fold the bottom edge up and over the filling, fold over the sides, and brush the sides with more butter. Roll up the *briwat* like an egg roll; if the dough is at all brittle, brush on a bit more butter as you roll to soften it. Before making your final fold, brush the last flap of *warqa* or phyllo with egg white to seal it. Place seam side down on the cooling rack or one of the parchment-lined baking sheets. Repeat to form the remaining *briwat*.

If frying, cook the rolls in batches so you don't overcrowd the pan. Fry for 2 to 3 minutes, turning the rolls from time to time, until they are crisp and a rich golden brown. Drain on the cooling rack and keep them warm in the oven while you fry the remaining rolls.

If baking, brush the tops with clarified butter and bake for 30 to 35 minutes, or until the rolls are hot and a rich golden brown.

Arrange 3 rolls on each serving plate and serve with the sauce on the side.

SERVES 6 (MAKES 18 ROLLS)

CORONA BEANS
TOMATO SAUCE
FETA

Loubya, a long-simmered stew of beans and tomatoes, is the baked beans of Morocco. It's served either cold as one of the seven salads or hot as the centerpiece of a meal, with bread for dipping in the soupy sauce, and sometimes a bit of preserved beef added to the mix for extra substance. When I opened Aziza, I wanted to serve it as a warm starter, but I knew it needed something more, and I decided that something was fat. A topping of creamy melted feta and herbed bread crumbs turned out to be the magic combo that has made this rustic dish into one of those runaway-hit appetizers we can never take off the menu.

Serve this as a starter or a side, or puree some of the beans before proceeding with the feta and crumbs, and take it to a party to serve as a hot dip. We sometimes make it with lima beans, navy beans, or cannellini, but coronas remain my favorite because, cooked right, they're as creamy as a bean can be. To make a (very Moroccan) version with fresh shell beans (like cranberry beans or butter beans), just cook about 3 cups of them (about 4½ pounds/2 kilos in the shell) in the sauce, and top with the cheese and crumbs.

beans
8 ounces (226 grams) dried corona beans
1 large carrot, peeled and quartered lengthwise
1 celery stalk, cut into 2-inch pieces
1 garlic clove
2 tablespoons (24 grams) brown sugar
1 tablespoon (9 grams) kosher salt

sauce
1½ cups (375 grams) diced canned tomatoes preferably San Marzano, with their juices
¾ cup (213 grams) tomato puree, preferably San Marzano
2¼ cups (527 grams) water
¼ cup (17 grams) coarsely chopped cilantro
¼ cup (17 grams) coarsely chopped flat-leaf parsley
1 tablespoon (12.5 grams) granulated sugar
1 tablespoon (12 grams) minced garlic
2 teaspoons (6 grams) kosher salt
1½ teaspoons (4 grams) sweet paprika
1½ teaspoons (3.8 grams) ground cumin
1 teaspoon (2.6 grams) dried oregano
¾ teaspoon (1.3 grams) ground coriander
¼ teaspoon (0.5 gram) ground black pepper
⅛ teaspoon (0.3 gram) cayenne

onions
1 tablespoon (13 grams) grapeseed or canola oil
1¾ cups (185 grams) thinly sliced onions
Pinch of kosher salt
1 teaspoon (5 grams) balsamic vinegar

One 4-ounce (112-gram) piece dry-packed feta cheese, such as Mt. Vikos or Redwood Hill, crumbled
1 cup (41 grams) Dried Bread Crumbs (page 378)
3 tablespoons (40 grams) extra virgin olive oil
1½ teaspoons (2 grams) minced oregano

FOR THE BEANS: Put the beans in a large container and pour in enough cold water to cover them by 2 inches. Leave them to soak overnight at room temperature.

Preheat the oven to 375°F.

CONTINUED

the dance
of the
seven salads

Watch a group of women putting together a meal in a Moroccan kitchen and you'll be confused. You'll see the main dish coming together, the chickens being cleaned and braised, the *basteeya* being assembled, or whatever.

But what's all that other activity? It's like a ritual dance, the young women moving fast, the older ones barely moving at all, as herbs are chopped, vegetables fried, spices pummeled and sprinkled into little pots and pans. They navigate around each other, seasoning here, tasting there, as if they're all being told what to do on headsets. And as you watch, all of this action comes together and turns into a single, quintessentially Moroccan institution: the seven salads.

They're served at the start of the meal, and they say a lot about the culture—about the importance of generosity, abundance, and making a good first impression. Seven being a "perfect" number associated with wholeness in a lot of Muslim cultures, it's the preferred number for the salads. But depending on the workload of the cooks, and who's at the table, there may not always be seven of them. Sometimes there are five, sometimes nine, sometimes even only one if it's just family, but it's always an odd number. And the salads are always set out on small plates.

Like *mezze* in some parts of the Middle East or antipasto in Italy, the idea is to offer a contrasting selection of warm and room-temperature foods, some spicy, some pickled, some sweet, and some savory. It's mostly vegetables, but spreads and even some meat dishes round out the array, and there's always bread to eat them with. This happens six days a week. On Fridays, when it's couscous day, we cut to the chase and skip the salads altogether.

Everyone loves and expects the seven salads, even if, at our house, as I imagine is the case in most homes, someone was always yelling at someone else not to fill up on them and spoil their appetite for the meal ahead.

In an odd way, the salads are both infinitely different and remarkably similar. Cumin tends to be the common denominator. There's a whole category of fried vegetables—beans, eggplant, squash, beets, tomatoes, sweet peppers, cabbage, leeks, yams—seasoned with cumin, paprika, parsley, garlic, olive oil, and other spices. These are generally the territory of the older cooks, whose instincts for complex seasoning have become second nature. Simpler salads—the fresh ones made with diced or sliced carrots, cucumbers, tomatoes, radishes, and other vegetables—are entrusted to the girls and younger women. Then there are savory jams (like Carrot Jam, page 358; Herb Jam, page 166; and Tomato Jam, page 108), creamy dips and spreads, and dressed-up olives. And it's all made from whatever's in season and whatever fits the weather and the mood of the household.

That's the spirit I'm going for when I plan a first course at home or at the restaurant. I don't serve seven salads, but I do love putting that same kind of array of flavor-packed sensations on a single small plate that welcomes people with the abundance of beautiful things I find at the farmers' market.

BRAISED ARTICHOKES
CIPOLLINI ONIONS
CUMIN BROTH

Even a Moroccan might not guess that this combination started with the flavors of a popular dish: a lamb tagine cooked with artichoke hearts and preserved lemons. But when I eat this little salad, that's definitely the memory I taste.

I'm always intrigued by the idea of turning heavier meat-based dishes into lighter vegetable-based appetizers. Here I cook the main elements separately, as I almost always do, so you get to enjoy all kinds of very distinctive flavors, depending on how you compose each bite, rather than eating a dish in which everything ends up tasting the same. I leave the spices whole and wrap them in a sachet, so the broth stays clean and clear. The artichokes, onions, and lemons each get their due in individualized preparations. And when you bring them together on the plate (warm or at room temperature is best here, not hot) along with their various cooking liquids, you get a very finely tuned kind of harmony.

Pistachio oil isn't always easy to come by. You can use hazelnut oil instead (in which case, swap out the pistachios with toasted, skinned, chopped hazelnuts). For another harmonious appetizer, puree the artichokes with a splash of their cooking liquid; top the puree with carrots cooked in stock, sherry vinaigrette, sugar, and salt; and garnish it all with a sprinkling of toasted hazelnuts.

1 tablespoon (10 grams) shelled pistachios

artichokes
3 lemons
6 globe artichokes (10 ounces/283 grams each) or
   9 small artichokes (6 ounces/170 grams each)
One 750-ml (746-gram) bottle Riesling
6 cups (1.4 kilograms) water
½ carrot

½ large onion
2 tablespoons (18 grams) kosher salt
6 garlic cloves, smashed
4 (4 grams) thyme sprigs
3 (0.5 gram) bay leaves
¼ cup (29.6 grams) cumin seeds
2 tablespoons (7.6 grams) coriander seeds
1 tablespoon (9 grams) Tellicherry peppercorns
1½ tablespoons (20 grams) extra virgin olive oil
1 teaspoon (1 gram) chopped flat-leaf parsley

cipollini onions
24 cipollini onions (1½ inches in diameter), unpeeled
8 tablespoons (4 ounces/113 grams) unsalted butter
½ teaspoon (0.5 gram) saffron threads
Kosher salt

lemon slices
Grapeseed or canola oil for deep-frying
24 thin (¹⁄₁₆-inch) lemon slices, preferably Meyer, seeded
Kosher salt

1 tablespoon (13 grams) pistachio oil
Crunchy sea salt

Preheat the oven to 300°F.

   Toast the pistachios in the oven for about 11 minutes, until light golden. Set aside.

FOR THE ARTICHOKES: Fill a large container with cold water. Cut the lemons in half. Squeeze the juice of 5 halves into the water, and add the 5 lemon rinds. To trim the artichokes, working around each artichoke one at a time, bend back the lower leaves until they snap and break, then pull them off, leaving the meat of the leaf attached to the heart. Continue until you reach the yellow inner leaves, rubbing the remaining lemon half over the exposed surfaces as you work to keep the artichoke from oxidizing. Repeat with the remaining artichokes. Turn each artichoke on its side and cut off the top two-thirds of the leaves, down to the meaty heart. Cut off the tough bottom ends of the stems.

Hold an artichoke heart in your hand stem side down and use a sharp paring knife to trim away the tough dark green parts around the heart. Turn the artichoke stem side up and trim the outside of the artichoke, creating a smooth line from the stem to the heart. Be sure that you go deep enough to reach the tender part of the artichoke. There shouldn't be any dark green, tough, or stringy sections left. Use a spoon to scrape out the fuzzy choke and discard it. Cut the artichoke heart into wedges—4 for small artichoke hearts, 6 for large. Drop into the lemon water and repeat with the remaining artichokes. Put a plate over the artichokes to keep them submerged.

Pour the wine into a large saucepan, bring to a simmer, and simmer for 15 to 20 minutes, or until reduced by half.

Add the water, carrot, onion, and salt to the wine. Wrap the garlic, herbs, and spices in a piece of cheesecloth and tie to make a large sachet. Add it to the pan and bring the liquid to a simmer. Simmer for about 5 minutes to infuse the flavors.

Drain the artichokes, add them to the cooking liquid, and simmer for about 20 minutes, or until just tender when tested with the tip of a paring knife. With a skimmer or slotted spoon, transfer the artichokes to a container. Remove the sachet from the pan and simmer the liquid for about 20 minutes to reduce it by about one-third. Pour the broth over the artichoke hearts. (The artichokes can be prepared 3 to 4 hours in advance.)

FOR THE CIPOLLINI: Trim the tops of the onions to create a flat top, with the layers of onion exposed. Peel the onions and trim the roots flush, leaving enough of the roots to hold the rings together as the onions cook.

Melt the butter over medium heat in a frying pan large enough to hold the onions in a single layer. Add the saffron and arrange the cipollini in the pan, top side down. Sauté, basting the onions frequently, tilting the pan and spooning the butter over the onions, for about 8 minutes, until golden brown on the first side. Turn them over and continue to baste with the butter for another 1 to 2 minutes, or until they are completely tender. Remove the onions from the pan and sprinkle each with a pinch of salt. Reserve the butter remaining in the pan.

FOR THE LEMON SLICES: Heat 1 inch of grapeseed oil to 350°F in a medium saucepan fitted with a thermometer. Dry the lemon slices. Add a small batch, in a single layer, to the pan and fry for about 1½ minutes. The flesh will become quite dark but the rind should only be lightly browned. Drain on paper towels and sprinkle with salt. Skim the oil and fry the remaining slices.

TO SERVE: Toss the artichokes with the olive oil and parsley.

Cut the cipollini in half through the root end. Divide the artichokes and cipollini among individual serving bowls and add about ¼ cup (60 grams) of the broth to each bowl. Arrange the lemon slices on and around the artichokes and sprinkle with the pistachios. Garnish each serving with ½ teaspoon (2 grams) of the reserved butter from the onions and ½ teaspoon of the pistachio oil, spooning them in droplets over the broth. Sprinkle with crunchy sea salt.

SERVES 6

BEETS
AVOCADO PUREE
PUMPKIN SEED CRUMBLE

Americans are funny about beets. I've had them on the menu at my restaurant since day one, and I've always gotten a kick out of how surprised people are when it turns out they like them. For a while, we served them in the classic "seven salads" way: boiled, cubed, and tossed with cumin, salt, and olive oil. But I got tired of that and came up with a thousand other ideas, including a single gigantic beet (I'm talking five pounds), salt-roasted, carved to order tableside like prime rib, and drizzled with a cumin vinaigrette.

I also like to use beet juice to color and flavor other things—a slice of peach, or a baby carrot—to add a little element of surprise. And I love to slice baby beets transparent-thin as a garnish.

I think the musty, earthy quality of beets calls for something fluffy and creamy. I've paired them with everything from crème fraîche and yogurt to goat cheese. Eventually I arrived at whipped avocado, and I'm happy to be here.

You can make this salad with one kind of beet, but an assortment of colors (and their respective, quite distinctive flavors) is more fun. Have you checked out Chioggias (pronounced "*kyo*-juh") and golden beets? Both have the excellent advantage of not bleeding all over you and everything they touch. When you use red beets as part of a mix of beets, cook them separately (as directed here), dividing the seasoned liquid accordingly. This way, they won't turn the other beets red. You can be fairly casual about this; the beets don't have to be completely submerged in liquid. Just make sure the pan is well sealed with aluminum foil.

beets

6 cups (1.4 kilograms) warm water

½ cup (120 grams) sherry vinegar

2 tablespoons (18 grams) kosher salt

6 (6.5 grams) star anise

2 teaspoons (6 grams) Tellicherry peppercorns

2 teaspoons (4.9 grams) green cardamom pods

2 teaspoons (2.5 grams) coriander seeds

12 small golden beets (1.5 ounces/43 grams each)

12 small Chioggia beets (1.5 ounces/43 grams each)

12 small red beets (1.5 ounces/43 grams each)

pumpkin seed crumble

6 tablespoons (58 grams) pumpkin seeds

¼ cup (28 grams) Dried Bread Crumbs (page 378)

2 tablespoons (24 grams) dark or light brown sugar

1½ teaspoons (3 grams) grated lemon zest

About 1 tablespoon (13 grams) extra virgin olive oil

Kosher salt

(MAKES ¾ CUP/126 GRAMS)

avocado puree

1 ripe avocado, halved, pitted, and peeled

⅓ cup (83 grams) whole milk

Kosher salt

2 teaspoons (10 grams) fresh lemon juice

2 tablespoons (14 grams) crème fraîche

(MAKES 2¾ CUPS/458 GRAMS)

2 pink grapefruits

Extra virgin olive oil

Micro-greens, preferably bull's blood, chickweed, or chervil

Crunchy sea salt

FOR THE BEETS: Preheat the oven to 400°F.

Combine all the ingredients except the beets in a bowl, stirring to dissolve the salt. Pour two-thirds of the mixture into a 9-by-13-inch baking pan and the rest into an 8-inch square pan.

Leave the roots on the beets and trim the greens to ¼ inch. Add the golden and Chioggia beets to the large pan and the red beets to the smaller one. Cover the pans tightly with aluminum foil and cook for 1 hour. Test the beets with a paring knife—the centers should be tender but not mushy. If your beets are larger than 1.5 ounces, they may need to cook longer.

Remove the pans from the oven, remove the foil, and let the beets cool to room temperature in the cooking liquid. Reduce the oven temperature to 350°F.

FOR THE CRUMBLE: Toast the pumpkin seeds in the oven for about 8 minutes, or until they are lightly browned. Set aside.

Put the bread crumbs, brown sugar, and lemon zest in a food processor and pulse a few times to combine. Add the pumpkin seeds and pulse a few times to break them up. With the machine running, slowly pour in enough olive oil so the mixture comes together into a moist crumble. Season to taste with salt.

FOR THE AVOCADO PUREE: Put the avocado, milk, and a pinch of salt in a blender and blend to a smooth puree. With the machine running, add the lemon juice. Transfer the puree to a bowl and fold in the crème fraîche. Add salt to taste if necessary.

Cut away the peel and white pith from the grapefruits, then cut between the membranes to release the segments. Set aside.

TO SERVE: Starting with the golden and Chioggia beets, rub each one gently with a paper towel to remove the skin. Gently rub the roots as well—if some of the delicate roots break off, that's fine, but keeping some of them intact will give you a more interesting presentation. Repeat with the red beets. Leave some of the beets whole and cut the rest into halves or wedges, so you have a variety of shapes. Trim off some of the stems, so that you can stand those beets up when you plate them.

Put each type of beet in a separate small bowl and toss with a light coating of olive oil. Dip the trimmed ends of some of the beets in the crumble.

Place a generous spoonful of avocado puree on each serving plate. Pull a small offset spatula through part of the puree to form a thinner base of puree. Arrange a variety of beets over and around the puree on each plate. Garnish with the grapefruit sections, a sprinkling of crumble, a few greens, and a bit of crunchy sea salt.

SERVES 6

CHEF TO CHEF: I confess, at the restaurant I can't bring myself to simply poach beets. Once they're cooked, I compress them (meaning I vacuum-seal them in a Cryovac bag) with some of their poaching liquid, which concentrates them and infuses them with more of the flavor of the aromatics.

FAVA BEANS AND RAMPS
5½-MINUTE EGGS
CHICKEN CRACKLINGS

I think of the word *fava,* and the image that comes to mind is my great-grandma, sitting cross-legged on the floor with a huge pile of pods filling her skirt front, shelling them for hours in a trance-like state. Or I think of the guys in Marrakesh who make their living getting bushels of whatever vegetable has just come into season, boiling it, carrying it up and down the alleyways in a steaming pot, and selling it in paper cones, sprinkled with cumin and salt. I popped a lot of slippery, salty favas into my mouth that way, walking home from school.

In California, fava beans and ramps come in at around the same time in the spring, and this is one of the best ways I've found to enjoy them together. The favas are blanched, the ramps pan-grilled, and the sauce that brings it all together is a full-flavored chicken jus that gets enriched in the moment by the oozing yolk of a soft-cooked egg.

The key is getting the egg just right, and this is one of those rare things for which eggs that are a few weeks old are better than very fresh ones, because they peel much more easily. I use large eggs, bring them to room temperature, and simmer them for 5 minutes and 30 to 45 seconds (you might want to do a trial run to determine the perfect timing for your batch of eggs).

Because I don't eat pork, my "bacon" is often chicken cracklings, and here the chickeny bacon-and-egg effect they create makes them a perfect crispy garnish.

fava beans

3 pounds (1.36 kilograms) fava beans in the pod
2 teaspoons (9 grams) extra virgin olive oil
½ teaspoon (3 grams) fresh lemon juice
1 teaspoon (1 gram) finely chopped flat-leaf parsley
Kosher salt and freshly ground black pepper

ramps

12 ramps
Canola oil
Kosher salt
1 teaspoon (4.5 grams) extra virgin olive oil
1 teaspoon (2 grams) grated lemon zest
Freshly ground black pepper

About ¾ cup (180 grams) Chicken Jus (page 366)
About ¼ cup (53 grams) Shallot Oil (page 375) or extra
　　virgin olive oil
Six 5½-Minute Eggs (page 376)
Crunchy sea salt and coarsely ground black pepper
Chicken Cracklings (page 372)

FOR THE FAVA BEANS: Bring a large pot of salted water to a boil. Fill a large bowl with ice water.

Shell the beans but do not peel them (the skins will protect the beans from losing too much flavor when chilled in the ice water). Add the beans to the boiling water. The cooking time will vary, depending on their size and the stage of the season. Small favas picked early in the season can be tender in 30 seconds, while larger end-of-season favas, with more starch, can take as long as 3 minutes. The only way to tell is to taste them. When they are tender, drain them and put in the ice water to cool completely.

Drain the favas, peel them (pinch the skin at one end of each bean, and pop out the bean), and put in a medium bowl. Set aside.

FOR THE RAMPS: Although you could cook the ramps on the grill, because they are small, it's easier to cook them in a cast-iron grill pan. Preheat the pan over medium heat. Brush the ramps with canola oil and sprinkle with salt. Grill for about 1 minute per side, or until lightly marked and tender; to avoid burning the greens, once they begin to darken, position the ramps so that the greens hang over the edges of the pan.

Transfer the ramps to a bowl and toss with the olive oil, lemon zest, and pepper to taste.

TO SERVE: If the chicken jus has solidified, warm it gently to melt about half the sauce, then remove from the heat and stir until it has all liquefied.

Toss the favas with the olive oil, lemon juice, parsley, and salt and pepper to taste.

Spoon a nest of fava beans into each serving bowl. Add about 2 tablespoons (30 grams) of the chicken jus and spoon drops of shallot oil over the jus, creating small pools. Add the ramps, and place an egg in the center of each nest. Sprinkle the eggs with crunchy salt and coarse pepper and garnish with the cracklings. Make a small cut in the center of each egg to break the yolk, and serve immediately.

SERVES 6

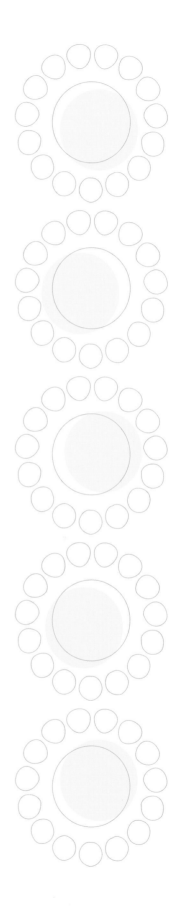

FIGS
CRÈME FRAÎCHE
ARUGULA
MINT

Northern California chefs have been praised, imitated, and even ridiculed for serving very simple dishes, like a few figs on a plate. I generally tend to go for more complex combinations, but with fresh figs, well, if you could taste the northern California figs I get, you'd agree that almost nothing should be done to them.

Figs, yogurt, and honey make perfect sense together. For a first course, crème fraîche instead of yogurt gives the combination a little more savory sophistication. And a piece of honeycomb instead of a drizzle of honey adds a cool visual reference point and a little waxy textural interest. The presentation can be miniaturized into a finger-food nibble. Just top a piece of fig with a dollop of crème fraîche, a small mint leaf, and a bit of pepper.

Tasmanian peppercorns are wonderful, but about ten times as hot as ordinary black pepper. They really work here, but be sure to season with a light hand and taste as you go.

1 cup (110 grams) crème fraîche
Kosher salt
A small handful of small mint leaves
12 Black Mission figs
12 Adriatic figs
3 cups (27 grams) arugula, any large stems removed
1 tablespoon (10.5 grams) Red Wine Vinaigrette
    (page 361)
One 6-ounce (170-gram) piece honeycomb,
    cut into pieces
Extra virgin olive oil for finishing
Crunchy sea salt and ground black pepper, preferably
    Tasmanian

Whisk the crème fraîche with a pinch of salt in a medium bowl until it has the consistency of lightly whipped cream.

Put the mint leaves in a bowl of ice water to crisp, then drain on a paper towel.

Cut the figs into rounds, wedges, or other shapes as you like.

Spoon some crème fraîche onto each serving plate, and drag the bottom of a spoon through it to form an elongated teardrop. Toss the arugula with just enough vinaigrette to coat, and stack some leaves on each plate. Arrange the figs, mint leaves, and honeycomb on the plates. Drizzle a few drops of olive oil over each fig and sprinkle with crunchy sea salt and pepper.

SERVES 6

CHICORY SALAD
ANCHOVY VINAIGRETTE
AGED BALSAMIC

In the winter, when tender baby greens aren't available, I get all kinds of amazing baby chicories (and by that I mean the whole chicory clan, including radicchio, endive, Treviso, and frisée) from David Retsky at County Line Harvest in northern Marin County. Each has its own distinctive flavor and texture, and the result is baby greens with a very adult attitude. I soak the leaves in ice water to crisp them and tone down their bitterness, and then I dress them with an anchovy-lemon vinaigrette, adding balsamic cranberries for an occasional burst of extra bittersweetness.

It's nice to dress a salad in a layered way—like first drizzling the plate with aged balsamic, an intense, pricey elixir that's best left unadulterated, then mounding vinaigrette-tossed greens on top. The same technique of "dressing the plate" can work well with a puree, a flavored oil, a jus, or a little reduced cooking liquid from any element of the dish.

To turn this into a substantial dinner salad, top it with warm "pulled" pieces of *Berbere*-Cured Confit Duck Legs (page 246).

croutons

Grapeseed or canola oil

1½ cups (54 grams) ¾-inch cubes country bread without crusts

4 garlic cloves, smashed but not peeled

Pinch of finely chopped rosemary

Pinch of Marash pepper

Kosher salt

anchovy vinaigrette

2 tablespoons (30 grams) fresh lemon juice, preferably Meyer lemon

2 tablespoons (29 grams) champagne vinegar

1 teaspoon (7 grams) Dijon mustard

1 small garlic clove

9 (28 grams) oil-packed anchovy fillets, rinsed

½ large egg yolk (optional)

½ cup (106 grams) extra virgin olive oil

(MAKES 1 CUP/185 GRAMS)

salad

16 cups (14 ounces/396 grams) mixed chicories (see headnote)

Aged balsamic vinegar, preferably 30 to 40 years old

2 tablespoons (18 grams) Balsamic Cranberries (page 359)

Shavings of Parmigiano-Reggiano or Grana (cut with a vegetable peeler)

FOR THE CROUTONS: Heat a generous film of oil in a medium frying pan over medium-high heat. Add the bread cubes and cook for about 1½ minutes, until beginning to brown. Add the garlic, rosemary, and Marash and cook until the croutons are crunchy on the outside but still soft on the inside, about 2 minutes. Drain on paper towels and sprinkle with salt.

FOR THE VINAIGRETTE: Put the lemon juice, vinegar, mustard, garlic, anchovies, and egg yolk, if using, in a blender and blend on low speed to break up the anchovies, then increase the speed to high and puree. With the blender running, drizzle in the oil until emulsified.

FOR THE SALAD: Pick over the chicory and discard any bruised leaves. Soak the leaves briefly in a large bowl of ice-cold water to crisp them. Swish gently and allow any dirt to sink to the bottom of the bowl, then lift the greens from the water and dry in a salad spinner. Layer the greens with paper towels to remove any remaining moisture.

Drizzle some balsamic over each serving plate. Toss the chicories with a light coating of the dressing. Toss the croutons with a little dressing as well. Arrange the greens, croutons, cranberries, and cheese on the plates.

SERVES 6

BABY LETTUCES
DATE LEATHER

Sweet and savory is, of course, an essential Moroccan concept. But sometimes I like to take that idea in directions that are a little less expected than the classic sweet-spice and caramel flavors of a slow-cooked sauce or a *basteeya*. With a salad, you can play with crunchy, tangy, fresh elements to get to sweet-savory in a lighter, more delicate way.

Here the sweetness comes from dates. For years, I slivered them and tossed them into salads or rolled them into balls (see page 179) and scattered them on top, but I was never really satisfied with either approach. The dates would fall to the bottom, and by the time you got to them, you'd be left with a plateful of date bits you no longer wanted to eat. So I came up with this simple technique for making thin sheets of date leather.

What I love about it, besides its intriguing tortoiseshell appearance on the plate, is the way it puts the date element right out there, like a carpaccio or a slice of gravlax, inviting you to jump right in and compose every bite of date and salad just the way you want it. The dressing is a classic shallot vinaigrette, but made without black pepper, because I add arugula to the mix for a more subtle peppery presence. I like wild arugula, because its small leaves mean that you don't get too much "pepper" in any single bite. If your arugula is large or very spicy, consider tearing it into smaller pieces.

Be sure to dry salad greens very thoroughly before you dress them. I mention this because even in my professional kitchen, people still slip up on this score from time to time. You can have the nicest greens and a great dressing, but if the leaves are wet, it'll throw everything out of balance and ruin your salad. That's why I recommend the technique of putting a paper towel in the salad spinner.

2 tablespoons (19 grams) skin-on almonds or salted Marcona almonds
18 Medjool dates
Extra virgin olive oil
12 cups (125 grams) mixed baby greens
2 cups (18 grams) arugula, preferably wild
About ¼ cup (40 grams) Red Wine Vinaigrette (page 361)
Crunchy sea salt
Edible wildflowers (optional)

If you are using skin-on almonds, toast them in a 350°F oven for about 10 minutes. Set aside.

FOR THE DATE LEATHER: Cut a lengthwise slit down one side of each date, then open it as you would a book and remove the pit. Spread a piece of plastic wrap about 16 inches long on the work surface and brush with a light coating of olive oil. Press 6 dates side by side, cut side down, onto the plastic in 2 rows of 3; it's fine if there are small spaces between the dates. Lightly oil a second sheet of plastic wrap and lay it, oiled side down, over the dates. Using a rolling pin, press down on the dates to flatten them slightly, then roll them into a thin rectangular sheet about 6 by 9 inches and ¹⁄₁₆ inch thick. If the dates separate or there are gaps, push them together and continue rolling. Set aside, still in the plastic wrap, and repeat 2 more times with the remaining 12 dates. (The sheets can be refrigerated in the plastic wrap for up to a week.)

Fill two large bowls with ice water and put them in or near the sink. Put the mixed greens and the arugula in one bowl and swish them gently in the water (the ice will help crisp the greens). Lift up a handful of the greens at a time and rinse them under cold running water, picking through them and

Arrange the sardine fillets skin side down in a container just large enough to hold them in a single layer. (If you only have a smaller container, they can be arranged in 2 layers; arrange the second layer at a 90-degree angle to the layer beneath it.) Pour in the cold pickling liquid and let sit at room temperature for 1 hour.

Remove the sardines from the liquid, rinse them under cold water, and drain them flesh side down on paper towels. Turn flesh side up and sprinkle with kosher salt. The sardines can be eaten at this point, drizzled with olive oil and sprinkled with salt, when they have the most pickled flavor, or they can be refrigerated covered in olive oil for up to 2 weeks, which will mellow the pickling flavor. If you want to store them in olive oil, clean the container and arrange the sardines as before. Pour in enough olive oil to cover and add the sliced garlic. Cover with plastic wrap and refrigerate. (The oil will congeal when the sardines are refrigerated; bring to room temperature before serving.)

FOR THE HERB JAM: Heat a light film of oil in a large sauté pan over medium heat. Add the onions and spices and cook, stirring often, for about 10 minutes, until the onions are translucent and the spices have toasted. Add the braising greens and stir to combine. Cover the pan and cook for about 10 minutes, turning the greens from time to time as they wilt and adjusting the heat as necessary so the spices do not burn. Add the sweet pickling liquid, cover, and cook for about 8 minutes, or until most of the liquid has evaporated. Remove the lid, reduce the heat to medium-low, and cook, stirring often for about 10 minutes, or until the greens and pan are dry. Season to taste with salt, and let cool.

FOR THE BRIOCHE TOASTS: Preheat the oven to 325°F. Line a baking sheet with parchment paper.

Put the slices of brioche on the parchment. Cover with another piece of parchment and another baking sheet and bake for 12 minutes, or until golden on the first side. Turn the bread over, rotate the pan, and bake for another 12 minutes, or until golden. Remove from the pan and let cool on a cooling rack.

TO SERVE: Fill a large bowl with ice water. Cut the fronds off the fennel bulb and remove any tough outer layers. Cut the fennel lengthwise in half. Place each flat side on a Japanese mandoline and cut into thin slices. Soak the fennel in the ice water for about 10 minutes.

Drain the fennel on paper towels, put into a bowl, and squeeze the lemon over the top. Toss with a drizzle of olive oil, some chives, and 2 pinches of kosher salt.

Cover each crouton with a ³/₈- to ½-inch-thick layer of the herb jam, spreading it in an even layer. Trim the sardines so they will fit crosswise on the croutons, and arrange about 5 pieces of sardine, skin side up, on each crouton.

Put a small spoonful of herb jam in the center of each serving plate to anchor the croutons. Put the croutons on the jam and garnish the dish with the slices of fennel and the preserved lemon. Drizzle with olive oil and sprinkle with crunchy sea salt.

SERVES 6

CHEF TO CHEF: For an unexpected garnish, deep-fry the sardine backbones, with all the bones intact, in grapeseed or rice bran oil. Heat the oil to 400°F and fry until the bones are browned and completely crisp.

SQUID AND NAPA CABBAGE
THAI-STYLE *HARISSA* SAUCE

Our restaurant is right at the epicenter of San Francisco's Richmond District, the fog-blanketed grid of numbered avenues that stretches along the north side of Golden Gate Park all the way out to the Pacific. The neighborhood is very Asian, so we've got an incredible choice of family-owned Chinese, Korean, Thai, and Vietnamese places to hit for a quick bite before or after service. For me, that quick bite is often a fiery Thai squid salad, and late one night, while chewing happily on it, I decided I wanted to try serving something along the same lines.

I started with *harissa,* since it's remarkably similar to Thai chile paste. And then I added fish sauce, because, even though there's nothing like it in the Moroccan pantry, I love how it works with sugar, lime, mint, and chiles. The rest of the ingredients could be straight out of my mom's kitchen.

I blanch the squid rings and then grill the tentacles at the last minute, so they add a warm element that makes a nice contrast to the cool salad. If you like, you can cook the tentacles ahead and serve them at room temperature.

squid

2 pounds (907 grams) squid, cleaned, tentacles reserved and bodies cut into ½-inch-wide rings
1 tablespoon (7.2 grams) Quick *Harissa* (page 82)
½ lemon
Crunchy sea salt

harissa *sauce*

2 tablespoons (14.4 grams) Quick *Harissa* (page 82)
1 tablespoon (15 grams) fish sauce
1 tablespoon (12.5 grams) granulated sugar
6 tablespoons (90 grams) fresh lime juice
1 teaspoon (3 grams) kosher salt

garnish

3 cups (113 grams) shredded Napa cabbage (tough ribs removed)
6 tablespoons (10 grams) thinly slivered mint leaves
3 tablespoons (5 grams) thinly slivered cilantro leaves
A handful of micro-greens, preferably bull's blood

FOR THE SQUID: Preheat a grill to high heat. Fill a large bowl with ice water.

Bring a large saucepan of water to a boil. Drop the squid rings into the boiling water for 10 seconds, then quickly drain them and submerge in the ice water. Drain again and set aside.

Put the tentacles in a small bowl, toss them with the *harissa,* and let them sit at room temperature for about 15 minutes. Just before grilling, scrape off excess *harissa.*

Although it may seem as if the tentacles will fall through the grill grates, if placed correctly, they will curl almost immediately when they hit the heat, preventing this. Lay the tentacles across the grates and grill for about 30 seconds. Turn them over and grill for another 15 seconds. Put in a medium bowl and toss with a squeeze of lemon juice and a sprinkling of crunchy sea salt.

FOR THE *HARISSA* SAUCE: Mix all the ingredients together in a small bowl.

TO SERVE: Put the cabbage in a bowl and toss it with a light coating of the sauce. Don't overdress it; you can always add more dressing. Toss in the mint, cilantro, and squid rings.

Arrange a stack of the salad on each serving plate. Garnish with the tentacles and micro-greens.

SERVES 6

if soup
could talk

You might be surprised to learn that soup is just not very Moroccan. Yes, there's the famous lentil *harira* (see page 177), but that's really in a category of its own. There are grain-based porridges, eaten at breakfast or late at night. And there's *chorba,* a kind of Moroccan minestrone. But the whole idea of a soup being *about* something in particular, like carrot, spinach, corn, or mushrooms, isn't one that interests Moroccan cooks much. That kind of thinking is more likely to show up in the seven salads department, where the soul of a single ingredient is beautifully showcased.

Me, I'm for soups that are unmistakably about something. I want the essence of the main ingredients to stand up and wave at you. If it's about carrots, I'll intensify their flavor with carrot juice; corn, I'll enrich with corn stock; tomatoes, I'll roast them in a salt crust. And because I serve soups as starters, I like them to be light and clean without a lot of spice and seasoning. I'd rather add more assertive flavors and textures with the garnish or in a separate element that sits on the sidelines—a crunchy, savory granola; a spice blend; or a little salad that half-floats in the bowl—so the soup can be its best self, and the "soupees" can compose each spoonful with whatever balance of elements they like.

I also love to play with meat stocks and vegetables, flipping the usual meat-center/veg-side equation, so the stock becomes the stage and the vegetable the star. No doubt that's a response to growing up in a culture where the idea of stock doesn't exist. Moroccan cooks add water, not broth, to meat (or poultry or seafood), vegetables, and spices, and that *becomes* a broth, which is often cooked down until it turns into a sauce. But I'm all about extracting the essences of ingredients to make concentrated stocks and then using those as building blocks to construct a dish. Very often that takes me right back to something that ends up tasting Moroccan, but in a surprising, sneak-up-on-you kind of way.

LENTIL SOUP
DATE BALLS
CELERY SALAD

This is my version of *harira,* the national soup of Morocco, which shows up in unending variations from city to city, street stall to street stall, and family to family. It can be vegan, vegetarian, or made with meat—usually lamb. Some cooks add chickpeas, chicken gizzards, or broken-up bits of angel hair pasta. But the result is always unmistakably *harira,* and that's what makes it so comforting and satisfying.

Harira has the inexplicable quality of being both light and filling at the same time, making you feel perfectly content. That's why, besides being the national soup, it's also a religious institution: it's what every family in Morocco eats to break their daily fast all through the monthlong observance of Ramadan. All over the country, for an entire month of sunsets, the first thing the entire population tastes is *harira,* and breaking the fast with anything else would be like serving Thanksgiving dinner without turkey.

During Ramadan here in the States, I fast all day, even though I keep up my normal schedule, shopping in the farmers' market and working in the kitchen. As soon as the sun goes down, I step away from my expediting station and have a quick bowlful of *harira* to get me through the evening. And on days off, I take home a quart of it to break the fast at my house.

The first time you make this, try making a light meal of it, with just some bread and maybe a simple salad. You'll understand what I'm talking about. It's weirdly, wonderfully satisfying—in a way that fills your soul more than your stomach.

I make *harira* with water, not stock, because I think this vegetarian (actually, vegan) version is lighter and cleaner tasting, but you can make it with chicken or lamb stock or half stock and half water.

While its flavor is very true to the original, I've played with its preparation. For example, I cook the lentils separately, to keep them from breaking down too much. (My mom called that crazy, but she smiled when she tasted the result.) And if you cook them in the soup, they darken the cooking liquid and give the soup a muddy appearance. The yeast-and-flour mixture is my version of the traditional starter made from fermented flour and water, used exclusively for *harira,* that you'll find in every Moroccan kitchen. It's easier to manage but has the same effect as that sourdough original, thickening and lightening the soup, and keeping it from separating, while adding a rich, tangy flavor. I wanted to give people a little crunch without adding an extra element, so I took the celery out of its usual place in the sautéed soup base and reintroduced it at the end as a raw garnish.

In Morocco, *harira* is classically served with dates, which add sweetness to balance the soup's acidity. Taste it without the dates, and then try it with them. You'll find it's an entirely different experience. When I first started serving this soup at the restaurant, I'd accompany it with a few beautiful (and expensive) California Medjools on the side. The dates kept coming back uneaten. People just didn't get the idea of savory soup and sweet dates, which drove me nuts. So I thought of a way to work the dates into the soup, rolling them into little balls and adding them as a garnish. People get it now. The date balls are never left uneaten. They're a part of the bigger idea, as they should be.

This makes a big batch. That's how I always do it, even at home, because we love to eat it over several nights, and it keeps for up to a week.

spice mix

3 tablespoons (27 grams) kosher salt

1 tablespoon (7.6 grams) ground cumin

1 tablespoon (5.5 grams) ground coriander

1 teaspoon (2.6 grams) ground white pepper

1½ teaspoons (4 grams) sweet paprika

1 teaspoon (2 grams) ground ginger

½ teaspoon (1.4 grams) ground turmeric

¼ teaspoon (0.2 gram) saffron threads

soup

2 cups (484 grams) tomato paste
   (not double concentrate)

8 quarts plus 1 cup (7.6 kilograms) cold water

2 bunches (8 ounces/224 grams) cilantro, leaves and
   tender stems only

1 bunch (4 ounces/112 grams) flat-leaf parsley,
   leaves and tender stems only

1½ pounds (680 grams) yellow onions

Green leaves from 1 bunch celery, about 3 cups
   (35 grams); stalks reserved for garnish

⅓ cup (44 grams) all-purpose flour

2 cups (468 grams) warm water (about 110°F)

⅛ teaspoon (0.4 gram) active dry yeast
   (not quick-rising)

Kosher salt

3 tablespoons (45 grams) fresh lemon juice,
   or to taste

date balls

12 Medjool dates

Extra virgin olive oil

1½ cups (288 grams) dried green lentils,
   preferably French, picked through and rinsed

celery salad

Reserved bunch of celery (from above)

2 tablespoons (27 grams) extra virgin olive oil

2 tablespoons (8 grams) minced flat-leaf parsley

Kosher salt and freshly ground black pepper

FOR THE SPICE MIX: Mix all the ingredients together in a small bowl. Set aside

FOR THE SOUP: Put the tomato paste and 7 quarts (6.6 kilograms) cold water in a large nonreactive stockpot over high heat. Whisk occasionally as the water comes to a boil, then reduce the heat to maintain a gentle boil and cook for about 1 hour, or until it has reduced by about one-quarter. (Remove from the heat if the onions aren't ready.)

Meanwhile, rinse the cilantro and parsley well and set aside. Cut the onions into large chunks. Put the chunks in a food processor and pulse until they are becoming a mush. Add as much of the herbs as fit into the food processor. Pulse the machine, adding small amounts of cold water if necessary to allow the blade to spin. As the herbs decrease in volume, add the remaining herbs and the celery leaves and continue to pulse. Stop from time to time to scrape the sides with a rubber spatula and mix the herbs to redistribute them. Run the machine for up to 10 minutes, until the mixture is almost liquefied.

Transfer the mixture to a large saucepan and stir in the spice mix.

Add the remaining 5 cups (1.2 kilograms) cold water to the onions and bring to a gentle boil over high heat, then reduce the heat and boil gently for about 1 hour or until the liquid is reduced by half.

Stir the onion mixture into the stockpot, return to a simmer, and cook for 1½ to 2 hours, skimming any impurities that rise to the top, until the soup has reduced by about one-third to just over 4 quarts (4 kilograms).

MEANWHILE, FOR THE DATE BALLS: Cut a lengthwise slit down one side of each date, open it as you would a book, and remove the pit. Cut the dates lengthwise in half, then cut each half lengthwise into 4 strips. Using your fingertips, shape each strip into a rough ball. If you keep the skin side facing out, the ball will be less sticky and will hold together better.

Pour a shallow pool of olive oil into a small bowl. Rub a little of the oil on the center of one palm, put a date ball on it, and use the index finger of your other hand to roll the date into a smooth ball. Put the ball in the bowl of oil, and repeat with the rest of the dates, adding more oil to the bowl as needed to keep the date balls covered. Set aside.

FOR THE LENTILS: Put the lentils in a saucepan, add 6 cups (1.4 kilograms) cold water, and bring to a simmer over medium heat. Cook the lentils for 10 to 12 minutes, stirring them from time to time.

Meanwhile, fill a large bowl with cold water. Taste a lentil. When they have started to soften but are still firm in the center, drain them in a fine-mesh strainer, rinse them with cold water, and submerge them in the bowl of cold water until ready to use.

FOR THE CELERY SALAD: Remove the tough outer celery stalks and reserve them for another use. Pinch off the leaves from the inner stalks and place the leaves in a bowl of ice water. Cut the stalks into ⅛-inch dice; you need 1 cup (120 grams). Put the diced celery in a small bowl, toss with the olive oil and parsley, and season to taste with salt and pepper.

TO FINISH THE SOUP: Once the soup has reduced, add the lentils; keep warm over low heat.

Whisk together the flour, water, and yeast in a small bowl and let sit at room temperature until foamy and bubbling, about 10 minutes.

Whisking constantly, add the flour mixture to the soup, then stir with a flat-bottomed wooden spoon, scraping the bottom of the pot, as you bring the soup to a simmer over medium heat. (High heat could cause the flour to stick to the bottom of the pot.) Simmer the soup gently, stirring often, for 10 minutes. Season to taste with salt, remove the soup from the heat, and stir in the lemon juice.

Drain and dry the celery leaves. Using 2 soupspoons, form the celery salad into a quenelle or football shape and place toward the rim of each soup bowl. Stack about 8 date balls alongside each quenelle. (If you end up with extra date balls, keep them in the refrigerator and add them to salads.)

Carefully ladle the soup around the garnishes so that a bit of the celery salad and the date balls remain visible. Drizzle some of the olive oil that remains in the bowl of celery salad over the soup and garnish with the celery leaves.

SERVES 12 TO 14 (MAKES 5 QUARTS/5 KILOGRAMS)

SUNCHOKE PUREE
Z'HUG GRANOLA

Sunchokes, or Jerusalem artichokes, are underappreciated in America. Not so in Morocco. My Aunt Samira makes a mean tagine of lamb and sunchokes, and my mom stews them and dresses them with salt, pepper, cumin, and olive oil to make a quick salad.

I get mine toward the end of summer from my potato guy, David Little, who runs the aptly named Little Organic Farm in Petaluma. When they're young and as tiny as your finger, you can eat sunchokes raw without even peeling them, or shave them right onto a salad. When they are larger, I slice them and fry them as chips.

I was delighted to discover that when you run sunchokes through a juicer, you get a white milky liquid that you can blend with cream to make ice cream. A quenelle of that ice cream floated in a warm artichoke soup is my kind of garnish. (By the way, though Jerusalem artichokes certainly go well with artichokes, they're not related to them.)

Here I sauté sunchokes with leeks and simmer them in stock to make a pretty straight-ahead puree. I season it sparingly to hold on to the delicate flavor of the sunchokes and then bring in the spice factor with a sprinkling of *z'hug* granola.

4 pounds (1.8 kilograms) medium sunchokes
3 medium leeks, white and light green parts only
½ pound (229 grams) unsalted butter
Kosher salt
1 cup (232 grams) Riesling
8 cups (1.87 kilograms) Chicken Stock (page 365)
Z'hug–Pumpkin Seed Granola (page 377)

Peel the sunchokes and cut them into ¼-inch-thick slices. For this recipe, you'll need about 9 cups (2.7 pounds/1.2 kilograms).

Cut the leeks lengthwise in half, then cut them crosswise into thin slices. Swish them in a bowl of cold water to remove any dirt, lift them out (leaving the grit behind), and place in a colander to drain. You should have about ¾ cup (150 grams).

Melt the butter in a large saucepan over medium-high heat. Add the leeks and a pinch of salt and cook for 3 to 4 minutes, or until they have softened. Add the sunchokes and ¼ teaspoon (0.75 gram) salt and cook, stirring occasionally, for 20 minutes, or until the sunchokes begin to stick to the bottom of the pan.

Add the wine and deglaze, using a flat-bottomed wooden spoon to scrape the bottom of the pan. Continue to cook for about 5 minutes, until the wine evaporates and the sunchokes begin to stick to the pan again. Add the chicken stock, bring to a simmer, and cook for 30 to 45 minutes, until the stock has reduced by one-quarter.

Working in batches, transfer the solids and liquid to a blender and puree (or use an immersion blender). For the silkiest texture, strain the soup through a fine-mesh strainer. Season to taste with salt.

TO SERVE: Pour the soup into serving bowls and mound a spoonful of granola to one side of each serving.

**SERVES 8 TO 10
(MAKES 2½ QUARTS/2.5 KILOGRAMS)**

CHICKEN BOUILLON
WHEAT BERRIES
SALT-BAKED TOMATO

Soup becomes experience. In this case, the experience of *chorba,* a Moroccan chicken, vegetable, tomato, and noodle soup. First you smell essence of chicken, as the steam rises from the intense, fortified bouillon. Then you cut into the taut-skinned, shiny tomato, and it turns out to be not solid, but filled with sauce, which mixes with the bouillon and the chewy wheat berries, creating a *chorba* effect right in your bowl.

The secret of the surprising tomato is that it's a dry-farmed Early Girl (truly the only kind I've found that works for this purpose) that has been buried in salt and roasted, so that it becomes a "water balloon" filled with a soft cooked tomato sauce. Dry-farmed tomatoes are given as little water as possible. They stay on the vine until late in the season, soaking up the sun as their roots dig deep for moisture. The result is a fruit that's richly concentrated, sweet, and meaty and a skin that's unusually firm—and thus perfect for balloon making.

tomatoes

About 2 pounds (907 grams) kosher salt

6 Early Girl tomatoes (4 ounces/113 grams each), with stems

Four 6-inch (24 grams) rosemary sprigs

6 (6 grams) thyme sprigs

½ cup (106 grams) extra virgin olive oil, plus enough to cover the tomatoes

wheat berries

1 cup (228 grams) wheat berries

1 tablespoon (9 grams) kosher salt

1 tablespoon (12 grams) minced preserved lemon rind (see page 45)

3 tablespoons (40 grams) extra virgin olive oil

(MAKES ABOUT 2½ CUPS/525 GRAMS)

Chicken Bouillon (page 366)

Extra virgin olive oil for finishing

Crunchy sea salt

Dill sprigs, fennel fronds, or fennel pollen for garnish

FOR THE TOMATOES: Preheat the oven to 250°F.

Choose an ovenproof container large enough to hold the tomatoes in one layer without them touching and deep enough so they can be covered in salt. Pour in a ½-inch-thick bed of salt and shake the container to spread it into an even layer. Add the tomatoes, stem side up, leaving space between them. Add enough salt to come to the top of the tomatoes. Place the herb sprigs on top and drizzle with the ½ cup (106 grams) olive oil.

Cover the container tightly with aluminum foil and put in the oven. The cooking time can vary considerably depending on the ripeness of the tomatoes. Begin checking after 25 minutes. Remove the salt covering one tomato and press the top;

the skin will be taut, but the interior should feel completely softened, like tomato sauce encapsulated in the skin. If necessary, cover the tomato with the salt again and return the tomatoes to the oven, checking every 20 to 30 minutes, for up to another 1 hour. Let the tomatoes cool completely in the salt.

Remove and discard the herbs. Remove enough salt to expose the tomatoes and gently lift them from the salt. Discard the salt, wash and dry the container, and return the tomatoes to it. Pour in enough olive oil to cover the tomatoes. The tomatoes should sit in the oil for at least 30 minutes; the olive oil will dissolve any excess salt clinging to them (or, the tomatoes can be refrigerated for up to 2 weeks).

FOR THE WHEAT BERRIES: Spread the wheat berries on a pale work surface or a piece of parchment paper and remove and discard any stones, dark seeds, or shells, then rinse them.

Put the wheat berries, salt, and 8 cups (1.8 kilograms) water in a large saucepan. Bring to a boil, and remove and discard any missed shells that have risen to the top. Reduce the heat and simmer for 1 hour and 45 minutes. If the water level drops below the top of the wheat berries, add water to keep them covered. Taste the wheat berries. They shouldn't taste at all raw, but they should still have a chewy texture. Remove them from the heat and let cool in the cooking liquid.

Drain the wheat berries and taste one or two. If they are too salty for your taste, rinse them with water. Drain thoroughly and put into a bowl. Toss them with the preserved lemon rind and olive oil.

TO SERVE: If the tomatoes have been refrigerated, see the Note below.

Heat the chicken bouillon until hot. The wheat berries can be served slightly warm or at room temperature.

Place a spoonful of wheat berries in each of six shallow soup bowls. Nestle a tomato in one side of the wheat berries and ladle the bouillon around the tomatoes. Pour some olive oil into a large soupspoon and, holding the spoon very close to the surface of the bouillon, add drops of oil all around the broth; they will form large pools—the closer the spoon is to the surface, the larger the pools will be. Sprinkle with salt and garnish with the dill sprigs.

SERVES 6

NOTE: If the tomatoes have been refrigerated, remove them from the refrigerator and let sit (in their oil) at room temperature for 1 hour. Preheat the oven to 325°F. Put the tomatoes and oil in the oven and heat, uncovered, for about 20 minutes, or until the tomatoes have softened again and are warm. Serve warm or let cool to room temperature.

CHEF TO CHEF: If you can't get Early Girl tomatoes, you can achieve a somewhat similar effect with tomato water, thickening it with xanthan gum and then using alginate, calcium chloride, and sodium chloride to "spherify" it into a balloon.

daily bread

On our morning walks through the medina, my grandpa would sometimes see a piece of bread lying on the ground. He'd pick it up, dust it off, kiss it, and whisper a prayer of gratitude. If it was large—a half-eaten loaf, or a roll that had fallen from someone's shopping bag—he'd set it somewhere prominent, so a hungry passerby would find it. If it was just a scrap, he'd hold on to it until he found a cat or some birds to feed it to.

At the table, bread was no less sacred. It was, and still is, served at absolutely every meal with absolutely every food except *basteeya* and couscous (which is, in a sense, a kind of giant mound of bread). It's deliberately simple and plain, because it's there for one reason only: in a culture where silverware is not traditional, plain white bread is an edible spoon for picking up food and sopping up all the flavors of the salads and sauces.

When the main eating is done, the big bread bowl is placed in the center of the table, and everyone tosses their uneaten bread back into it. The bread is taken back to the kitchen to be eaten later, turned into bread crumbs, given to poor people, or fed to animals. Throwing it away is never an option.

In our house, we had an oven, but it was generally regarded as "that box that came with the stove," not good for much more than storing a few pots, and certainly not up to the task of baking eight loaves of bread a day. In the 1970s, in the medina of Marrakesh, bread still happened one way only. You made your dough and took it to the neighborhood bakery. And that bakery didn't sell bread or baked goods. It sold baking.

Taking the rounds of dough to the bakery on a long wooden board was generally my job. I'd drop them off in the morning on the way to school. Sometimes families would mark their dough with a particular symbol to identify it, but somehow, symbol or no symbol, the bakery rarely mixed up anyone's loaves. The bakers would spend the morning whisking bread in and out of the brick oven in neat rows, and when you came back a few hours later, you'd find your board with your warm, freshly baked loaves waiting for you.

No matter where my cooking goes, that grounding warmth of daily bread stays with me. Every morning, Haddi Rih, who has been with us since we first opened, starts his day by making all of our bread doughs. They're proofed, punched down, and baked throughout the day and right through service. It's not just a routine. It's a sacred ritual I know I'll never change.

GRILLED FLATBREADS

From the time I opened my first restaurant, I'd wanted to serve small, simple flatbreads that could be baked throughout service—something with the texture of wood-fired pizza to go with our spreads. But we've never had a brick oven, and our main convection oven is completely turned over to baking *basteeya* all night, so I had to come up with a different plan. I thought of the little breads we would sometimes have at home when I was a kid, made on a flat earthenware griddle over a wood or charcoal fire, and that gave me the idea of using our grill.

Eventually we came up with this dough recipe, which has exactly the right texture: soft enough to puff up nicely but stiff enough to firm up on contact with the grill grates, so it doesn't fall through. I love the grill marks, not just because they look cool, but because they add that element of charred dough you get with great Neapolitan pizza. You'll notice that the grill marks don't happen on the second side, because the dough has become bubbly and irregular at that point, so serve the breads crosshatch side up for best effect.

At first we made these plain, but I wanted to add a bit of seasoning. We tried all kinds of herbs, spices, and seeds, without success—everything seemed to burn or fall off. But then we turned to *za'atar,* with its blend of sumac, oregano, and sesame seeds, and that's what stuck, literally and figuratively. The sumac adds sourness, the oregano blooms with the heat, and the seeds get smoky and toasty. We found that sprinkling one side only was just right.

At the restaurant, we make these on a gas grill, which gives us very good control of the heat, but I've made them many times on charcoal grills. If you do that, bank the coals to create a fairly low pile of embers and cook over that.

In our kitchen, these are the after-service snack of choice. We make them into tacos with leftover grilled or braised meat. Or we top them with tomato or tomato sauce, mozzarella, creamy feta, sautéed mushrooms, and caramelized onions, bake them for about 8 minutes in a very hot oven, and then throw on some arugula for an incredible pizzetta. Leftovers? Cut them into batons and fry them in olive oil, then toss them with tomato, red onion, and vinaigrette to make a kind of "pizzetta panzanella."

yeast mixture
1 teaspoon (3 grams) active dry yeast (not quick-rising)
1 teaspoon (4.2 grams) granulated sugar
2½ tablespoons (37 grams) warm water (about 110°F)

dough
2 large eggs
½ cup (106 grams) extra virgin olive oil, plus additional as needed
3½ cups (459 grams) all-purpose flour, plus additional as needed
1 cup (171 grams) semolina flour
4 teaspoons (12 grams) kosher salt
4 teaspoons (16.7 grams) granulated sugar
1 cup (234 grams) warm water (about 110°F)

Za'atar (page 38) for sprinkling
Kosher salt for sprinkling

FOR THE YEAST MIXTURE: Combine the yeast and sugar in a small bowl. Stir in the warm water and let proof in a warm spot for about 10 minutes, or until the mixture is foamy and bubbling.

FOR THE DOUGH: Combine the eggs and oil in a bowl.

Put the two flours, salt, and sugar in the bowl of a stand mixer. Spray the hook attachment with nonstick cooking spray to keep the dough from sticking to it, and fit the hook on the mixer. Turn the mixer to low and add the egg and oil mixture, mixing to moisten the flour and stopping the machine to scrape down the sides of the bowl as necessary. Mix in the warm water and the yeast mixture to combine. As a dough begins to form around the hook, turn the speed to medium-low. (I mix bread doughs at lower speeds than you might expect. Mixing at high speeds can heat up the machine and adversely affect the bread. Don't rush the process!) Knead the dough for another 10 minutes, stopping the mixer occasionally to release any dough sticking to the hook. The finished dough will wrap around the hook and should feel smooth and silky. It will feel somewhat tacky, but it shouldn't stick to your fingers when you touch it. If it does, add a bit more flour. The dough should be elastic when you stretch it; it shouldn't break in two or collapse in the center.

Dust a board with flour, turn the dough out, and knead for about 2 minutes. Then lift the dough and tuck the edges under to form a round ball.

Rub a large metal bowl with a light coating of olive oil. Add the dough and cover the bowl tightly with plastic wrap. Let rise in a warm spot for 1½ to 2 hours, or until it has doubled in size.

TO SHAPE THE DOUGH: Lightly dust the cleaned board with flour. Return the dough to the board and knead it to work out any air bubbles. Form the dough into a ball.

Line two baking sheets with parchment paper and brush lightly with olive oil. Cut the dough into 12 equal portions (about 95 grams each). Using the palm of your hand, roll each portion against the board to form a ball. (When you become good at this, you'll be able to use both hands and roll 2 balls at a time.)

Space the balls evenly on the sheets. Cover tightly with plastic wrap and let rise in a warm spot for about 1 hour, or until doubled in size.

TO BAKE THE BREADS: Preheat a grill to high heat, or heat a grill pan over high heat.

Coat your work surface with olive oil. Place the balls on the surface and oil the tops of the balls. Using your fingertips, press the dough into 5- to 6-inch rounds.

Sprinkle the tops of the flatbreads lightly with za'atar and salt.

Reduce the heat of the grill (or under the grill pan) to medium-high. To test the heat, cook 1 flatbread: Carefully lift a flatbread and place it spice side down on the grill (or in the pan). Cook for 45 seconds. Turn the flatbread 90 degrees and cook for an additional 45 seconds to mark with a crosshatch. The marks should be well browned but not burned. Flip the bread over and repeat on the second side. Adjust the heat if necessary, and cook the remaining breads. Serve the flatbreads warm.

MAKES 12 FLATBREADS

NOTE: The flatbreads are best the day they are made, but they can be baked several hours ahead. To reheat the breads, brush the tops lightly with olive oil and reheat them in a 350°F oven for about 5 minutes.

BEGHRIR

About a year after I got to the United States, a fellow starving student took me to this Ethiopian place in Berkeley called The Blue Nile. I had never had Ethiopian food and didn't know what to expect. Out came the stew, and with it, some *injera,* the spongy bread you scoop it up with. I absentmindedly stuck a piece of *injera* in my mouth and freaked out. I called the waiter over and asked if he could bring me some honey and butter. He was puzzled, but complied. And a moment later, I was happily lost in a familiar dream: *beghrir,* the tender little yeasted pancakes I grew up eating for breakfast, on holiday mornings, and with afternoon tea.

Just like *injera,* or, if that image isn't speaking to you, crumpets, *beghrir* are cooked on one side only, and their tops are covered with tiny holes, which soak up the butter and honey you smother them with. A great *beghrir* is about warm butter and honey, trapped in a barely there matrix of flour and yeast.

In Morocco, not everyone dares to make homemade *beghrir.* In a culture that's not big on written recipes, some dishes require a lifetime's worth of skill and cooking wisdom. *Beghrir* are my mom's signature, but even though she's made them a million times, she's superstitious about the process. The holes, you see, are thought of as eyes. And the superstition is that the more eyes that are watching you as you make *beghrir,* the fewer holes you'll get. So my mom chases everyone out of the kitchen and makes them in hiding.

Once I tasted that *injera,* I knew I had to master *beghrir,* so I started experimenting. I played with

buttermilk, eggs, and even carbonated water, and this recipe is where I ended up. The batter has to have just the right consistency and "liveliness," so that when it hits the pan, the bubbles start to rise immediately and make "tubes." If it's too thin, the tubes seal over on top; too thick, and the bubbles gets trapped on the bottom and never tunnel through. That tube effect is the key, and you may need to adjust the flour and the water a little in order to achieve it. The first few won't turn out (what pancakes ever do?), but once you get this, you'll be blown away.

In Morocco, *beghrir* are usually about 6 inches in diameter. My mom makes hers on a square tile griddle with a black circle in the middle, the same one she's been using all my life. I like them a bit smaller, and I found a cast-iron Swedish pancake pan with 3-inch-wide indentations that's just right; a silver-dollar pancake pan will work, or you can cook the pancakes in a small skillet. Nonstick spray is a must, giving you a perfectly browned, omelety bottom crust.

The classic finishes for *beghrir* are butter and honey or jam, but I also like to make miniature *beghrir* and serve them as finger-food tidbits, topped, like blini, with crème fraîche and caviar or smoked salmon, or with Carrot Jam (page 358), Charred Eggplant Puree (page 115), or *Berbere*-Cured Chicken Liver Mousse (page 123). For dessert, try stacking *beghrir* with crème fraîche or Greek yogurt, maple syrup, and lightly sweetened berries, like the ones used with the Lavender-Almond Roulade (page 311).

WHITE BREAD WITH SESAME SEEDS

WHOLE WHEAT ROLLS

HARISSA ROLLS

HARISSA ROLLS

For quite a while, I would send each table an assortment of freshly baked bread with homemade butter or really good olive oil at the start of a meal. But half of it would come back uneaten because people didn't want to spoil their appetites. So I wanted to offer a one- or two-bite bread moment, rich enough to eat without butter or oil, as an *amuse bouche*.

I tried *harissa* churros, and later a feta version, both of which were a big hit, but a real challenge to deep-fry to order for every table. So I came up with these little rolls. They're made with a bit of extra fat so they're moist and soft, like a fresh-baked pretzel, with a moderate level of heat and extra flavor from the *harissa*. We bake them before service, and then as soon as a table is seated, we brush the rolls with clarified butter, sprinkle on some *harissa* powder, warm them in oven for 2 minutes, and season them with crunchy salt. That same bake-ahead strategy makes them good for entertaining at home.

At events, I've used these to make mini-sandwiches, like Lamb BLTs (page 269), or sliders with *Merguez* (page 270) or *kefta* (see page 139) patties with yogurt, *harissa,* and Gruyère. If you have leftover Braised Oxtail (page 282) or Beef Cheeks (page 274), pile the meat on the split rolls along with a bit of Carrot Jam (page 358).

yeast mixture

1½ teaspoons (4.5 grams) active dry yeast (not quick-rising)

1 teaspoon (4.2 grams) granulated sugar

2 tablespoons (30 grams) warm water (about 110°F)

dough

3¼ cups plus 2 tablespoons (426 grams) all-purpose flour, plus additional as needed

2 teaspoons (8 grams) light brown sugar

2 teaspoons (6 grams) kosher salt

2 teaspoons (4.8 grams) *Harissa* Powder (page 85)

1 teaspoon (3.4 grams) granulated garlic

1 teaspoon (1.8 grams) ground coriander

½ teaspoon (1.3 grams) ground cumin

¼ teaspoon (0.6 gram) cayenne

1 cup (234 grams) hot tap water (about 120°F)

2 tablespoons (24 grams) Clarified Butter (page 375), melted and cooled

1 tablespoon (16 grams) warm whole milk (about 110°F)

2 cups (468 grams) boiling water

¼ cup (62 grams) baking soda

¼ to ½ cup (48 to 95 grams) Clarified Butter (page 375), melted

2 to 4 teaspoons (4.8 to 9.6 grams) *Harissa* Powder (page 85)

Crunchy sea salt

FOR THE YEAST MIXTURE: Combine the yeast and sugar in a small bowl. Stir in the warm water and let proof in a warm spot for about 10 minutes, or until foamy and bubbling.

FOR THE DOUGH: Put all of the dry ingredients in the bowl of a stand mixer. Spray the dough hook with nonstick cooking spray to keep the dough from sticking to it, and fit the hook on the mixer. Turn the machine to low and add the yeast mixture. Once it is combined, add the water, butter, and milk. As a dough begins to form around the hook, turn the speed to medium-low. (I mix bread doughs at lower speeds than you might expect. Mixing at high speeds can heat up the machine and adversely affect the bread. Don't rush the process!) Knead the dough for another 10 minutes, stopping the mixer occasionally to release any dough that is sticking to the hook. The finished dough will wrap around the hook and should feel smooth and silky. It will feel somewhat tacky, but it shouldn't stick to your fingers when you touch it; if it does, add a bit more flour. The dough should be elastic if you stretch it; it shouldn't break in two or collapse in the center.

Dust a board with flour, turn out the dough, and knead for about 2 minutes. Then lift the dough and tuck the edges under to form a round ball of dough.

Spray a large bowl with nonstick spray. Add the dough and cover the bowl tightly with plastic wrap. Let rise at room temperature in a warm spot for about 1 hour, or until doubled in size.

TO SHAPE THE DOUGH: Lightly dust the cleaned board with flour. Return the dough to the board and knead it to work out any air bubbles. Form the dough into a ball.

Line a baking sheet with parchment paper and lightly spray with nonstick cooking spray.

Cut the dough into 18 equal portions (about 45 grams each). Using the palm of your hand, roll each portion against the board to form a ball. (When you become good at this, you'll be able to use both hands and roll 2 balls at a time.)

Space the balls evenly on the sheet and cover with plastic wrap. Place in a warm spot to rise for about 1½ hours, or until 1½ times their original size.

TO BAKE THE ROLLS: Preheat the oven to 325°F.

Lay a towel near the work surface. Line a baking sheet with parchment paper and lightly spray with nonstick cooking spray. Combine the boiling water and baking soda in a medium bowl.

One at a time, dip the rolls into the baking soda mixture, drain briefly on the towel to absorb the excess moisture that will run off the roll, and place on the prepared baking sheet, spacing them evenly on the sheet.

Bake for 22 minutes, or until lightly browned and tender to the touch.

You can serve the rolls at this point, brushing them with butter and sprinkling with the *harissa* powder and crunchy sea salt. Or, for a crunchier crust, increase the oven temperature to 425°F and bake the rolls for 2 more minutes, or until crisp, then brush with the butter and sprinkle with the *harissa* and salt. The rolls can also be baked ahead and held at room temperature for up to 4 hours. To serve, brush with the butter and *harissa* and crisp in a 425°F oven for about 2 minutes.

MAKES 1½ DOZEN SMALL ROLLS

RYE BREAD

Berbers, the original "native Moroccans," favor rustic brown breads made with whole wheat and other hearty grains, like rye or durum wheat semolina. I'm very drawn to this kind of bread even though (or maybe because) I almost never had it growing up.

I came up with this dark, soft, molasses-enhanced rye bread because I wanted something sweet to serve with our *Berbere*-Cured Chicken Liver Mousse (page 123). It's moist and rich with a delicate crumb, almost like a cross between a bread and a spice cake, and vaguely reminiscent of the sweet Moroccan anise-sesame buns called *ghrissat*. Use it to make sandwiches with thinly sliced maple ham or maple-roasted turkey, butter lettuce, and mayo. Or toast it for breakfast and serve it with eggs.

yeast mixture
1 tablespoon (9 grams) active dry yeast
    (not quick-rising)
1 teaspoon (4.2 grams) granulated sugar
½ cup (117 grams) warm water (about 110°F)

dough
2 tablespoons (15 grams) caraway seeds
2¼ cups (295 grams) all-purpose flour, plus additional
    as needed
½ cup (44 grams) unsweetened alkalized cocoa
    powder, preferably Cacao Barry Extra Dark
    Extra Red
2 cups (272 grams) rye flour
¾ cup (246 grams) unsulfured blackstrap molasses
¼ cup (48 grams) Clarified Butter (page 375),
    at room temperature
1 large egg, at room temperature
2 teaspoons (6 grams) kosher salt
2 teaspoons (8.3 grams) granulated sugar
1 cup (250 grams) warm whole milk (about 110°F)

Unsalted butter, at room temperature,
    for the loaf pan
1 large egg, beaten with 1 tablespoon (15 grams)
    water, for egg wash

FOR THE YEAST MIXTURE: Combine the yeast and sugar in a small bowl. Stir in the warm water and let proof in a warm spot for about 10 minutes, or until foamy and bubbling

MEANWHILE, FOR THE DOUGH: Put the caraway seeds in a small frying pan and toast over medium heat, swirling the pan and flipping or stirring the seeds occasionally so they toast evenly, until fragrant, 2 to 3 minutes. Transfer to a plate and set aside to cool.

Lay a large piece of parchment paper on a work surface. Sift together the all-purpose flour and cocoa onto the paper, then mix in the rye flour and caraway seeds. (The paper will make it easier to add the dry ingredients to the mixer bowl.)

Put the molasses, clarified butter, egg, salt, and sugar in the bowl of a stand mixer. Fit the dough hook on the mixer, turn the machine to medium-low, and mix for about 3 minutes, or until well combined. Add the yeast mixture, drizzle in the milk, and mix for about 3 minutes, or until combined. Turn the machine to low, lift the edges of the parchment paper, and slowly add the dry ingredients to the bowl. As a dough begins to form around the hook, turn the speed to medium-low. (I mix bread dough at lower speeds than you might expect. Mixing at high speeds can heat up the machine and adversely affect the bread. Don't rush the process!) Knead the dough for another 6 to 8 minutes, stopping the mixer halfway through to scrape the sides and bottom of the bowl. The finished dough will wrap around the hook and should feel smooth. It will feel somewhat tacky, but it shouldn't stick to your fingers when you touch it; if it does, add a bit more all-purpose flour. The finished dough should be elastic if you stretch it; it shouldn't break in two or collapse in the center.

Dust a board with all-purpose flour, turn out the dough, and knead for about 2 minutes. Then lift the dough and tuck the edges under to form a round ball of dough.

Oil a large bowl with nonstick cooking spray. Add the dough and cover the bowl tightly with plastic wrap. Let rise in a warm spot for about 1½ hours, or until doubled in size.

TO SHAPE THE DOUGH: Butter a 5-by-9-by-2¾-inch loaf pan. Lightly dust the cleaned board with flour. Return the dough to the board and knead it to work out any air bubbles. Flatten the dough into a rectangular shape to fit the pan.

Put the dough in the pan, pressing it into the corners for a snug fit. (This may seem like a lot of dough for the pan, but I like to make a large loaf that rises over the top of the pan.) Cover the pan loosely with plastic wrap and place in a warm spot to rise for about 1½ hours, or until the dough has doubled in size.

TO BAKE THE BREAD: Preheat the oven to 325°F.

Brush the top of the bread with the egg wash. Put the loaf pan on a baking sheet and bake for 30 minutes. Rotate the pan and bake for 15 to 20 minutes more, or until a skewer inserted in the center of the loaf comes out clean. Unmold onto a cooling rack and cool completely.

MAKES 1 LARGE LOAF

fish story

When the summer sun turned the whole medina into a blazing brick oven, everyone in Marrakesh would move en masse to El Jadida on the coast. My grandpa had a condo there, right on the beach. And all summer long, like sea lions gorging for the winter ahead, we'd feast on fish, squid, mussels, clams, and sea urchins. You could buy them all at the busy fish market, from kids with trays strapped around their necks on the beach, or from the fishermen, right off the back of the boat. And for next to nothing, you could sit down at one of the many beachside stands, point to whatever you wanted, watch as it was grilled, and then sprinkle it with lemon juice, salt, and cumin and devour it with a bottle of soda to wash it down.

DUNGENESS CRAB
MEYER LEMON
HARISSA BUTTER

Moroccans don't eat a lot of crab, looking down on it as a lowly scavenger. But I like to think that if they appreciated it more, this is how they'd want it—with the lemon and butter so popular in San Francisco and much of the rest of the world, plus a dash of spicy *harissa*. If you want even more toasty, roasted flavor, you can start by making Brown Butter (page 64) and then use that to steep the *harissa* and lemon.

This is a simple first course, best served Moroccan-family-style from a central dish. Roasting crab gives it a sweeter, more concentrated flavor than boiling. The texture is springier too, and more lobster-like. If you don't want to cut up live crabs, you can make the dish by boiling them first for a minute, then cutting them up and roasting them, but you'll lose a

lot of flavor to the cooking water. Or, if you know any particularly accommodating fishmongers who sell live crab, you could ask them to cut it up for you, in which case, I recommend racing home and cooking it within an hour.

½ pound (227 grams) unsalted butter
1½ tablespoons (10.8 grams) *Harissa* Powder
  (page 85)
1 teaspoon (3 grams) kosher salt, or to taste
2 Meyer lemons, cut into 8 wedges each and seeds
  removed
2½ tablespoons (20 grams) thinly sliced garlic
Two 2-pound (907-gram) live Dungeness crabs
Baguette or other crusty bread

Put the butter, *harissa* powder, and salt in a medium saucepan and set over medium heat. When the butter is melted, add the lemon wedges and garlic and bring to a simmer. Turn the heat to the lowest setting, or put the pan on a diffuser to keep the butter at just below a simmer, and cook for about 40 minutes to infuse the flavors. Taste the butter and add more salt if necessary. Remove from the heat and set aside in a warm spot.

If you feel squeamish about cutting up live crabs, bring a large pot of water to a boil. Drop the crabs headfirst into the water, leave them in for about 1 minute, and then remove them.

Start by cutting the crabs in half down the center of the shells with a chef's knife. Pull off the top shells, remove the gills from each side, and scoop out any gray or yellow matter, then cut off the mouths. (These can all be discarded.) Cut the crabs into smaller sections, cutting between the legs. Use the back of the knife to crack the shells, which will make the crabs much easier to eat.

Preheat the oven to 500°F. Heat a gratin dish, preferably enameled cast iron, in the oven for about 15 minutes, or until very hot.

Put the crab in a large bowl and toss with the lemon butter. Spread the crab in the hot gratin dish and pour any butter remaining in the bowl over it. Roast for 12 to 14 minutes, or until the crabmeat is opaque and the shells have begun to brown.

Serve the crab directly from the gratin dish, with bread for dipping in the butter.

SERVES 4

BERBERE-CRUSTED SCALLOPS
CAULIFLOWER COUSCOUS
VADOUVAN FOAM

This is a real "sum of the parts" kind of dish. Take the scallops, for example. I use Hokaido scallops, because they're phosphate-free and sweeter and drier than other commercial scallops, which are often soaked to plump them. These are the scallops used by good sushi bars, and that's important here, because I barely cook them. I want a nice seared crust on the outside, but I like them just warmed through inside. Making sure they're very dry and dipping them in *berbere* helps with that crusting, and so does browning them in duck fat. If you don't have duck fat, use grapeseed oil or another neutral oil with a high smoke point—but not extra virgin olive oil, which will burn before you get a nice crust.

I like serving scallops with a creamy puree, and I've tried them all—celery root, potato, parsnip, you name it. I also like them with couscous. So I thought I'd combine those two ideas using a single vegetable, cauliflower. First there's a creamy puree. (Xanthan gum helps give it an amazing sheen and texture, but it's okay to leave it out.) Then there's cauliflower "couscous." It's actually just finely chopped raw cauliflower warmed with a little *vadouvan* butter—an idea based on a cauliflower couscous I heard about from my friend and fellow chef James Ormsby, who got it from Charlie Trotter, by way, he thinks, of Ferran Adrià. Whoever thought of it, thank you! It's really good, and a nice couscous alternative in a kitchen where real couscous has been served every way you can imagine. I've made carrot, radish, and even Armenian cucumber "couscous" in the same way, but cheddar (orange) cauliflower remains my favorite because of its uncanny trompe l'oeil resemblance to the original.

The pickled raisins and *vadouvan* foam give the whole thing a curry-and-chutney accent without overpowering the scallops. This makes a great starter too; serve 1 large or 2 medium scallops per person.

pickled raisins

1 tablespoon (3.8 grams) coriander seeds
2 tablespoons (21.3 grams) yellow mustard seeds
2 tablespoons (21.3 grams) brown mustard seeds
3 (1.8 grams) chiles de árbol
2 (0.3 gram) bay leaves
One 6-inch rosemary sprig
6 (6 grams) thyme sprigs
1 (1.1 grams) star anise
6 (1 gram) green cardamom pods, cracked
8 (0.6 gram) cloves
One 3-inch cinnamon stick
1 teaspoon (1.2 grams) pink peppercorns
1 teaspoon (3 grams) Tellicherry peppercorns
2 cups (465 grams) water
⅔ cup (133 grams) granulated sugar
½ cup (120 grams) sherry vinegar
1½ cups (240 grams) golden raisins

(MAKES ABOUT 2 CUPS/448 GRAMS)

cauliflower

1 head cheddar (orange) or white cauliflower
    (2 to 2.5 pounds/907 grams to 1.1 kilograms)
4 tablespoons (2 ounces/57 grams) unsalted butter
2 teaspoons (6 grams) kosher salt, or to taste
½ cup (125 grams) whole milk
½ cup (117 grams) water
½ teaspoon (1.7 grams) xanthan gum (optional)
1½ tablespoons (18 grams) *Vadouvan* Brown Butter
    (page 36), strained

(MAKES 1 CUP/138 GRAMS COUSCOUS AND
ABOUT 3 CUPS/970 GRAMS PUREE)

About ¼ cup (50 grams) *Vadouvan* Brown Butter
   (page 36)
About 2 tablespoons (16 grams) *Berbere* (page 36)
24 large scallops (U8 to U13; 2½ pounds/
   1.14 kilograms total weight, each 1.5 to 2 ounces/
   43 to 56 grams), muscles removed
Kosher salt
2 tablespoons (28 grams) duck fat or (26.5 grams)
   grapeseed oil

FOR THE PICKLED RAISINS: Put the coriander seeds
in a medium frying pan and heat over medium heat,
swirling the pan and flipping or stirring the seeds
occasionally so they toast evenly, until fragrant, about
2 minutes. Remove them from the pan and set aside.
Add the mustard seeds to the pan, cover, and swirl the
pan, flipping or stirring the seeds occasionally so they
toast evenly, until they begin to pop, about 2 minutes.
Toast for 30 seconds more, then remove from the pan.

   Wrap the coriander seeds, chiles, bay leaves,
rosemary, thyme, star anise, cardamom pods,
cloves, cinnamon stick, and peppercorns in a piece
of cheesecloth and tie to make a sachet.

Combine the water, sugar, and vinegar in a
medium saucepan and bring to a simmer over medium
heat, stirring to dissolve the sugar. Add the mustard
seeds and sachet and simmer for about 8 minutes to
reduce the liquid until syrupy.

   Add the raisins and bring to a simmer. Cover
the pan, remove from the heat, and let sit at room
temperature for 30 minutes to infuse the flavors.
Discard the sachet. (The pickled raisins can be
refrigerated in an airtight container for up to 1 month.)

FOR THE CAULIFLOWER COUSCOUS: Cut the
cauliflower into florets. Hold a floret over a bowl
and use a paring knife to shave away the surface
of the floret. Repeat until you have a cup or so of
shavings, then put the shavings in a food processor
and pulse into pieces that resemble fine couscous.
You need about 1 cup (120 grams) "couscous." Set it
aside, and reserve the remaining florets for the puree.

CONTINUED

FOR THE FISH: Score both sides of the fish with 3 shallow diagonal cuts, no more than ¼ inch deep. Cut 1 of the preserved lemons into quarters. Cut 2 of the quarters into chunks and stuff them into the cavity of the fish. Remove the flesh from the rind of the remaining 2 pieces and cut the rinds into 3 lengthwise pieces each. Insert them into the diagonal cuts. Rub about ¼ cup of the *charmoula* on each side of the fish. Stand the fish upright on its belly (the way it swims) in a flameproof baking dish or roasting pan large enough to hold all the vegetables in one layer. It will help the fish stay upright if you open up the cavity a bit to give it more of a base. Let it sit at room temperature until it is no longer cold to the touch, about 45 minutes.

Meanwhile, preheat the oven to 425°F.

FOR THE VEGETABLES: Remove the fronds and outer layer from the fennel bulb. Cut the fennel into 8 wedges. If you like, for a more finished look, trim the sharp edges for more rounded wedges.

Peel the turnips with a paring knife. (Because they have thick skin, a vegetable peeler won't cut deep enough to remove all the tough peel.)

Put all the vegetables, the olives, and garlic in a large bowl and toss with the remaining *charmoula*. Arrange around the fish. Drizzle any *charmoula* remaining in the bowl over the fish and vegetables.

Cut the remaining preserved lemon into quarters. Remove and discard the flesh. Cut the rind into 8 petals (2 per quarter) and arrange in the vegetables. If you have a remote thermometer, insert the probe in the thickest part of the fish.

Set the baking dish over medium-high heat, bring the liquid to a simmer, and simmer for a minute to heat the dish. Put in the oven and roast for about 20 minutes, until the fish has an internal temperature of 130°F and the vegetables are tender (if you don't have a probe thermometer, check the temperature with an instant-read thermometer). If the fish is cooked before the vegetables are tender, carefully transfer the fish to a parchment-lined baking sheet and cover with aluminum foil; return the vegetables to the oven until tender.

Turn the heat to broil. Return the fish to the vegetables if you removed it. Broil for about 3 minutes to caramelize the vegetables slightly and brown the fish.

TO SERVE: Run a knife down the backbone of the fish and carefully lift off the fillet, then remove the backbone and lift off the remaining fillet. Arrange the fillets on a serving platter or divide them into individual servings and arrange on plates. Arrange the vegetables around the fish and drizzle with the sauce.

SERVES 4

BLACK COD
POTATOES
SAFFRON BROTH

If the preceding recipe sits at one end of the fish spectrum, this one would be way at the other end. It's like a fish haiku—pristine, spare, understated, and pure. To me, black cod demands that kind of approach. It's meltingly buttery and best appreciated without a lot of seasoning, crusting, or "transformational" cooking. Potatoes, saffron, and fish are classically Moroccan, but here I want the flavors to go into the potatoes, not the fish. That's why I steam the fish in a clay pot over, not in, the potatoes and broth. The result is moist fish that remains firm but falls into tender flakes when you touch it with a fork. A hint of green from the peas and olives makes the white-on-white elegance of the dish even more pronounced.

saffron broth
Clam Stock (page 364)
2 teaspoons (1.8 grams) saffron threads
2 (0.3 gram) bay leaves
1 tablespoon (15 grams) fresh lemon juice

potatoes
1 pound (453 grams) small fingerling potatoes (about 18)
2 garlic cloves, smashed
3 (3 grams) thyme sprigs
2½ tablespoons (22.5 grams) kosher salt

18 green olives, preferably Castelvetrano
One 1½-pound (680-gram) piece Alaskan black cod fillet, skin removed
Kosher salt
24 snap peas
12 pea shoots
About 6 tablespoons (80 grams) extra virgin olive oil, for finishing

FOR THE SAFFRON BROTH: Pour the stock into a saucepan, add the saffron, bay leaves, and lemon juice, and bring to a simmer over medium-low heat. Skim any impurities that rise to the surface. (Putting the pot to one side of the burner will move the impurities to one side, making it easier to skim them.) Simmer for about 15 minutes to reduce the stock by half. Remove from the heat and strain through a fine-mesh strainer.

MEANWHILE, FOR THE POTATOES: Put the potatoes, garlic, thyme, and salt in a medium saucepan, add enough water to cover the potatoes by 1 inch, and bring to a simmer. Cook for 12 to 15 minutes, or until the potatoes are almost tender. Do not overcook them; they will cook again in the oven. Drain the potatoes, and when they are cool enough to handle, cut each one lengthwise in half.

TO FINISH THE DISH: Preheat the oven to 425°F.

Cut 2 pieces from each olive by cutting a slice from either side of the pit. Set aside.

Cut the cod into 6 pieces and sprinkle lightly with salt.

You can cook the cod in individual clay pots or in a gratin dish that will hold the potatoes covered with the cod in a single layer. Arrange the potatoes in the bottom of the serving vessel(s) so that they form a base for the fish. Arrange the fish over the potatoes. Add enough broth to come just to the top of the potatoes.

Cover the clay pots with their lids. Or, if you are using a gratin dish, cover the fish with a parchment lid (see page 379), brush with water to keep the edges from curling up, and cover tightly with aluminum foil. Put in the oven and cook for about 15 minutes for individual servings, or about 20 minutes longer for the gratin dish, until the fish begins to flake.

Meanwhile, fill a medium bowl with ice water. Bring a small pot of water to a simmer.

Add the snap peas to the simmering water and cook for 2 minutes, or until they are almost tender but still have some bite. Transfer to the ice water. Blanch the pea shoots for a few seconds, just until they turn bright green. Add them to the ice water to cool quickly. Drain the peas and shoots and dry on paper towels.

Lay a snap pea on the cutting board. If you are right-handed, cut off the tip of the pea pod on the diagonal, with the tip pointing to 11 o'clock (if you are left-handed, cut the tip to face 1 o'clock). Flip the pea top to bottom and cut the other tip off the same way. Find the dark green string running the length of the pod. With the tip of a small paring knife, cut through the pod just above the seam and remove the top half of the pod. Select the 12 pods where the peas are most uniform in size. (Reserve the other pods for a cook's treat or other use.)

If you used a gratin dish, arrange the potatoes and fish in serving bowls and ladle in some stock. Or serve directly from the clay pots. Drizzle each fillet with about 1 tablespoon (13.3 grams) olive oil and garnish with 6 olive slices, 2 snap peas, and some pea shoots.

SERVES 6

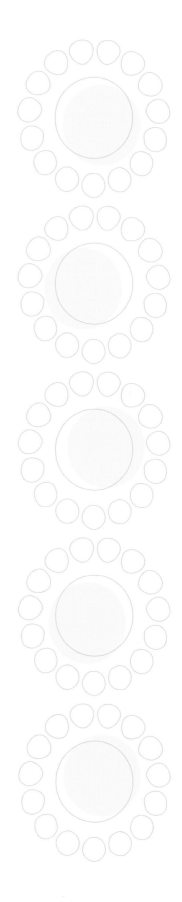

back to *beldi*

The chickens in Morocco slowly began to change right around the time I was born. Until the 1970s, chickens were raised by families or grown on small farms and sold live. We'd go to the market and pick out a brown-feathered chicken from a wall of cages. And that bird would be big, with tough meat that really had to be braised.

But since then, a poultry industry has developed that now produces thirty times as much chicken as the country consumed annually when I was a kid. Today, for the most part, chicken in Morocco has become a product in a package. You can still find those big brown-feathered chickens in market stalls, though. They're referred to as *beldi* chickens, a word used the way we might say "heirloom" or "artisan" to mean authentic, free-range, traditional, and real.

For my mom, my aunts and uncles, and everyone else I know of their generation, the commercial stuff, *roumi* chicken (always said with an air of weary disdain), is not an option. It's got to be *beldi*.

If chicken's on the menu for lunch at one of their houses, and you peer into the kitchen, you'll see a big vat of chicken parts—what looks like far too much for a single family, but leftovers are always mandatory—soaking in salted water with lemons and olives. This brining isn't just for flavor and moistness. It's also how Moroccan cooks clean chickens, working their fingers under the skin to remove the mucilaginous substance that accumulates there, and it's done with real vigor. I've seen chickens rubbed and massaged for up to a quarter of an hour. The skin gets trashed in the process, but that's not a problem; it's never about perfect crispy skin in Morocco. Once the cleaning and brining has happened, the chicken parts are slow-cooked, surrendering their chickeny essence to the sauce.

When I came to the United States in the late 1980s, *beldi* chicken was the only kind I knew, and I was stunned by how quickly my first supermarket chicken cooked and how flavorless it turned out. A few decades later, we're lucky to have some fantastic poultry growers here in California, like Field to Family and Marin Sun Farms. Their *beldi*-esque birds taste more like what I remember from childhood, and I encourage you to find good suppliers with integrity wherever you live. Also seek out air-chilled poultry, which is less waterlogged and cooks up crisper with a more concentrated flavor than the typical water-processed kind.

I make all sorts of poultry dishes, some clearly Moroccan inspired, some that just follow an idea that interests me. But whatever I'm doing, whether the techniques are simple or a complex series of texture- and flavor-enhancing steps, for me it has to be about getting back to that remembered poultry purity—the beauty of *beldi*.

CONFIT CHICKEN WINGS
BRUSSELS SPROUTS
APPLE PUREE

To me, chicken wings have the perfect ratio of meat to skin and bone, and confiting them—slowly simmering them in fat (ideally duck fat, for the richest flavor)—is by far my favorite way to bring out the best of every part of that ratio. The meat becomes rich and moist, and there's no risk of the dryness you sometimes get with baked or fried chicken wings. The bones gradually infuse the meat with flavor. And the skin slowly renders its own fat, so that when you brown the wings in a pan as a finishing step, the skin is light, crisp, and not at all fatty.

I like these wings as a plated first course with all the different elements working together—the slightly bitter Brussels sprouts, the sweet-tart apple puree and gastrique, and the contrasting creamy and chewy textures. But for a party or a family-style dinner, you can serve the wings as finger food on a platter, with the apple puree in a bowl for dipping.

You can confit and bone the wings up to a day in advance and then crisp them at the last minute. Deboning the wings makes them a bit more elegant, but if it's just you and some close friends, you might want to leave the bones in so everyone can enjoy gnawing on them.

chicken wings
18 chicken wings (4 ounces/113 grams each)
1½ tablespoons (11.5 grams) ground cumin
1 tablespoon (7.2 grams) Marash pepper
1 tablespoon (9 grams) kosher salt
About 4 cups (896 grams) duck or chicken fat, or
    (848 grams) canola oil

red wine gastrique
6 tablespoons (87 grams) champagne vinegar
2 tablespoons (25 grams) granulated sugar
¼ cup (59 grams) water
½ cup (50 grams) minced shallots
2¼ cups (268 grams) dry red wine, preferably
    Pinot Noir
2 tablespoons (50 grams) liquid glucose
3 tablespoons (45 grams) red wine vinegar
Kosher salt

apple puree
2 lemons
2 pounds (907 grams) Granny Smith apples
Four 6-inch rosemary sprigs
¼ teaspoon (0.8 gram) kosher salt
½ teaspoon (3 grams) fresh lemon juice,
    preferably Meyer, or to taste
⅛ teaspoon (0.4 gram) xanthan gum
Pinch of citric acid

(MAKES 2 CUPS/485 GRAMS)

brussels sprouts
12 medium Brussels sprouts
Kosher salt
½ lemon, preferably Meyer

A handful of frisée lettuce and celery leaves for
    garnish
About 1 tablespoon (10 grams) Red Wine Vinaigrette
    (page 361)
Crunchy sea salt
¼ cup (38 grams) salted Marcona almonds

FOR THE WINGS: Cut off the wing tips and discard. Cut through the wing joint to separate the wings into 2 sections. Cut off the soft bottom end of each "drumstrick"; be careful not to cut off too much, or the bone could shatter. Push the meat upward, twisting it around the bone to form a "lollipop."

Put the wings in a large bowl. Toss with the cumin, Marash, and salt. Let stand at room temperature for 1 hour, or even better, refrigerate overnight.

Preheat the oven to 325°F.

Arrange the wings in a large cast-iron pot or other heavy pot with a lid, standing the drumsticks meat end down around the edges of the pot and arranging the remaining wings in a single layer in the center. Add enough fat to completely cover the wings and bring to a simmer over medium-high heat. Cover the wings with a parchment lid (see page 379) and brush it with water to keep the edges from curling up. Cover with the pot lid and put in the oven to cook for about 1½ hours, or until the wings are completely tender, almost falling from the bones.

MEANWHILE, FOR THE RED WINE GASTRIQUE: Stir the champagne vinegar, sugar, and water in a small saucepan over medium-high heat to dissolve the sugar. Put the shallots in a bowl, pour the hot liquid over them, and let stand at room temperature for 1 hour; drain.

Pour the wine into a small saucepan, bring to a simmer, and simmer for about 10 minutes to reduce by half. Stir in the glucose, red wine vinegar, and drained shallots and simmer for about 15 minutes to reduce the liquid by half.

Strain the liquid into a small saucepan, bring to a simmer, and simmer for about 20 minutes, or until reduced to 2 tablespoons (32 grams), lowering the heat as necessary to avoid burning the sauce. Stir in a pinch of salt and set aside.

FOR THE APPLE PUREE: Fill a large bowl with cold water and squeeze in the juice of the 2 lemons. Peel and core the apples. Cut into 1-inch pieces and submerge them in the lemon water to keep them from discoloring.

Fill a medium pot with cold water. Wrap the rosemary sprigs in a piece of cheesecloth and tie to make a sachet. Add to the pot and bring the water to a simmer. Drain the apples, add them to the pot, and simmer for about 5 minutes, or until they are tender enough to puree.

Drain the apples, put them in a blender, and blend until smooth. With the motor running, add the salt and lemon juice. Taste and add additional lemon juice if desired. Add the xanthan gum and citric acid, and blend on high to incorporate. For the finest texture, pass the puree through a fine-mesh strainer. (The apple puree can be refrigerated in an airtight container for up to 3 days. Bring it to room temperature before serving.)

TO DEBONE THE CHICKEN WINGS: Remove the wings from the oven and let them cool in the fat for about 45 minutes, until you are able to handle them; they should still be warm. Remove them from the fat. Strain the fat and reserve. Set the "drumsticks" aside and bone the remaining wing sections: Cut off both ends of each piece, squaring them off. Hold each piece in one hand and carefully pull out the two bones that run the length of the wing. Set aside.

FOR THE BRUSSELS SPROUTS: Trim the bottom of each sprout. Remove a few outer leaves and discard. If you have a small melon baller, use it to scoop out the core of each Brussels sprout to make separating the leaves easier; otherwise, use a paring knife to cut out the core. Remove the leaves, cutting out more core as necessary, until the leaves are so small that you are unable to separate them without breaking them. Discard the core.

TO SERVE: Heat a film of the reserved fat in a medium nonstick frying pan. Add the Brussels sprout leaves and sauté, tossing often, for about 3 minutes, or until they are tender and have caramelized around the edges but still hold their shape. Drain on paper towels and sprinkle with salt.

Add another film of the reserved fat to the pan and heat over medium-high heat. Brown the wings for about 1½ minutes on each side to crisp, then drain on paper towels.

Toss the greens with a light coating of the vinaigrette. Toss the Brussels sprouts with lemon juice to taste.

Place a large dollop of apple puree on each serving plate. Drag a small offset spatula through the puree to form a sweep. Sprinkle the wings with crunchy sea salt. Arrange the Brussels sprouts and wings on the plates. Garnish with the greens and almonds, and drizzle with the red wine gastrique.

SERVES 6

CHICKEN SKEWERS

If you're browsing for a totally simple recipe in this book to start with, here you go: quick, tasty chicken skewers with a marinade and finishing vinaigrette that work together to give you an easy approximation of the pleasures of red *charmoula*. If you're having people over, you can prepare the skewers in advance so you'll have only a few minutes of grilling to do when it's time to eat. For a barbecue picnic at the beach or in a park, pack the skewers, uncooked, in the marinade so you can grill them on the spot. They work well as a starter, or as a main course over couscous with some grilled asparagus, drizzled with the vinaigrette.

marinade

3 tablespoons (24 grams) sweet paprika
1 tablespoon (7.7 grams) ground cumin
¾ teaspoon (1.5 grams) ground ginger
1 tablespoon (12 grams) finely chopped garlic
3 tablespoons (8 grams) coarsely chopped thyme
1½ tablespoons (7 grams) coarsely chopped flat-leaf
    parsley
1 tablespoon (4 grams) coarsely chopped cilantro
1½ cups (318 grams) extra virgin olive oil

6 boneless, skinless chicken breasts
    (6 ounces/170 grams each)
Kosher salt and freshly ground black pepper

vinaigrette

¼ cup (48 grams) finely diced preserved lemon rind
    (see page 45)
¼ cup plus 3 tablespoons (93 grams) extra virgin
    olive oil
2½ tablespoons (11 grams) finely chopped flat-leaf
    parsley
1 tablespoon (15 grams) fresh lime juice

FOR THE MARINADE: Mix all the ingredients in a large bowl.

Trim the chicken breasts of excess fat. Remove the tenders and reserve for another use. Cut the meat into 1½-inch pieces. Add the chicken to the marinade and refrigerate for at least 6 hours, or as long as overnight.

FOR THE VINAIGRETTE: Whisk all the ingredients together. Set aside.

FOR THE CHICKEN: Soak 6 long wooden skewers in cold water for 30 minutes.

Lift several pieces of the chicken at a time from the marinade and squeeze them over the bowl to drain the extra marinade. Skewer the chicken, leaving ¼ inch between the pieces to allow all sides of the chicken to cook evenly. Season the chicken lightly with salt and pepper.

Preheat a grill to medium-high heat.

Place the skewers on the grill and cook for 2 to 3 minutes without moving them, to mark the chicken. Turn the skewers 90 degrees to mark with a crosshatch pattern and grill for another 1 minute. The marks should be well browned but not burnt. Turn the skewers over and cook for about 2 minutes to finish cooking the chicken.

Carefully remove the chicken from the skewers and place in a bowl. Toss with a light coating of the vinaigrette, and serve the extra vinaigrette on the side.

SERVES 6

ROAST CHICKEN
PRESERVED LEMONS
ROOT VEGETABLES

If chicken legs braised in a tagine with preserved lemons and olives (see page 247) is my faithful adaptation of a Moroccan institution, this recipe takes that dish one step further. I'm extremely fond of the not-at-all-Moroccan idea of roast chicken—that and some buttered couscous would be my pick for a last meal—and I love how when you buy a great air-chilled bird and roast it, the flavor that really comes through is unmistakably chicken. In Morocco, between the slow braising and the assertive seasonings that generally go into any chicken dish, that comforting, brothy poultry flavor is sacrificed, along with the thrill of crispy skin, for the greater good of the dish.

But sometimes I want both—chicken that tastes like peak-experience, crisp-skinned chicken *and* sauce with Moroccan richness, depth, and intensity—and that's when I make this recipe. I brine whole chickens just like they do in Morocco with plenty of salt, lemon, and olives. But then, instead of braising them, I roast them whole over a bed of vegetables, with preserved lemons and thyme tucked under the skin.

I promise you, it's worth the effort. Also, not that you would, but don't compromise on the vegetables. The nicest ones you can find at the farmers' market will make a great difference as they caramelize and their sweetness comes out. If you have very small vegetables, you can leave them whole; larger ones should be cut and trimmed to even shapes with a paring knife. Use burgundy carrots if you can find them; they're great here. Peel them lightly so you don't remove too much of their color. And if you've got time to make the spiced prunes, go for it. They add a lot.

brine

4 quarts (3.7 kilograms) cold water
¾ (150 grams) granulated sugar
1½ cups (216 grams) kosher salt
2 lemons, cut into quarters
1 cup (220 grams) cracked green olives, with their brine
12 (42 grams) flat-leaf parsley sprigs
3 tablespoons (24 grams) sliced garlic
1 tablespoon (9 grams) Tellicherry peppercorns
8 thyme sprigs
10 (1.7 grams) bay leaves
4 quarts (1.96 kilograms) ice cubes

chicken

3 (450 grams) Preserved Lemons (see page 43)
2 air-chilled chickens (3½ pounds/1.58 kilograms each), excess fat removed
8 (8 grams) thyme sprigs
Kosher salt
8 tablespoons (4 ounces/113 grams) unsalted butter, at room temperature

vegetables

12 medium turnips
3 small rutabagas
4 small parsnips
12 medium carrots
8 cipollini onions, about 1½ inches in diameter, left unpeeled
2 tablespoons (27 grams) extra virgin olive oil
2 teaspoons (2 grams) coarsely chopped thyme
18 garlic cloves
Kosher salt

12 Spiced Prunes (page 360; optional)

1 tablespoon (16 grams) preserved lemon liquid
  (see page 45)

2 tablespoons (1 ounce/28 grams) cold unsalted
  butter, cut into pieces

2 teaspoons (3 grams) coarsely chopped flat-leaf
  parsley

FOR THE BRINE: Put the water in a 10- to 12-quart
stockpot and bring to a simmer. Add the brine
ingredients (except the ice) and stir to dissolve the
sugar and salt. Turn off the heat and let sit at room
temperature for 20 minutes to infuse the flavors.

   Add the ice to chill the brine. If the brine isn't
completely cold, refrigerate it until it is. Add the
chickens to the cold brine and weight them with a
plate or smaller pot lid to keep them submerged.
Refrigerate for 8 to 12 hours.

FOR THE CHICKENS: Cut the preserved lemons into
quarters. Cut the flesh away from the rinds and
reserve both the rinds and flesh. Remove the chickens
from the brine (discard the brine), rinse them, and dry
well with paper towels. Place 1 chicken on a work
surface with the legs facing you. Starting at the cavity,
work the handle of a wooden spoon between the skin
and one breast to create a pocket, working slowly and
gently to avoid tearing the skin. Repeat on the other
side. Holding the chicken in place with one hand, slide
the index and middle fingers of your other hand into
each pocket to enlarge it, then slide your fingers down
to create a pocket over the thigh. Repeat with the
second chicken.

   Insert the pieces of preserved lemon rind, white
pith side down, and thyme sprigs into the pockets
over the thighs and breasts. Sprinkle the cavities with
salt, and rub the chickens with the reserved flesh from
the preserved lemons.

I like to truss poultry without using kitchen twine, which saves tying and untying them and makes for a more natural presentation. Position 1 chicken breast side up, with the legs facing you. Cut a vertical slit in one side, about 1 inch back from the cavity, alongside the thigh. Cross the end of the opposite drumstick over the drumstick on this side and poke the end of the top drumstick through the slit. (Depending on the condition of the chicken's skin, it may rip as you try to poke the drumstick through it, so have some kitchen twine on hand just in case, and tie the legs together if necessary.) Repeat with the other chicken. Sprinkle the chickens with salt.

Preheat the oven to 500°F.

FOR THE VEGETABLES: Peel the turnips and rutabagas with a paring knife. (Because they have thick skins, a vegetable peeler won't cut deeply enough to remove all the tough peel.) Cut them into pieces of about the same size—I usually cut small turnips in half from the top to bottom and quarter small rutabagas lengthwise.

Peel the parsnips and carrots with a vegetable peeler. If the carrots are small, leave them whole. Cut large carrots and parsnips into 1½-inch pieces. If you'd like the vegetables to have a less rustic appearance, they can be trimmed (turned) into oval shapes, cutting away the sharp edges. Peel the onions and trim the root ends.

TO FINISH THE DISH: Put all the vegetables in a large bowl and toss them with the olive oil, thyme, garlic cloves, and 3 pinches of salt. Spread them in a large roasting pan. Put a roasting rack in the pan and set the chickens breast side up on it, leaving a space between the chickens. They should rest just above the vegetables, not touching them.

Roast for 15 minutes. Spread the room-temperature butter over the breasts. Roast for another 30 minutes. Add the prunes, if you are using them, to the pan and roast the chickens for another 15 to 20 minutes, or until the skin is richly browned and the temperature in the meatiest sections registers 160°F. Remove from the oven and put the chickens on a carving board to rest for 20 minutes.

Meanwhile, remove the rack, set the roasting pan on the stove so that it spans two burners, and bring the cooking liquid to a simmer. Whisk in the preserved lemon liquid and simmer for 2 minutes. Stir in the butter bit by bit to emulsify the sauce and glaze the vegetables. Stir in the parsley.

Present the chickens whole or carved, arranged over the vegetables in the roasting pan or on a large platter.

SERVES 6 TO 8

BERBERE-CURED CONFIT DUCK LEGS

Duck isn't really a Moroccan bird, but it should be. When I started experimenting with all kinds of game birds in the United States, like partridge, pheasant, and guinea fowl, I found that more than any of them, duck is a natural with Moroccan spices and seasonings, especially the toasty brown ones that go into *berbere*.

Confit—slow-cooking in fat—is one of my favorite techniques. I use it not just for duck, but for all kinds of poultry and many vegetables (carrots, potatoes, parsnips, rutabagas, turnips, fennel, and garlic, to name a few).

Stored in their cooking fat, confit duck legs keep for months in the refrigerator, and they take just a few minutes to brown in a pan. The meat is lusciously rich and soft, and the exterior crisps up beautifully. A panful tucked away in your fridge means you can make something incredible for dinner at a moment's notice.

You can serve these legs whole as a main course with Rainbow Chard (page 294) or other slow-cooked greens. Or shred the warm meat and serve it over Chicory Salad (page 158) as a complete meal. For an elegant dinner, serve it over mashed potatoes, drizzled with Duck Sauce (page 369).

cure
6 tablespoons (54 grams) kosher salt
2 tablespoons (25 grams) granulated sugar
2 tablespoons (12 grams) grated orange zest
1 tablespoon (3 grams) finely chopped thyme
2 tablespoons (16 grams) *Berbere* (page 36)
1 tablespoon (7.2 grams) Marash pepper
3 (0.5 gram) bay leaves, crumbled

6 duck legs (8 ounces/220 grams each), preferably Moulard
7 to 8 cups (1.56 to 1.79 kilograms) duck fat or (1.48 to 1.69 kilograms) canola oil
4 thyme sprigs

FOR THE CURE: Mix all the ingredients together in a bowl. Spread a thin layer of the mixture in the bottom of a baking dish that will hold the duck legs in a single layer. Top with the duck legs and sprinkle the remaining mixture over the tops of the legs. Cover with plastic wrap and refrigerate for 10 hours.

FOR THE CONFIT: Rinse the legs well under cold water to remove all the cure. Dry thoroughly with paper towels and let come to room temperature.

Preheat the oven to 200°F.

Choose a Dutch oven or other deep heavy pot that will hold the duck legs in one layer, or slightly overlapping. Melt 7 cups (1.6 kilograms) of the duck fat (or warm the oil) in the pot over low heat. Dry the duck legs again and add them to the pot, along with the thyme sprigs. Add more fat (or oil) as needed to completely cover the legs. Top with a parchment lid (see page 379) and brush it with water to keep the edges from curling up. Increase the heat to medium-low. When a few bubbles begin to appear, cover the pot with its lid, transfer to the oven, and cook for 4 hours.

Check the duck: test the meat with a paring knife or skewer—it should be completely tender but not falling off the bone. If necessary, cook for a bit longer. Remove from the oven, discard the parchment lid, and cool the duck in the fat.

Carefully transfer the duck legs to an airtight container (they can overlap or be stacked). Let the fat (or oil) sit for about 30 minutes, so any juices settle on the bottom of the pot.

Hold a fine-mesh strainer over the duck and ladle in enough fat to cover the legs. (Any leftover fat can be strained and used for cooking.) Cover the surface of the fat with plastic wrap and seal the container well. The legs will keep in the refrigerator for up to 3 months.

TO FINISH: Preheat the oven to 275°F. Bring the container of duck legs to room temperature, to soften the fat. (You may damage the legs if you try to remove them from the hardened fat.)

Remove the legs and wipe away most of the fat. Heat a large ovenproof frying pan (or use two pans) over medium heat. Working in batches if necessary, place the legs skin side down in the pan(s) and cook until the skin is a rich golden brown, about 2 minutes. Turn the legs and repeat on the other side. Turn them skin side up and place the pan(s) in the oven. Or, if you are cooking the legs in batches, place the first batch on a rack set over a rimmed baking sheet and put it in the oven. Heat the legs for about 6 minutes, or until they are warmed throughout.

SERVES 6

CHEF TO CHEF: *Taste the juice that has settled below the duck fat in the pot to see how salty it is and decide if you want to save it for a vinaigrette or for enriching sauces.*

CHICKEN LEGS
PRESERVED LEMONS
GREEN OLIVES

If you're looking for an ultraclassic Moroccan chicken dish—and a great starter recipe for test-driving your new tagine—this is it. In Morocco, where until fairly recently the idea of "chicken parts" didn't exist, it would be made with a whole chicken—or several chickens—sometimes cut into pieces, but more often than not cooked whole. I've eaten this a thousand times, and I remember how we'd all avoid the breast pieces, which were always dry and overcooked, and fight over the legs and thighs. Now I make the dish with dark meat only.

In Morocco, the bird would be placed in a tagine or a big pot with water, spices, and oil and cooked for a few hours. Then the chicken would be removed and the olives and preserved lemons added. The sauce would be cooked way down, and the chicken would be put back in at the end to warm it through. I approach it in a more European way, browning the meat in duck fat to build flavor, sautéing the onions with the spices, simmering the legs in stock, and then adding a final enrichment of butter. If you don't have a stainless steel tagine, a heavy Dutch oven (fitted with a cone of aluminum foil as described on page 97) will also work well.

6 chicken legs with thighs (8 ounces/226 grams each), trimmed of excess fat
Kosher salt
1 to 3 tablespoons (14 to 42 grams) duck or chicken fat
5 cups (530 grams) thinly sliced yellow onions
2 tablespoons (11 grams) ground coriander
2 teaspoons (5.3 grams) ground white pepper
2 teaspoons (4.1 grams) ground ginger
1 teaspoon (0.9 gram) saffron threads
½ teaspoon (1.4 grams) ground turmeric
1½ cups (352 grams) Chicken Stock (page 365)

TO GRILL THE POUSSINS: Preheat one area of the grill to medium-high heat and another to low heat. Oil the grill grates with a kitchen towel dipped in oil.

Brush the leaves and zest from the poussins (or they will burn on the grill). Rub the birds with a light coating of canola oil. Place breast side down on the hot side of the grill and cook undisturbed for 3 to 4 minutes to mark the skin. If at any point the skin is getting too dark, reduce the heat to medium. Turn the poussins 90 degrees to mark the skin in a crosshatch pattern and grill for another 3 to 4 minutes. Brush with the glaze, move the poussins to the cooler area of the grill, breast side up, and brush with the glaze again. Cook for another 5 minutes. If the skin is getting too dark, turn off this part of the grill (or move the birds away from the coals); the hotter side will continue to cook the poussins with indirect heat. Brush the birds again with glaze and cook for another 2 to 3 minutes, or until the juices run clear when a leg is twisted or the meat is lightly pierced with a small paring knife. Remove the poussins from the grill and let them rest for about 15 minutes.

Meanwhile, pour any remaining glaze into a small saucepan and bring to a simmer; remove from the heat.

Arrange the poussins on a serving platter, with the glaze drizzled over the top, and season with black pepper.

SERVES 4

rite of spring

It started like any other holiday morning. I woke up to early spring sunshine and the smell of my mom's *begrhir* pancakes, and there was a huge dish of the sweet barley porridge called *herbel* and a spread of *briwat* and other treats laid out on the table. In honor of the occasion, I got the new pair of running shoes I'd been asking for, and put them on right away. Then, after a huge breakfast, it was time to slaughter the lamb.

I was thirteen, and I'd seen the ritual happen ever since I could remember. It was always the same, whether it was the weekly chicken or the lamb that marked five or six special days throughout the year. In Morocco, slaughtering has to be done by a man, and it has to be done expertly, so that the animal suffers as little as possible. My grandpa, being the head of the household, was the only person permitted to do it, and he'd made a point of having me by his side to witness the act from the time I could stand up.

The whole family, easily thirty of us in all, gathered in a circle in the courtyard. The lamb, tethered to a tree, was munching on weeds. Three men from Grandpa's farm approached it. One held its head, the others held its legs. I stood near them, Grandpa embracing me from behind. He was holding the special razor-sharp knife used only for this purpose.

As he said the prayer of thanks for this animal and the sacrifice it was about to make, I felt nervous. We all did. It's not a sight you ever get used to. The air became strangely thick and still. The men brought the lamb closer. And then, before I knew what was happening, Grandpa put the knife in my right hand, closed his hand firmly around mine, and guided it toward the lamb's neck. In a second, it was over. Grandpa grabbed me and squeezed me tighter than he ever had. He said another prayer of thanks and then leaned down and whispered in my ear, "Congratulations." My mom rushed over in tears and held me, rocking back and forth.

There were many older boys and men in the family, all my uncles and cousins. But Grandpa had chosen me over his own sons. To be honest with you, I felt terrified, less by the experience itself and more by the responsibility I'd been given. But I trusted Grandpa and felt comforted by his strength. And from that day on, I was the only other person in the house allowed to slaughter chickens, rabbits, and even a few more lambs.

No doubt your reaction to this is that it seems barbaric. But I'm telling you that it's the opposite, not simply because the slaughter is done in a humane way, but because the act of witnessing it is a reminder that we can never take a life for granted. When you've seen an animal give its life for you, you don't take it lightly. You cook it with care. You eat it with respect. And perhaps the greater barbarism is never coming face to face with that, and pretending that meat comes from a market, not an animal.

Grandpa understood that. "We cared for that lamb and gave it a good life," he told me, "and now we thank it for sustaining our lives." It's a lesson I have never forgotten. When I prepare meat, or any food that once walked, swam, flew, or swayed in the breeze, I would never dare to waste or spoil it. I cook it with a grateful heart and the steady guidance of my grandpa's hand.

LAMB SHANK
SPICED PRUNES
BROWN BUTTER FARRO

Whenever I mentioned that I was writing this book, it seemed like nine out of ten people would ask, "Are those lamb shanks gonna be in there?" These are those lamb shanks. Their classic model is lamb with honey, a dish that starts by braising lamb shoulder with onions, *ras el hanout,* saffron, cinnamon, cloves, and nutmeg. Once the meat is cooked, honey and, sometimes, prunes are added and the sauce is reduced down to a shiny spiced-honey glaze. To me, it's like the baklava of lamb dishes—very sweet and very much about the honey. I've reduced the honey over the years, to the point where I finally eliminated it altogether, adding sweetness by way of separately cooked spiced prunes. I serve the lamb with a rich, tangy red wine gastrique, but here I've also given the simpler option of a more rustic sauce made from the braising liquid.

There's a lot of enthusiasm out there for French prunes, but to me, Moyers are the go-to choice. Moyer prunes are plump and meaty, with large pits that give them an almondy flavor when you cook them. Look for them at farmers' markets or mail-order from Bella Viva Orchards.

Even if you're not a chef, check out the Chef to Chef at the end of the recipe for making a "log" of braised shank meat. This is a fantastic thing to do with any braised meat. The gelatin in the meat holds it together in a form that's easy to store (for up to 5 days in the refrigerator) and cook. And, like duck confit, once you have it on hand, you can make an amazing meal in a few minutes. (You can skip the Activa RM, and the technique will still work well.)

When you order lamb shanks, ask for the meatier foreshanks, rather than the rear shanks, and ask the butcher to french the shanks, removing the fat and tendons that surround the bone.

lamb

6 lamb foreshanks (1 pound/453 grams each), trimmed and frenched

Kosher salt

8 cups (1 kilogram) coarsely chopped onions

¼ cup (32 grams) sliced garlic

¾ cup (159 grams) grapeseed or canola oil, plus more for browning the lamb

¼ cup (22 grams) ground coriander

1½ tablespoons (9.3 grams) ground ginger

1 tablespoon (7.7 grams) ground cumin

2 teaspoons (3.7 grams) ground black pepper

2 teaspoons (3.7 grams) ground turmeric

1 teaspoon (0.9 gram) saffron threads

8 to 10 cups (1.88 to 2.35 kilograms) Lamb Stock (page 369), (1.87 to 2.35 kilograms) Chicken Stock (page 365), or (1.86 to 2.34 kilograms) water

farro

3 tablespoons (27 grams) kosher salt

2¼ cups (450 grams) farro, picked over and rinsed

1 cup (134 grams) finely diced red onion

¼ cup (53 grams) grapeseed or canola oil

¾ cup (130 grams) Brown Butter (page 64), melted and still warm

4 tablespoons (2 ounces/57 grams) unsalted butter, (for the braising-liquid sauce)

1 teaspoon (1 gram) finely chopped parsley (for the braising-liquid sauce)

About 3 tablespoons (36 grams) Clarified Butter (page 375), melted, or (39.8 grams) extra virgin olive oil, for brushing the shanks

Red Wine Gastrique Lamb Sauce (page 371), warmed (optional)

6 Spiced Prunes (page 360)

Small spinach leaves, preferably New Zealand
Edible wildflowers, preferably radish and mustard
  blossoms
Crunchy sea salt

(MAKES ABOUT 7 CUPS/1.17 KILOGRAMS)

FOR THE LAMB SHANKS: Put a cooling rack on a baking sheet lined with paper towels. Salt the lamb shanks on all sides and put on the rack. Cover with a damp towel and refrigerate overnight.

Preheat the oven to 350°F.

Put the onions and garlic in a large bowl and toss with the oil.

Heat a large heavy roasting pan over medium heat for several minutes. Add a film of oil, then add the shanks in a single layer. Brown the lamb evenly on all sides for about 12 minutes, adjusting the heat as necessary.

Transfer the shanks to the baking sheet and pour off any fat remaining in the pan. Add the onion mixture and cook, stirring constantly, over medium heat, until the onions are an even golden brown; adjust the heat as necessary. Increase the heat to high, add 2 tablespoons (18 grams) salt, and the remaining spices and cook for about 2 minutes, stirring constantly, to bring out the flavors of the spices.

Nestle the shanks, smoother side down, in the onions and cook for 2 to 3 minutes. Turn the shanks over. (The side with the most connective tissue will be facing down; the meat will be more tender cooked this way.) Add enough stock to come three-quarters of the way up the shanks and bring to a simmer. Cover with a parchment lid (see page 379), brush it with water to keep the edges from curling up, and cover the pan tightly with aluminum foil. Put in the oven and cook for 2 hours and 45 minutes, or until the meat is completely tender.

MEANWHILE, FOR THE FARRO: Pour 5 quarts (4.65 kilograms) water into a small stockpot, add the salt, and bring to a boil over high heat. Stir in the farro, reduce the heat, and boil gently for about 30 minutes, until the farro is tender but not mushy. Drain the farro in a large strainer, shaking the strainer to remove the excess water.

Meanwhile, put the onions and oil in a large saucepan and set over medium-high heat. When the onions begin to sizzle, decrease the heat to medium and cook, stirring occasionally, for 15 minutes, or until the onions have softened and are slightly caramelized. Set aside.

TO FINISH THE LAMB: Carefully remove the shanks from the braising liquid, place them meaty side up on a baking sheet, and cover with aluminum foil to keep warm.

If you want to make a sauce from the braising liquid, rather than serving the gastrique sauce, preheat the oven to 200°F and transfer the shanks to the oven to keep them warm.

Pour the braising liquid, with the onions, into a large saucepan. Let sit for about 5 minutes, then ladle off the fat that has risen to the top and discard. Bring to a boil and boil gently for about 15 minutes to reduce the sauce to 5 to 6 cups (1.2 to 1.4 kilograms). If the flavor seems weak, continue to reduce it to intensify the flavor. Blend in the butter, preferably with an immersion blender, and stir in the parsley.

Stir the prunes into the sauce you have chosen.

Turn on the broiler. Brush the shanks with the clarified butter and put under the broiler for a few minutes to brown.

TO SERVE: Reheat the onions over medium heat, and stir in the farro. Add the brown butter, stirring to coat the farro.

Spoon some farro and sauce onto each serving plate. Set the lamb shanks over them. Garnish each plate with a prune, some spinach leaves, and edible flowers. Sprinkle the shanks with crunchy sea salt.

SERVES 6

CHEF TO CHEF: Pulling the cooked lamb from the bones, adding a bit of Activa RM to help it hold together, and rolling it tightly in plastic wrap will give you another way of using the meat. I usually make large rolls about 7 inches long by 2 inches thick, or narrow rolls about 10 inches long by 1 inch thick (pictured below). Six lamb shanks will make 2 large logs or 2 to 3 smaller logs. Roll and knot the ends tightly against the meat. The logs need to be chilled, and the best way to do this is in ice water. (It will maintain the round shape.) Fill a deep rectangular pan with ice water (a bowl would bend the ends) and add the logs. They should float; if not, add more water. Refrigerate for at least several hours, or up to 5 days.

If you are cooking slices from a large log, preheat the oven to 400°F. Cut the ends off the rolls. Cut large rolls, through the plastic, into 1-inch-thick rounds, or cut the smaller rolls into 3 pieces about 3 inches long. Remove the plastic wrap. Heat a film of grapeseed oil in a nonstick pan (ovenproof if you're cooking larger rounds) over medium heat. Let it get really hot, then add the large rounds to the pan and brown well on both sides, about 4 minutes. Put in the oven to heat all the way through. If cooking small rounds, roll them in the hot oil for about 2 minutes to crisp and heat through.

RACK OF LAMB
EGGPLANT-DATE PUREE
RED CABBAGE

Lamb is the meat of choice on the Moroccan table. When I was growing up, we would eat lamb three or four times a week, chicken maybe twice, and beef once or not at all.

In traditional Moroccan butcher shops, you buy lamb by the kilo, not the cut, and you get a mix of cuts, all of which, for the most part, get braised together. And because in Morocco meat is always eaten fully cooked, with no sign of blood, rack of lamb, lamb chops, and lamb loin are culinary concepts that don't exist there.

Here in the United States, of course, it's just the opposite. The lean "middle meats"—the steaks, chops, and tenderloin—are prized and cooked simply to showcase their flavor, while the tougher cuts are often ground to make hamburger.

Personally, I'd take a good braised lamb dish over a chop any day, not just because that's what I grew up on, but because between the slow-cooking and the opportunities to infuse other flavors, braising is where the real art of meat cooking happens. Having said that, I must admit that I do also love a good lamb chop, especially when it's prepared in a clean way, so that the flavor of the lamb really comes through, and served with interesting flavor partners. That's the idea here. Eggplant, fruit, and lamb are classically Moroccan, so I work those flavors in by way of the eggplant puree, which is slightly sweetened with dates. A light coating of *ras el hanout* on the rack gives great flavor just on the outside, keeping the balance right.

I like cooking whole racks because you get beautiful medium-rare meat throughout, and because a rack gives you the added bonus of the fat cap, the flap that covers one side of the rack. When you order your racks, ask your butcher to french them if you like, and to remove the fat caps and include them with your order, so you can use them to make Lamb Bacon (page 267).

Racks vary quite a bit in size, depending on the age of the lamb and which end they're cut from. My advice for making great rack of lamb is to treat it more like lamb chops and less like a roast—in other words, pansear it and then finish it in a hot oven as directed here.

lamb

Two 8-bone racks of lamb (2 pounds/907 grams each), cleaned and frenched, fat caps reserved for Lamb Bacon (page 267), if desired
Grapeseed or canola oil
1 tablespoon (8.5 grams) *Ras el Hanout* (page 29)
1 teaspoon (3 grams) kosher salt
2 tablespoons (1 ounce/28 grams) unsalted butter

eggplant puree

Grapeseed or canola oil for deep-frying
4 Medjool dates, pitted
1½ pounds (680 grams) eggplant, preferably Rosa Bianca or globe
¾ teaspoon (2.3 grams) kosher salt
1 teaspoon (2.3 grams) Aleppo pepper
⅛ teaspoon (0.3 gram) cayenne
2½ teaspoons (13 grams) sherry vinegar
½ cup plus 1 tablespoon (132 grams) heavy cream

(MAKES 1¾ CUPS/403 GRAMS)

red cabbage

2 pounds (907 grams) red cabbage

¼ cup (50 grams) canola oil (if not using the fat cap)

Kosher salt

1¼ teaspoons (4.4 grams) yellow mustard seeds

½ cup (50 grams) minced shallots

4 garlic cloves, finely chopped

1 cup (235 grams) port, preferably ruby

½ cup (108 grams) dry red wine, preferably
   Zinfandel

2 tablespoons (25 grams) granulated sugar

¾ cup (118 grams) prunes, preferably Moyer,
   pitted and roughly chopped

3 Medjool dates, pitted and roughly chopped

3 tablespoons (50 grams) whole-grain mustard

¼ cup (60 grams) sherry vinegar

(MAKES ABOUT 4 CUPS/965 GRAMS)

Six 8-inch (2.5 grams each) summer savory sprigs or
   six 6-inch (6 grams each) rosemary sprigs

Crunchy sea salt

FOR THE LAMB: If you have reserved the fat caps, cut enough fat into ⅛-inch dice to make ½ cup (48 grams). Set aside.

The lamb looks best with a uniform shape, so tie the meat between each set of bones with a piece of kitchen twine. Rub the lamb with oil and season with the *ras el hanout* and salt. Place on a tray and refrigerate, uncovered, overnight.

CONTINUED

FOR THE EGGPLANT: Pour 2 inches of oil into a small stockpot fitted with a thermometer and heat to 400°F.

Soak the dates in a bowl of hot water to loosen the skins.

Meanwhile, cut off and discard the ends of the eggplant. Peel the eggplant and cut into ¾-inch pieces.

Drain and peel the dates.

Line a baking sheet with paper towels. Working in 4 batches, fry the eggplant for about 3 minutes, using a skimmer to hold any floating piece under the oil so it browns evenly. Transfer to the paper towels.

Put the eggplant, dates, salt, Aleppo pepper, cayenne, and vinegar in a food processor and process until smooth. Pass through a fine-mesh strainer, and set aside.

Whip the cream to soft peaks and refrigerate.

FOR THE CABBAGE: Cut the cabbage into quarters. Cut out the core and cut the cabbage crosswise into ¼-inch-wide strips.

If using lamb fat, put ¼ cup (24 grams) of the reserved lamb fat in a large sauté pan over medium-high heat. As soon as the fat begins to render, add a pinch of salt and the mustard seeds and cover the pan (the mustard seeds will begin to pop). Lift the lid occasionally to check, and when the fat begins to color, turn the heat to medium-low to render the remaining fat slowly. After about 3 minutes, when the fat has lightly browned, add the shallots and garlic, stir to coat in the fat, and cook for about 6 minutes, or until tender.

If using canola oil, heat the oil in a large sauté pan over medium heat. Add a pinch of salt and the mustard seeds, cover the pan (the mustard seeds will begin to pop), and swirl the pan, flipping or stirring the seeds occasionally so they toast evenly, until they begin to pop, about 2 minutes. Toast for 30 seconds

more, then add the shallots and garlic and cook for about 6 minutes, or until tender.

Increase the heat under the pan to medium and add the cabbage. Cook for about 4 minutes to wilt, stirring to coat the cabbage with the shallots and seeds. Increase the heat to medium-high and cook for 1 to 2 minutes to lightly color to the cabbage. Add the port, wine, sugar, prunes, and dates and cook for 8 to 10 minutes, or until most of the liquid has evaporated and the cabbage is tender. Reduce the heat to medium-low and stir in the mustard and sherry vinegar. Season to taste with salt and set aside.

TO COOK THE LAMB: Preheat the oven to 400°F.

If you have a 12-inch cast-iron skillet or other heavy ovenproof pan, you will be able to cook the racks together; if your pan is smaller, brown the racks individually. (In the latter case, return the first rack to the pan before proceeding to roast them in the oven.)

Heat the skillet over high heat. When the pan is smoking hot, add the remaining ¼ cup (24 grams) of the reserved lamb fat or a film of oil. Let the fat render, or heat the oil. Add the racks, standing the eye of the rack up against the side of the pan with the bones extending upward; the curve of the pan will help brown the meat evenly. Lower the heat to medium-high and cook, holding the meat against the side of the pan as necessary to brown it evenly, for 5 to 7 minutes total. Baste the lamb with the fat in the pan from time to time.

Remove from the heat. If you have a remote digital thermometer, insert the probe in the center of one end of one rack, the smaller rack if they are not the same size. Roast in the oven for about 18 minutes, or until the internal temperature is 135°F for medium-rare (use an instant-read thermometer if you don't have a remote thermometer). Remove from the oven, add the butter to the pan, and baste the lamb several times with the fat. Transfer the lamb to a cutting board and let it rest in a warm place for 15 minutes, or until the temperature has reached 145°F.

Meanwhile, fold the whipped cream into the eggplant puree.

TO SERVE: To cut the racks into double chops with one bone in the center, make the first cut flush against the inside of the first bone, then flush against the third bone, to form the first chop. Cut flush against the other side of the third bone and repeat the process to form 3 double chops (the small end chops can be passed as seconds). Repeat with the remaining rack.

To serve individually, arrange a spoonful of eggplant puree, some red cabbage, and a lamb chop in the center of each large serving bowl or plate. Garnish with a sprig of savory and sprinkle with crunchy sea salt. *To serve family-style,* use a small offset spatula or the back of a spoon to spread a layer of the eggplant puree on a platter. Spoon the red cabbage over the puree. Arrange the double chops over the cabbage. Garnish with the savory and sprinkle the lamb with crunchy sea salt. Serve the remaining puree, cabbage, and the small chops on the side.

SERVES 6

STEAMED LAMB SHOULDER
SAFFRON BUTTER
CUMIN SALT

The next time you're thinking of making a roast, think again, and bust out the couscoussier. You'll need a 16-quart one for this recipe (or you can improvise with a large pot and a steamer rack).

In Morocco, a single big chunk of lamb is a special-occasion luxury. It's generally either simmered with water and vegetables in the bottom half of a couscoussier (with the couscous in the top half) or, as in this recipe, steamed *over* the water and vegetables, in the top half, with no couscous involved. Steaming makes lamb insanely moist and pull-apart tender, and, for added interest, I like to finish the meat in a hot oven to crisp the exterior.

Saffron is another luxury reserved for celebrations, and I've incorporated it here in the form of a saffron-cumin compound butter that gets rubbed both on the outside and in the cavity of the shoulder. It infuses the meat as it steams and also drips down to enrich the broth. I like the blue-cheese flavor that aged butter adds here, but you can use unsalted butter.

Ask the butcher to bone the shoulder, leaving the meat in one piece. There will be skin and fat on the top of the shoulder; ask the butcher to trim it without removing it completely, so a thin protective layer remains. The larger pieces of fat on the inside can be removed, but here again, you don't want to cut into the meat. And have the butcher cut the bone into a few pieces for you, so you can fit it in the bottom of the couscoussier to add more flavor to the broth.

I add vegetables to the broth to enrich it but simmer other vegetables separately to serve with the meat. And I reduce the broth way down to make a rich sauce. Neither of these approaches is traditionally Moroccan. There the broth is often served in bowls so you can sip it between bites of meat. If you'd like to try it that way, reduce it to about 4 cups (1 kilogram), which will take about 30 minutes.

lamb

½ teaspoon (0.45 gram) saffron threads
1 tablespoon (7.7 grams) ground cumin
½ pound (226.8 grams) Aged Butter (page 374) or unsalted butter, at room temperature
One 4-pound (1.8-kilogram) boneless lamb shoulder, bone reserved and cut into 3 or 4 pieces (have the butcher do this)
1 large onion, cut in half
2 carrots, cut into chunks
1 celery stalk, cut into chunks
12 (42 grams) flat-leaf parsley stems
3 garlic cloves
10 cups (2.35 kilograms) Lamb Stock (page 369) plus 6 cups (1.4 kilograms) water, or 4 quarts (3.72 kilograms) water
Kosher salt and freshly ground black pepper
2 tablespoons (24 grams) Clarified Butter (page 375)

carrots

6 medium yellow carrots
6 medium red carrots
1½ cups (352 grams) Chicken Stock (page 365)
1 tablespoon (15 grams) sherry vinegar
1 teaspoon (4.2 grams) granulated sugar
1 teaspoon (3 grams) kosher salt

marble potatoes

24 marble potatoes

2 teaspoons (6 grams) kosher salt

2 teaspoons (2 grams) chopped thyme

1 garlic clove

cipollini onions

12 cipollini onions, about 1½ inches in diameter, left
unpeeled

8 tablespoons (4 ounces/113 grams) unsalted butter

½ teaspoon (0.5 gram) saffron threads

Crunchy sea salt

Cumin Salt (page 26)

2 tablespoons (8 grams) chopped flat-leaf parsley
(optional)

FOR THE LAMB: Put the saffron in a spoon (saffron will
toast more evenly and be less likely to burn when
toasted this way), hold the spoon 4 to 5 inches above
a medium-low flame, and toast until fragrant, about
1 minute. Transfer the saffron to a large mortar and
grind to a fine powder with the pestle. Add the cumin
and butter and mix to incorporate the saffron. Or,
if you don't have a mortar, put the saffron in a bowl
and mix in the butter and cumin.

If the lamb shoulder is wrapped in butcher's
paper, leave the paper under the lamb when you trim
it, then throw away the paper, for easy cleanup. Trim
away any remaining sections of fat and sinew from the
lamb, leaving the fat cap intact. Add any trimmings to
the bottom of the couscoussier. Add the onion, carrots,
celery, parsley, garlic, and enough lamb stock (and/or
water) to fill the pot half-full. Bring to a simmer.

Meanwhile, cut a 4-layer piece of cheesecloth
large enough to enclose the lamb generously and
spread it on the work surface. Generously season both
sides of the lamb with salt and pepper. Lay the lamb
fat side down on the cheesecloth and unfold the
meat. Smear the inside of the lamb with a generous
coating of the saffron butter. Fold the shoulder back
together and smear the outside of the lamb with the
remaining butter. Wrap the lamb in the cheesecloth
and tie the roast at 1-inch intervals with kitchen
twine. Turn the lamb 90 degrees and repeat.

Place the lamb in the top of the couscoussier and
cover with the lid. If steam is escaping between the
top and bottom sections of the steamer, pull off a long
piece of plastic wrap and tie it around the pot, where
the top and bottom meet. Steam the meat for 2½
hours, or until very tender. The easiest way to test the
meat, without unwrapping the whole shoulder, is to
cut a small slit with scissors or a paring knife through

the layers of cheesecloth, then insert a paring knife through the hole.

MEANWHILE, FOR THE CARROTS: Put all the ingredients in a medium saucepan, bring to a gentle simmer over medium heat, and cook for 5 minutes, or until the carrots are tender. Drain and set aside.

FOR THE POTATOES: Put the potatoes in a medium saucepan, cover by ½ inch with cold water, and add the salt, thyme, and garlic. Bring to a gentle simmer over medium heat and cook for 12 minutes, or until the potatoes are tender. Drain the potatoes and set aside.

FOR THE ONIONS: Trim the tops to create a flat top with the layers of onion exposed. Peel the onions and trim the roots flush, leaving enough of them intact to hold the rings together as the onions cook. Melt the butter over medium heat in a frying pan large enough to hold the onions in a single layer. Add the saffron and arrange the cipollini in the pan, top side down. Cook, basting the onions frequently by tilting the pan and spooning the butter over them, for about 8 minutes, until golden brown on the bottom. Turn them over and continue to baste with the butter for another 1 to 2 minutes, or until they are completely tender. Remove the onions from the pan and sprinkle each with a pinch of crunchy sea salt.

FOR THE SAUCE: Carefully remove the lamb from the steamer and place it on a baking sheet. Remove and discard the cheesecloth, cover the lamb with a piece of aluminum foil, and set aside in a warm spot while you complete the dish.

Strain the broth in the bottom of the couscoussier into a large saucepan. Skim any fat from the surface of the broth and bring to a rapid simmer over medium-high heat. Cook for about 50 minutes, or until the sauce has reduced to 1 cup (250 grams).

Meanwhile, preheat the oven to 475°F.

TO SERVE: Brush the lamb with the clarified butter and place it in the oven for about 10 minutes to reheat it and brown the top.

Meanwhile, add the vegetables to the sauce and warm them for 3 to 5 minutes, stirring to coat them in the sauce.

Place the lamb on a large serving platter. Lift the vegetables out of the sauce and arrange them around the lamb, or place them in a bowl. Serve the remaining sauce and the cumin salt on the side.

My favorite way to eat this dish is to have everyone use their fingers to pull away pieces of lamb. The meat will pull off with the grain, and although normally meat should be cut against the grain, this is the one time it is acceptable! Dip the meat in the sauce, then in the cumin salt. If you prefer, you can slice the lamb, arrange it on the platter, and top the meat with the vegetables, sauce, and a sprinkling of parsley.

SERVES 4 TO 6

CHEF TO CHEF: Try a comfort-food version of this dish. Leave the bone in the shoulder and place it in the bottom of the couscoussier with a few tablespoons of aged butter. Cover the lamb with stock and/or water and simmer for about 2 hours, until tender; add the vegetables for the last 20 minutes.

LAMB BACON

At the restaurant, we buy whole lambs and put every last part to use. Not eating pork but wanting to experience the magic of bacon everyone's always talking about, I thought we'd try making lamb bacon with one of those "last parts," the fat cap that covers the racks. This confit-like method is a fair amount of work, but it's really worth the payoff.

I serve it as part of a warm appetizer that's kind of my answer to the pork-belly trend: a thick slab of crisped lamb bacon with romanesco, wheat berries, mustard blossoms, and a drizzle of chicken jus. At home, you can use it just like any bacon—sliced and fried with your morning eggs, cut into *lardons* for salads, diced and used in recipes, and as part of a truly outstanding Lamb BLT (see below).

lamb spice mix

⅓ cup (47.7 grams) kosher salt

1 tablespoon (8 grams) sweet paprika

2 teaspoons (3.7 grams) ground coriander

2 teaspoons (2.6 grams) finely chopped savory or rosemary leaves

2 teaspoons (1.9 grams) finely chopped thyme

¾ teaspoon (2 grams) smoked paprika

¾ teaspoon (1.8 grams) Aleppo pepper

½ teaspoon (1.3 grams) ground cumin

1½ teaspoons (5 grams) finely chopped garlic

2 lamb fat caps (2 to 3 pounds/907 grams to 1.36 kilograms total)

6 to 8 cups (1.27 to 1.69 kilograms) canola oil

(MAKES ABOUT ¾ CUP/108 GRAMS)

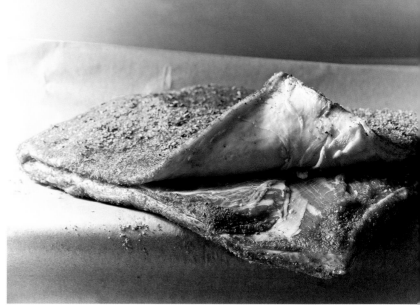

FOR THE SPICE MIX: Combine all the ingredients in a spice grinder and finely grind. Set aside.

Using your fingers, open the flaps on the wide (shoulder) end of each fat cap to expose the flat piece of cartilage. Cut it out and discard. Cut out and discard the long tendon that runs down the length of each cap.

Lay one cap meat side up on the work surface. Put the second cap meat side down over the first cap, matching the thicker side of one cap with the thinner side of the second cap. Press them together.

Rub and press a generous coating of the spice mix on all sides of the caps. Wrap in plastic wrap, place on a baking sheet, top with a second baking sheet, and put a weight on top. Refrigerate for at least 12 hours, or up to 24 hours.

Preheat the oven to 275°F.

Unwrap the caps. Tie a piece of twine around the center of the stacked caps and then one to each side; repeat in the other direction. Put in a Dutch oven, pour in enough oil to cover the meat, and rub the meat to loosen the spices and flavor the oil. Cover the pot and cook in the oven for 1 hour.

The meat will have shrunk and be loose in the twine. Carefully remove the bacon from the oil, cut off the twine, and tie again securely with new pieces of twine. Return it to the pot, cover, and cook in the oven until completely tender. The cooking time will be about 30 minutes to 1 hour, depending on the size of the fat caps. Allow the bacon to cool to room temperature in the oil, 1½ to 2 hours.

Remove the bacon from the oil, place on a baking sheet, and weight as before. Refrigerate overnight.

TO COOK THE BACON: Slice the bacon crosswise into ⅛-inch-thick slices. Lay the strips in a cold nonstick frying pan, set over medium heat, and cook for about 10 minutes, or until the bottom has browned. Turn and cook for about 5 minutes to brown the second side. Drain on paper towels

MAKES 1 TO 1½ POUNDS (453 TO 680 GRAMS) UNCOOKED BACON

CHEF TO CHEF: Before sandwiching the caps, dust the insides of the caps with Activa RM. This will help to glue the pieces together, keeping the braising liquid from entering the bacon.

LAMB BLTS

6 *Harissa* Rolls (page 202), sliced and toasted
Preserved Lemon Mayonnaise (page 49)
12 slices lamb bacon, cooked
Sliced tomatoes
Crunchy sea salt and freshly ground black pepper
Wild arugula

Spread the bottom of each bun with a smear of the mayonnaise. Top each with bacon, some tomatoes, a sprinkling of salt and pepper, and a small handful of arugula. Cover with the tops of the rolls.

MAKES 6 SANDWICHES

KEFTA TAGINE
CUSTARDY EGG YOLKS

Cooking is always serious business in Morocco, and for a real sit-down meal, there aren't a lot of shortcuts or quick-fix dishes. But this is one of them. It's a classic bachelor dish, one of the few things men cook. And it's what I remember eating whenever there was a lot going on in the house—preparations for a holiday or some big group activity like preserving lemons—and people needed something satisfying and hearty that didn't take hours to braise and could be entrusted to one of the younger women.

The meatballs would be simmered in the sauce without being browned first, and then eggs would be cracked into wells in the sauce and cooked until they were no longer runny. In this version, I brown the *kefta* separately so they're moister and more flavorful, and I use only egg yolks, cooked just long enough to warm them to a soft, custardy consistency. I don't think the egg whites really add anything, and the yolks mix wonderfully with the sauce and the meatballs.

I make a big batch of sauce and freeze what I don't use for other purposes (it's great on pasta). It will keep in the freezer for at least a month. If you can't find San Marzano tomato puree, you can make your own by pureeing canned chopped San Marzano tomatoes and their liquid in a blender.

This recipe is easily turned into great stuffed bell peppers. Cut off the tops of the peppers, clean out the ribs and seeds, and stuff them with the *kefta* mixture, lightened, if you like, with a cup of Fresh Bread Crumbs (page 378) or cooked rice. Put the tops back on the peppers, brush them with olive oil, and nestle them in a baking dish. Thin the sauce with a bit of water, ladle it around the peppers, and bake at 350°F until the peppers are soft and the filling is cooked through.

tomato sauce

Grapeseed or canola oil

2 cups (270 grams) diced (¼-inch) onions

2 tablespoons (19 grams) finely chopped garlic

4 cups (1.1 kilograms) tomato puree, preferably San Marzano

1 cup (234 grams) water

1 cup (255 grams) carrot juice

½ teaspoon (1.3 grams) sweet paprika

½ teaspoon (1.3 grams) ground cumin

¼ teaspoon (0.5 gram) ground black pepper

1/16 teaspoon (0.1 gram) cayenne

1½ teaspoons (4.5 grams) kosher salt

1½ teaspoons (2 grams) finely chopped thyme

1½ tablespoons (18 grams) diced (1/8-inch) preserved lemon rind (see page 45)

1½ teaspoons (2 grams) finely chopped flat-leaf parsley

1½ teaspoons (2 grams) finely chopped cilantro

(MAKES ABOUT 4 CUPS/1 KILOGRAM)

½ recipe (about ½ pound/234 grams) *Kefta* (page 139)

Grapeseed or canola oil

6 large egg yolks, at room temperature

2 quarters preserved lemon rind (see page 45), cut into 9 strips each

Urfa pepper

Fennel fronds (optional)

Extra virgin olive oil for finishing

FOR THE TOMATO SAUCE: Heat a film of oil in a large saucepan or small stockpot over medium-high heat. Add the onions and sauté, lowering the heat as needed, for 12 to 14 minutes, until golden and just beginning to caramelize around the edges. Add the garlic and sauté for another 2 minutes to soften.

Add the tomato puree and bring to a simmer. Stir in the water, carrot juice, paprika, cumin, pepper, cayenne, salt, and thyme, and simmer gently for about 40 minutes, until the sauce is reduced by about one third.

Stir in the diced preserved lemon, parsley, and cilantro and remove from the heat.

TO COOK THE *KEFTA*: Divide the mixture into 20 portions and shape into balls. Flatten them slightly to form 1½-inch patties. Heat a film of oil in a large nonstick frying pan over medium-high heat. Add the lamb patties, in batches, and cook for 1 to 1½ minutes on each side, or until browned and cooked to medium. Drain on paper towels.

Pour a ½-inch layer of the tomato sauce into a tagine or a round wide flameproof baking dish with a lid (any remaining sauce can be refrigerated or frozen for another use). Bring to a simmer over medium heat. Arrange the egg yolks in a circle in the pan. Cover the pan and cook for 1½ to 2 minutes to warm the yolks. Remove the lid and arrange the *kefta* around the egg yolks. Garnish the dish with the strips of preserved lemon, a sprinkling of Urfa, and a scattering of fennel fronds, if using. Drizzle with olive oil.

SERVES 6

BEEF CHEEKS
CARROT JAM
HARISSA EMULSION

Beef cheeks are the ultimate meat for braising. They're rich in gelatin but leaner than other more typical braising cuts like short ribs, so they have a wonderful mouth-coating texture and flavor. Cheeks vary tremendously in size, depending on the size and age of the animal they came from. I get small ones that weigh 6 to 8 ounces and will serve one person, but I've seen them in butcher shops weighing as much as a pound.

You should be able to get trimmed beef cheeks from the butcher, but if you get untrimmed cheeks, here's what you'll need to do. There's a large fatty flap of tissue over the top of the meat that's easily removed and discarded. What's left is a heart-shaped piece of meat. Trim off all excess fat on the surface.

You'll see that there is a membrane that runs through the cheek. This can't be removed, but don't worry about that—it will break down as the meat cooks. Once all the excess fat is trimmed, the cheek will range from 6 to 12 ounces. Your target portion size for this recipe is 5 to 6 ounces; small cheeks should be left whole and large ones cut in half lengthwise.

If you don't have time to make *harissa* emulsion or Carrot Jam, Horseradish Mint Sauce (see page 276) is a good alternative here.

I like to serve braised dishes with a fresh raw green or vegetable element for contrast. In this case, the slightly slippery quality of purslane bridges nicely with the textures of the meat and the jam.

beef cheeks

Kosher salt

6 pieces trimmed beef cheeks (5 to 6 ounces/
141 to 170 grams each)

2 teaspoons (6 grams) Tellicherry peppercorns

1 tablespoon (3.8 grams) coriander seeds

4 (0.6 gram) allspice berries

4 (0.3 gram) cloves

2 (1.2 grams) chiles de árbol

Canola oil

3 pounds (1.36 kilograms) shallots, cut into large
pieces

1 large onion, cut into large pieces

10 garlic cloves, crushed

One 750-ml bottle dry red wine, preferably
Cabernet Sauvignon

5 cups (1.17 kilograms) Chicken Stock (page 365),
heated until hot

2 (0.3 gram) bay leaves

3 (3 grams) thyme sprigs

harissa *emulsion*

1¼ cups (293 grams) Chicken Stock (page 365)

2 tablespoons (32 grams) whole milk

2 tablespoons (28 grams) Quick *Harissa* (page 82)

4 tablespoons (2 ounces/57 grams) unsalted butter

¼ teaspoon (0.8 gram) kosher salt

½ teaspoon (1.1 grams) lecithin

(MAKES ABOUT 1¼ CUPS/225 GRAMS)

Brown Butter Couscous (page 64)

Carrot Jam (page 358)

Small greens, preferably purslane (optional)

TO BEGIN THE BEEF CHEEKS: Place a cooling rack on a baking sheet lined with paper towels. Salt the beef cheeks on all sides and place on the rack. Cover with a damp towel and refrigerate overnight.

TO COOK THE CHEEKS AND VEGETABLES: Preheat the oven to 275°F.

Wrap the peppercorns, coriander, allspice, cloves, and chiles in a piece of cheesecloth and tie to make a sachet. Set aside.

Dry the cheeks with paper towels. Heat a film of canola oil in a Dutch oven, preferably enameled cast iron, over medium-high heat. Add the beef cheeks and brown on all sides, for 10 to 12 minutes total, removing each piece as it is browned.

Pour off any fat from the pot and add a film of oil. (There will be browned bits in the bottom of the pot; however, if the bottom looks burnt, clean the pot, then add the film of oil.) Over medium heat, add the shallots, onion, and garlic, and cook, stirring often, for 12 to 15 minutes, until the onion is caramelized. Pour in the wine and scrape the browned bits from the bottom of the pot to deglaze. Simmer for 12 to 15 minutes, or until the wine has reduced and the onion is glazed.

TO BRAISE THE BEEF CHEEKS: Spread the vegetables out, and arrange the cheeks in a single layer over the vegetables. Pour in the chicken stock. Most of the meat should be covered by liquid, but it's fine if the tops stick out a bit. Add the sachet and bring to a simmer. Cover with a parchment lid (see page 379), brush it with water to keep the edges from curling up, and cover with the lid. Put in the oven and cook for 3 to 4 hours, or until the meat is completely tender.

CONTINUED

Meanwhile, tie the bay leaves and the thyme together with a piece of kitchen twine to make an herb bouquet.

Remove the pot from the oven. Transfer the meat to a large saucepan. Skim and discard any fat on the surface of the braising liquid. Strain the liquid over the meat. Add the herb bouquet, bring to a rapid simmer, and simmer for about 8 minutes to infuse the flavors of the herbs. Remove and discard the herb bouquet, and continue to simmer for about 20 minutes, until the sauce is reduced and the meat is richly glazed.

MEANWHILE, FOR THE *HARISSA* EMULSION: There will be more emulsion than you need, but it is difficult to make a smaller quantity. Pour the stock into a small saucepan, bring to a simmer, and simmer for 15 to 20 minutes, or until it has reduced to ½ cup (110 grams). Add the milk, *harissa,* butter, and salt and bring to a simmer, whisking to melt the butter.

Pour the mixture into a blender and add the lecithin. Start the blender slowly to release any steam, then blend at high speed for about 30 seconds to dissolve the lecithin. Strain through a fine-mesh strainer into a bowl.

TO SERVE: Using a frother, froth the *harissa* emulsion (if you don't have a frother, just drizzle it over the meat). Place a mound of couscous on each plate and top with a beef cheek. Place a spoonful of carrot jam by the meat and spoon some emulsion over the meat. Garnish with greens, if using.

SERVES 6

Z'HUG-RUBBED STANDING RIB ROAST
HORSERADISH-MINT SAUCE

For those times when you want something celebratory but uncomplicated, this standing rib roast is the ticket. It's simply rubbed all over with *z'hug* and roasted on a bed of onions to give it extra flavor. To complement the spicy heat of the *z'hug,* I serve the meat with a cooling twist on traditional horseradish sauce, made with yogurt and mint, along with some sautéed greens. Farro is my top pick for a side dish here, but potatoes—mashed, smashed, roasted, or even boiled, peeled, and smoked in a stovetop smoker—would also be right at home. So would either couscous or jasmine rice cooked with a bit of saffron and sprinkled with chives.

beef

One 3-bone standing rib roast (7 to 8 pounds/
  3.17 to 3.62 kilograms)
Kosher salt and freshly ground black pepper
6 tablespoons (48.6 grams) *Z'hug* (page 38)
4 large onions, peeled and sliced into 1-inch-thick slices

horseradish-mint sauce

Three 6-inch zucchini
Grapeseed or canola oil
1 cup (238 grams) whole-milk Greek yogurt
3 tablespoons (18 grams) finely grated fresh
  horseradish
1 teaspoon (1 gram) thinly slivered mint leaves
1 tablespoon (15 grams) fresh lemon juice
Kosher salt and freshly ground black pepper

(MAKES 1½ CUPS/352 GRAMS)

chicory
Grapeseed or canola oil
1½ pounds (680 grams) mixed chicories
1¾ teaspoons (9 grams) aged balsamic vinegar,
    preferably 30 to 40 years old
Crunchy sea salt

FOR THE BEEF: Place a cooling rack on a baking sheet lined with paper towels. Season the roast generously on all sides with salt and pepper, sprinkle with the *z'hug,* and put on the rack. Refrigerate, uncovered, overnight.

Preheat the oven to 450°F.

Line a roasting pan that will hold the roast (without its edges touching the sides) with the onions. The onion slices stand in for a roasting rack. Put the roast bone side down on the onions. If you have a remote thermometer, insert the probe into the thickest part of the roast.

Roast for 20 minutes, then lower the heat to 300°F and cook for about 1 hour and 50 minutes for rare meat, or until the internal temperature reaches 125°F; about 2 hours for medium-rare meat (130°F); or just over 2 hours for medium meat (135°F). Remove from the oven and let rest for 30 minutes.

MEANWHILE, FOR THE HORSERADISH SAUCE: You will use only the green outside part of the zucchini for this dish. Trim away the ends and cut off the sides in ⅛-inch-thick slices. Cut into ⅛-inch dice.

Heat a very light film of oil in a nonstick skillet over medium-high heat. Add the zucchini and sauté for 4 to 5 minutes, until tender and browned on the edges. Put in a fine-mesh strainer set over a bowl and set aside to cool.

Mix the remaining horseradish sauce ingredients together in a serving bowl. Stir in the zucchini.

FOR THE CHICORY: Cook the chicory in 3 batches. Heat a large cast-iron skillet until it smokes. Add a light film of oil, and when it begins to smoke, add one-third of the chicory and sauté for about 1 minute, until barely wilted. Remove from the pan and repeat with the remaining batches.

Combine all the batches of chicory in a serving dish and drizzle with the balsamic vinegar. Sprinkle with a pinch of crunchy sea salt.

TO SERVE: Cut the meat away from the bones by holding a slicing knife at the top of the roast next to the bone and slicing down around the meat, working close to the bones, until the meat is removed. Slice the meat, and cut between the bones to separate them. Arrange the meat and bones on a platter and serve with the horseradish sauce. Serve the chicory as a side dish.

SERVES 6

SHORT RIB *TANGIA*
AGED BUTTER
PRESERVED LEMONS

A *tangia* is a tall terra-cotta pot that looks like a cross between an ancient Greek amphora and a bean pot, with handles on either side that hold a loop of wire for carrying it. And, like a tagine, *tangia* is also the name of the stew you cook in it.

The *tangia* is uniquely associated with Marrakesh, and it's a guy thing. Men fill their *tangias* with lamb, aged butter, and *ras el hanout* (making it a no-brainer from the point of view of seasoning), throw in some preserved lemons and a bit of water, seal the top with the butcher paper from the meat, tie it with twine, and take it with them to the *hammam,* the steam bath.

They drop it off in the boiler room, where, for a small fee, the attendants bury the *tangia* in the warm ashes raked from the wood-fired boiler, and there it sits overnight. I like to think of this as the original *sous-vide*—food sealed with a minimal amount of liquid and slowly cooked at a very low temperature until it becomes meltingly tender and flavorful.

My grandpa would make it one day, then bring it home for lunch the next, holding the hot wire handle in a piece of folded newspaper. Visit a *hammam* in the medina of Marrakesh today, and if you sneak around to the boiler room, I promise you, you'll see *tangias*

nestled in the warm ashes, their paper coverings marked with a number or symbol to identify them.

This recipe will give you a very authentic-tasting version of that stew, without the need for boiler rooms or ashes. I make it with beef short ribs rather than the traditional lamb, because they braise so beautifully this way. The aged butter gives it a rich *umami* quality (think Roquefort sauce with braised beef), but you'll get great results with regular unsalted butter too.

When I trim the crust from a loaf of bread, I like to make croutons out of it, especially for a dish like this. They're extra-crunchy, so they really stand up well to the sauce and are a good contrast to the very soft meat. If you have leftover oil from making Garlic Confit (page 360), use that to make them even better.

brine

2 quarts (1.86 kilograms) water
2¼ cups plus 1 tablespoon (463 grams) granulated sugar
2¼ cups plus 2 tablespoons (342 grams) kosher salt
1 tablespoon (9 grams) Tellicherry peppercorns
1 tablespoon (7.4 grams) cumin seeds
1 tablespoon (6.6 grams) cloves
4 pieces (4.3 grams) star anise
2 teaspoons (3.7 grams) coriander seeds
4 (2.4 grams) chiles de árbol
5 (0.8 gram) bay leaves
8 cups (980 grams) ice cubes

short ribs

One 3-bone plate beef short ribs (4½ pounds/ 2.04 kilograms)
12 (42 grams) flat-leaf parsley sprigs
10 (35 grams) cilantro sprigs

Grapeseed or canola oil
2 tablespoons (1 ounce/28 grams) unsalted butter
One 3-inch piece (53 grams) fresh ginger, peeled and cut into ¼-inch pieces
10 garlic cloves
2½ teaspoons (6.4 grams) ground cumin
½ teaspoon (1 gram) ground ginger
2 quarters Preserved Lemon (page 43), halved lengthwise, rinsed, and seeds removed
8 cups (2.2 kilograms) Beef Stock (page 371), (1.87 kilograms) Chicken Stock (page 365), (1.88 kilograms) Vegetable Stock (page 364), or (1.86 kilograms) water
1 teaspoon (0.9 gram) saffron threads
2 tablespoons (1 ounce/28 grams) Aged Butter (page 374) or (1 ounce/28 grams) unsalted butter, at room temperature

croutons

Grapeseed or canola oil
1 cup (36 grams) 2½-by-¼-inch strips of crusts cut from a country loaf of bread
3 garlic cloves, smashed but not peeled
Pinch of finely chopped rosemary
Pinch of Marash pepper
Kosher salt

herb salad

1¼ cups (15 grams) flat-leaf parsley leaves
⅓ cup (5 grams) tarragon leaves
2 tablespoons (4 grams) 1-inch pieces chives
¼ cup (3 grams) chervil leaves
2 teaspoons (10 grams) fresh lemon juice
1 teaspoon (4 grams) extra virgin olive oil
Kosher salt

FOR THE BRINE: Bring the water to a simmer in a large stockpot. Add the remaining brine ingredients except the ice and stir to dissolve the sugar and salt. Turn off the heat and let sit at room temperature for 15 minutes to infuse the flavors.

Add the ice to cool down the brine. If it is not cold, refrigerate it until it is.

Add the short ribs to the brine and weight them with a plate to keep them submerged. Refrigerate for at least 6 hours, or for as long as overnight.

FOR THE SHORT RIBS: Preheat the oven to 275°F.

Remove the short ribs from the brine (discard the brine) and dry well with paper towels. Tie the parsley and cilantro sprigs together with kitchen twine.

Heat a film of oil in a roaster or Dutch oven, preferably enameled cast iron and oval (to echo the shape of the short ribs), over medium-high heat. Add the short ribs meat side down and sear for about 4 minutes, pressing them down from time to time. Once the bottom has browned, turn them over and brown for another 4 minutes. Lift the short ribs and brown each narrow side for about 1 minute. Remove from the pot.

If there are any burnt bits in the pot, clean the pot. Melt the unsalted butter in the pot, then add the fresh ginger and garlic and sauté for 2 minutes. Add the cumin and ground ginger and stir for 30 seconds to 1 minute, or until fragrant. Stir in the preserved lemon, then add the meat, bone side down, and the herb bundle. Pour in just enough stock to cover the meat (the bowed section of the meat may not be completely covered), add the saffron, and bring to a simmer over medium-high heat.

Cover the meat with a parchment lid (see page 379), brush it with water to keep the edges from curling up, and cover with the lid. Put in the oven and cook for about 4 hours, or until the meat is completely tender. Remove from the oven and let the short ribs rest in the pot for 30 minutes.

MEANWHILE, FOR THE CROUTONS: Heat a generous film of oil in a medium frying pan over medium-high heat. Add the bread crusts and cook for about 1½ minutes, until they begin to brown. Add the garlic, rosemary, and Marash and cook until the croutons are crunchy on the outside but still soft on the inside, another 2 minutes. Drain on paper towels and sprinkle with salt.

FOR THE SAUCE: Preheat the oven to 250°F.

Put a cooling rack on a baking sheet, remove the short ribs from the pot, and put them on the rack. Cover with aluminum foil and set in a warm spot.

Ladle off any fat that has risen to the top of the braising liquid. Strain into a large saucepan and bring to a simmer. Cook for 35 to 40 minutes, to reduce the sauce to about 2 cups (506 grams). Whisk in half of the aged butter.

Rub the remaining butter over the top of the short ribs and reheat in the oven.

FOR THE HERB SALAD: Toss all the herbs together, then toss with the lemon juice, olive oil, and salt to taste.

Spoon the sauce into a serving bowl or deep platter and set the short ribs on top. Stack the herb salad over the short ribs and scatter the croutons on top.

SERVES 6

BRAISED OXTAIL
ROASTED VEGETABLES
"FREGOLOTTO"

When I was growing up, once a year my family would butcher a cow and make a massive supply of the aged beef called *kh'lea*. We'd use the whole animal, and this recipe (with the exception of the wine) is a faithful recreation of the way we'd cook the tail. It would be served in lots of sauce, with bread to soak it up, and any leftovers would be picked from the bones, moistened with the sauce, and turned into a filling for *Rghaif* (page 129).

I serve it with fregola, a pasta similar to Israeli couscous with a nutty, toasted flavor. It's not something you find in Morocco, but I use it from time to time as an alternative to couscous. Rather than simply boiling it in the usual way, since I borrowed it from the Italians, I cook it with a borrowed Italian technique—the one used to make risotto. I sauté shallots, add wine and reduce it, toss in the fregola, and cook it in successive additions of stock. The result is a rich, flavorful "fregolotto" with a slightly creamy consistency. It goes with all things braised, especially the Chicken Legs (page 247) and the Beef Cheeks (page 274).

Oxtail is one of the most underappreciated items in the meat case, and I always encourage people to make it at home. Yes, it's all about bones, but that's the point. In addition to adding a lot of flavor, the bones protect the meat that's hidden between them. And oxtails are interactive, inviting you to pick them up and gnaw on them to get every last bit of succulent meat. Like all Moroccans, I don't believe oxtails should be a fork-and-knife thing (unless it's a fancy occasion, in which case you can follow my Chef to Chef instructions [page 284] for boning the meat and forming it into a *crépinette*). And if the conversation comes to a standstill because everyone's sucking out the marrow, that's the ultimate sign of success.

oxtails

8 pounds (3.6 kilograms) trimmed oxtails

Kosher salt

One 3-inch (3.3 grams) cinnamon stick, crumbled

4 (0.6 gram) bay leaves

2 teaspoons (2.5 grams) coriander seeds

1 teaspoon (2.5 grams) cumin seeds

1 teaspoon (3 grams) Tellicherry peppercorns

6 (1 gram) green cardamom pods, shelled and seeds reserved

1 (1.1 grams) star anise

2 (1.3 grams) chiles de árbol

Grapeseed or canola oil

4 large carrots, cut into 2-inch pieces

5 celery stalks, cut into 2-inch pieces

3 medium onions, cut into 2-inch pieces

⅓ cup (50 grams) garlic cloves

1 cup (216 grams) dry red wine, preferably Pinot Noir

5 cups (1.37 kilograms) Beef Stock (page 371), (1.17 kilograms) Chicken Stock (page 365), or (1.17 kilograms) water, or as needed

2 tablespoons (1 ounce/28 grams) unsalted butter

roasted vegetables

1 head garlic

1 cup (212 grams) extra virgin olive oil

12 large carrots, cut into 1-inch pieces, preferably obliques (see Note)

12 small shallots

8 (8 grams) thyme sprigs

Extra virgin olive oil

Granulated sugar

Kosher salt

fregola

Grapeseed or canola oil

1 cup (100 grams) minced shallots

½ cup (116 grams) Riesling

2 cups (375 grams) fregola

1 teaspoon (3 grams) kosher salt

3 to 3¾ cups (703 to 879 grams) Chicken Stock
  (page 365)

1 tablespoon (4 grams) minced flat-leaf parsley

2 tablespoons (1 ounce/28 grams) unsalted butter

(MAKES 5 CUPS/1.2 KILOGRAMS)

FOR THE OXTAILS: Set a cooling rack on a baking sheet lined with paper towels. Salt the oxtails on all sides and put on the rack. Cover with a damp towel and refrigerate overnight.

Put a piece of parchment paper on a work surface.

Combine all the spices and the chiles in a medium heavy frying pan, set it over medium heat, and swirl the pan, flipping or stirring the spices occasionally so they toast evenly, until fragrant, 2 to 3 minutes. Pour onto the parchment paper and let cool. Lift the edges of the parchment and pour the spices into a spice grinder. Finely grind them, and set aside.

Set a cooling rack on a baking sheet.

Heat a film of oil in a large frying pan over medium-high heat. Cook the oxtails in batches, without crowding the meat; sauté for 12 to 15 minutes per batch, turning and moving the oxtails to brown evenly on all sides. Transfer to the rack. (Set the pan aside.)

Preheat the oven to 325°F.

Add 3 tablespoons (36 grams) of the fat remaining in the frying pan to a large roasting pan set over two burners and heat over medium heat. Add the carrots, celery, onions, and garlic and sauté for 5 to 7 minutes, until lightly colored. Pour in the wine and cook for about 5 minutes, until evaporated.

Meanwhile, if the browned bits in the frying pan are not burnt, deglaze it: Pour off any remaining fat, add about ½ cup (140 grams) stock or (120 grams) water, and bring to a simmer, scraping up the bits stuck to the bottom of the pan.

Add the pan juices to the roasting pan, along with the remaining stock (or water). Bring to a boil and stir in the spices and 2 teaspoons (6 grams) salt. Nestle the oxtails in the vegetables. The liquid should come at least two-thirds of the way up the oxtails; if it doesn't, add more stock (or water) as necessary. Rest a parchment lid (see page 379) on the meat, brush it with water to keep the edges from curling up, and cover the pan tightly with aluminum foil.

Put in the oven and cook for 3 hours, or until the meat is completely tender.

MEANWHILE, FOR THE ROASTED VEGETABLES: Separate the garlic cloves, put them and the olive oil in a small saucepan, bring to a simmer over medium heat and simmer gently, stirring often, for about 20 minutes, until the garlic is soft and golden brown. Remove the garlic from the oil and set aside. The oil can be strained and reserved for another use (such as the croutons in the recipe on page 158).

Put a baking sheet in the oven and preheat the oven to 500°F.

Toss the carrots, shallots, and thyme together with a light coating of olive oil, a pinch of sugar, and a sprinkling of salt. Spread on the hot baking sheet and roast for 15 minutes, or until the vegetables are colored and almost tender. Add the reserved garlic and roast for another 5 minutes, or until the vegetables are tender. Remove from the oven and set aside.

CONTINUED

FOR THE FREGOLA: Pour a generous film of oil into a medium sauté pan (preferably with a rounded bottom). Add the shallots and sauté over medium heat for 7 minutes, or until tender and slightly caramelized. Add the wine and cook for about 4 minutes to evaporate it.

Add the fregola and salt and stir over medium-high heat for about 2 minutes to toast the fregola. Add 1½ cups (352 grams) of the stock and bring to a simmer. Reduce the heat to medium and cook for 3 to 4 minutes, until most of the stock has evaporated. Repeat two more times, adding ¾ cup (175.5 grams) stock each time. Taste the fregola; if isn't tender, add the remaining stock and cook until tender.

TO FINISH THE OXTAILS: When the oxtails are tender, put a cooling rack on a baking sheet, remove the oxtails from the roasting pan, and put on the rack. Cover with aluminum foil and set in a warm spot.

Ladle off any fat from the top of the braising liquid. Strain the liquid into a large saucepan, bring to a simmer, and simmer for about 15 minutes, until reduced to about 2 cups (506 grams). Whisk in the butter and remove from the heat. Drizzle a little of the sauce over the oxtails.

TO SERVE: Reheat the vegetables in ¼ cup (64 grams) of the sauce in a small saucepan for about 1 minute.

Reheat the fregola if necessary, and stir in the parsley and butter.

Spoon the fregola onto a platter and top with the oxtails, vegetables, and more sauce. Serve the remaining sauce on the side, if desired.

SERVES 6

NOTE: To cut carrots into oblique pieces, starting at the narrow end of each carrot, cut a diagonal piece about ½ inch long, with the blade of the knife pointing away from you at a 45 degree angle. Roll the carrot a quarter turn and cut another piece at the same angle. Repeat until the carrot widens. Slice it lengthwise in half and continue to turn and cut. If the pieces become too large, cut lengthwise again to keep the pieces equal in size.

CHEF TO CHEF: The meat from the oxtails can be made into a log. Pick the meat from the bones, chill, and then roll the cold meat into a log in plastic wrap. Keep refrigerated and then slice and sauté to serve.

Alternatively, to make a crépinette, *wrap the meat in caul fat and then brown in clarified butter.*

VEGETABLE STEW
EGGS
FRIED BEANS

Vegetarians often wind up having to make a restaurant meal from starters, salads, and sides. I wanted to offer them an entrée with some real substance and protein. So I came up with this hearty stew that reminds me a bit of a meatless version of a *Kefta* Tagine (page 272), in which the soft-cooked egg yolk blends with the sauce, adding luxurious richness.

To give it that little extra that french fries bring to a burger, I top the stew with spicy deep-fried beans. Butter beans or cranberry beans are ideal, but you can even use canned navy beans, chickpeas, or cannellini—before you fry them, rinse them, drain them on paper towels, spread them on a baking sheet, and put them in the oven set to its lowest temperature for about an hour, until they're completely dry. This will prevent splattering and give the beans a nice crisp texture when you fry them. The beans are a great way to introduce spicy heat to this dish without adding it directly to the vegetables and overpowering their delicate flavor. If you'd like to achieve the same effect in a more elegant way, you can replace the beans with the *Harissa* Emulsion from the Beef Cheeks (page 274).

spice mix
1 tablespoon (9 grams) kosher salt
1 tablespoon (8 grams) sweet paprika
1 tablespoon (5.5 grams) ground coriander
2 teaspoons (5.1 grams) ground cumin
1 teaspoon (2.7 grams) ground white pepper
1 teaspoon (2.4 grams) Aleppo pepper

stew
Eighteen 3-inch fingerling potatoes
6 large carrots
4 medium turnips
8 shallots

½ cup (106 grams) grapeseed or canola oil
¼ cup (37 grams) chopped garlic
4 cups (1 kilogram) diced canned tomatoes, preferably San Marzano, with their juices
¾ cup (213 grams) tomato puree, preferably San Marzano
⅔ cup (160 grams) tomato paste
6 tablespoons (25 grams) finely chopped flat-leaf parsley
3 tablespoons (13 grams) finely chopped cilantro
4 cups (930 grams) water
½ cup (96 grams) diced preserved lemon rind (see page 45)
1 tablespoon (7.2 grams) Marash pepper, plus more for garnish

beans
Grapeseed or canola oil for deep-frying
2 cups (360 grams) cooked butter beans or cranberry beans (see Cooking Beans, page 378), drained and dried well with paper towels
1 teaspoon (2.4 grams) *Harissa* Powder (page 85), or to taste
½ lemon
Kosher salt

Six 5½-Minute Eggs (page 376)
Minced chives
Crunchy sea salt and freshly ground black pepper
Extra virgin olive oil for finishing

FOR THE SPICE MIX: Mix the salt and spices together in a bowl; set aside.

FOR THE STEW: Using a paring knife, "turn" the fingerling potatoes, trimming them from top to bottom to shape them into ovals. They do not have to be perfect, but if there are any sharp edges, trim them to make them smooth. Cut the thicker ends of the carrots into 3-inch pieces. (You won't use the narrow ends for this recipe.) As you did with the potatoes, trim the pieces into oval shapes. Cut the turnips lengthwise into quarters, then trim as before. Cut the shallots lengthwise in half.

Heat the oil in a large pot over high heat. Stir in the garlic, canned tomatoes, tomato puree, tomato paste, and spice mix, then add the vegetables, ¼ cup (17 grams) of the parsley, the cilantro, and water. Bring the liquid to a simmer and cook for 30 minutes, or until the vegetables are tender and the sauce has thickened.

Add the preserved lemon and Marash and simmer for another 10 minutes to meld the flavors.

MEANWHILE, FOR THE BEANS: Pour 2 inches of oil into a stockpot fitted with a thermometer and heat to 350°F. Line a plate with paper towels.

Add a few of the beans to the oil to check the oil temperature and fry, stirring occasionally. The beans should be golden brown and crunchy in 3 to 5 minutes. Remove the beans with a slotted spoon or skimmer and drain them on the paper towels; adjust the heat as necessary. Cook the remaining beans in batches, without overcrowding the pot.

Transfer the drained beans to a bowl and sprinkle with the *harissa* powder, a squeeze of lemon juice, and salt to taste. Fold the remaining 2 tablespoons (8 grams) chopped parsley into the stew.

Spoon the stew into serving bowls and top with the fried beans. Nestle an egg in each bowl and sprinkle with chives, crunchy sea salt, and pepper. Drizzle the stew with olive oil.

SERVES 6

sides, front and center

In Morocco, vegetables are either part of the seven-salads course or are incorporated into main dishes. The idea of a simply prepared side of vegetables served with an entrée doesn't really exist. Just like meat, poultry, and seafood, vegetables get treated to the full menu of cooking techniques and flavoring possibilities. And the same goes for grains and starches, which are themselves full-fledged dishes, like couscous or porridges, not accompaniments.

In the United States, people tend to think of starchy sides as something relatively bland, designed to soak up the sauce. In Morocco, that's the role of bread, and I agree with that. When I serve vegetables or grains as side dishes, I make them quite bold, because I usually serve them in small portions. They're not afterthoughts, but mini-events in their own right that make a plate whole, assertively adding a critical element like sourness, spice, or sweetness.

FOR THE TOMATOES: Pour a film of oil into a large sauté pan set over medium heat, add the onions, and sauté for about 8 minutes, stirring from time to time, until almost tender. Add the garlic and stir frequently for another 5 minutes, or until the onion and garlic have softened and are just beginning to color.

Turn the heat to medium-high, add the *harissa,* the cumin, paprika, and jalapeño, and cook, stirring constantly, for about 1 minute, until fragrant. Add the tomatoes and their juices, the water, and salt and simmer for about 30 minutes, or until the mixture has thickened, the liquid has evaporated, and the tomatoes have melted. Add ¼ cup (53 grams) oil and "fry" the mixture for about 1 minute. Remove from the heat and stir in the pepper and parsley.

MEANWHILE, START THE OKRA: Rub the okra with a towel to remove the sharp spines. Trim the stems, but do not expose the seeds. Heat a large nonstick frying pan over high heat until smoking. Add a film of grapeseed oil. When the oil smokes, add the okra in one layer and cook, without moving them for 3 to 4 minutes, or until the bottoms are browned. Turn each piece to brown the second side. Transfer to a bowl, add the olive oil and *harissa* powder, and toss to coat.

TO SERVE: Spoon the melted tomatoes into a serving bowl and arrange the okra on top. Sprinkle with crunchy sea salt.

SERVES 6

LEEK GRATIN

When you're making a gratin, reinforcing the béchamel by simmering it with finely ground vegetables (and then straining them out) gives it a great deal of personality, and I recommend this technique for making any kind of vegetable gratin. You can generally use celery, leeks, carrots, onions, and parsley, and then add a bit of whatever you're making the gratin with. For a cauliflower gratin, for example, I include a little extra cauliflower in the chopped vegetable mix, and I also infuse the milk with a bit of saffron. For fennel, I use the fronds and add some toasted fennel seeds in the chopped mixture.

béchamel sauce
1 cup (125 grams) coarsely chopped yellow onion
1 cup (120 grams) coarsely chopped celery
1 cup (109 grams) coarsely chopped parsnips
1 cup (100 grams) coarsely chopped fennel bulb
¾ cup (100 grams) coarsely chopped carrots
¼ cup (25 grams) coarsely chopped leek
   (white and light green parts only)
3 (10.5 grams) flat-leaf parsley sprigs
2 cups (500 grams) whole milk
1½ teaspoons (2.7 grams) fennel seeds
1½ teaspoons (4.5 grams) kosher salt
3 tablespoons (1.5 ounces/42.5 grams) unsalted butter
3 tablespoons (24.5 grams) all-purpose flour
             (MAKES ABOUT 2 CUPS/450 GRAMS)

leeks
8 leeks (5 pounds/2.3 kilograms)
Kosher salt

1 cup (224 grams) Fresh Bread Crumbs (page 378)
Crunchy sea salt

FOR THE BÉCHAMEL: Process the onion, celery, parsnips, fennel, carrots, leek, and parsley in batches in a food processor until finely ground to a paste.

Bring the milk to a simmer in a large saucepan. Stir in the vegetables and fennel seeds and return to a simmer, then turn off the heat and let sit at room temperature for 30 minutes to infuse the flavors.

MEANWHILE, FOR THE LEEKS: Bring a large pot of salted water to a boil. Fill a large bowl with ice water.

Cut off the dark green ends of the leeks, leaving the white and light green parts only, about 5 inches in length. Rinse them under cold water to remove any surface dirt. Tie the leeks into a large bundle with a piece of kitchen twine. (Their combined weight will help to keep them submerged in the water as they cook.) Add the leeks to the water and simmer for 8 to 10 minutes, until tender. (If the bundle still rises to the top, put a plate on top of it to keep the leeks under the water.) Remove the bundle and place in the ice bath to chill. Cut the string and drain the leeks on paper towels.

TO FINISH THE BÉCHAMEL: Strain the milk through a fine-mesh strainer into a spouted measuring cup, pressing on the vegetables with a ladle to release all the liquid. Stir in the salt, and set aside.

Preheat the oven to 375°F.

Melt the butter in a medium saucepan over medium heat. Add the flour and whisk constantly for about 2 minutes, until the butter begins to separate from the flour and color lightly. Gradually whisk in the milk, whisking until smooth before adding the next addition. Bring to a simmer and cook until thickened. Strain through a fine-mesh strainer into a spouted measuring cup.

TO COMPLETE THE GRATIN: Cut the leeks into ½-inch-wide rounds. Arrange the rounds, overlapping them, in 4 long rows in an 8½-by-11-inch gratin or baking dish. Sprinkle lightly with kosher salt. Pour the béchamel sauce over the leeks. Only the very tops of the leeks should peek through.

Bake for 45 minutes, or until the béchamel sauce is bubbling lightly. Remove the gratin from the oven and increase the heat to 450°F.

Sprinkle the bread crumbs over the top of the gratin and return to the oven for 12 to 15 minutes, or until the top is golden brown. Sprinkle with crunchy sea salt.

SERVES 6

RAINBOW CHARD
RAS EL HANOUT
PRESERVED LEMON

Moroccans would take a hearty green like chard and cook it way down to make something like the Herb Jam on page 166. This version takes a more Italian approach, blanching the greens and stems and then sautéing them. Its flavors will go with just about anything in this book. If you have leftovers, squeeze the cooked greens lightly to remove excess moisture, toss them with some crumbled feta and toasted pine nuts, and use the mixture as a filling for *briwat*, following the method on page 134.

4 bunches rainbow chard (10 ounces/283 grams each) preferably with red and gold stalks

Kosher salt

¼ cup (53 grams) grapeseed or canola oil

½ cup (85 grams) diced (⅛-inch) onion

1 tablespoon (6.7 grams) *Ras el Hanout* (page 29)

1 tablespoon (15 grams) fresh lemon juice, preferably Meyer lemon

¼ cup (48 grams) diced preserved lemon rind (see page 45)

1½ teaspoons (3.6 grams) Urfa pepper

Extra virgin olive oil for finishing (optional)

Cut the stalks from the chard, and set the greens aside. Trim away the bottoms and narrow tops of the stalks. Trim away the two outer edges of the stalks (which are not tender). Cut enough stalks into 3-by-⅛-inch-thick matchsticks to give you 1½ cups (113 grams). Cut enough of the remaining stalks into 1/16-inch dice to give you 1 cup (108 grams).

Bring a large pot of heavily salted water to a boil. Fill a large bowl with ice water.

Working in batches, blanch the chard leaves for 2 to 2½ minutes, until tender. Remove the leaves and place them in the ice water. Once they are chilled, remove them from the water, squeeze them well to remove the excess water, and coarsely chop them. Set aside.

Heat the oil in a large sauté pan over medium heat. Add the onion and a pinch of salt and cook, stirring often, for 5 minutes, or until the onion begins to soften. Add the chard matchsticks, *ras el hanout*, and another pinch of salt and cook for 4 to 5 minutes, or until the matchsticks begin to soften. Stir in the diced stalks and cook until both matchsticks and stalks are tender, about 5 minutes. Stir in the leaves and cook for about 1 minute to warm them.

Remove from the heat and stir in the lemon juice, preserved lemon, and Urfa. Drizzle with olive oil, if desired.

SERVES 6

SUNCHOKE *SOUBRIC*

A *soubric* is one of my favorite ways to get both bread and vegetable on the plate in a surprising, delicate way. As I make them, *soubrics* are basically bread puddings made with pureed vegetables, custard, and bread crumbs. I bake them in a thin layer, then cool them under weights (or Cryovac them to compress them) and cut them into small firm pieces. Those pieces get browned in a pan to serve, and the result is a soft, warm vegetable custard with a crispy crust. If you're an experimenter, try making *soubric* with other vegetables, including carrots, turnips, or squash.

3 tablespoons (1.5 ounces/43.5 grams) unsalted butter, plus more for the pan and parchment paper
12 ounces (340 grams) sunchokes, peeled and cut into ¼-inch-thick slices
1½ teaspoons (6.3 grams) granulated sugar
1½ teaspoons (4.5 grams) kosher salt
3 tablespoons (44 grams) water
½ cup (125 grams) whole milk
½ cup (117.5 grams) heavy cream
2 large eggs
3 cups (672 grams) Fresh Bread Crumbs (page 378), prepared from brioche, processed until finely ground
Grapeseed or canola oil

Preheat the oven to 350°F. Butter the bottom and sides of a 9-by-5-by-2¾-inch loaf pan. Line the bottom with a piece of parchment paper. Butter it, then top with a second piece of buttered parchment. Cut a third piece of parchment the size of the pan, butter it, and set aside.

Melt the butter in a medium frying pan over medium-high heat. Add the sunchokes and cook for 12 to 15 minutes, stirring from time to time and scraping the bottom of the pan to keep the sunchokes from sticking, until they have caramelized on both sides.

Remove the pan from the heat and stir in the sugar and salt. Transfer the sunchokes to a blender, add the water, and puree until smooth, beginning on low speed and then increasing the speed; stop to scrape down the sides as necessary. Pour into a large bowl.

Whisk the milk, cream, and eggs together, then whisk into the puree. Whisk in two-thirds of the bread crumbs, then slowly add the remaining crumbs, whisking until the mixture has a texture like oatmeal.

Spoon the mixture into the prepared pan and smooth the top. Place the third piece of parchment paper buttered side down over the mixture. If you have a second loaf pan the same size, cover the bottom with a smooth layer of aluminum foil and lay it on top to help keep the top of the *soubric* flat as it bakes. If you don't have one, seal the top of the pan tightly with aluminum foil. Bake for 1 hour and 15 minutes, or until a skewer inserted in the center tests clean. Remove from the oven and let sit on a cooling rack for about 1 hour until it has cooled to room temperature (leave the *soubric* in the pan).

Cut a piece of cardboard the same size as the top of the loaf pan. Wrap it in plastic wrap and place it on the *soubric*. Set a second loaf pan over the cardboard and add some weights, such as heavy cans. Refrigerate overnight.

TO FINISH: Remove the weights, cardboard, and parchment. Loosen the sides by running a small knife around the edges, if necessary. Remove from the pan and trim the sides to straighten them. Cut the *soubric* widthwise into ¾-inch-thick slices. Cut the slices into cubes, strips, or other shapes, as desired.

Heat a film of oil in a medium nonstick frying pan over medium heat. Add the *soubric* pieces and cook, turning to brown them on all sides, about 6 minutes. Drain on paper towels and serve.

SERVES 4 TO 6

SALT-ROASTED POTATOES

The same technique I use to make the Salt-Roasted Thai Snapper (page 216) works with small potatoes. Salt-roasting cooks them evenly, so they're moist and creamy inside, and the spices and seasonings in the salt crust add just a hint of subtle flavor and mystery. Smashed and browned in oil, as described below, they make a nice passed appetizer, topped with crème fraîche and caviar. Once roasted, the potatoes can be stored in olive oil in the fridge for up to 3 days. The salt-roasting technique can also be used for carrots, parsnips, turnips, and beets.

12 ounces (340 grams) 1-inch marble potatoes or 2-inch fingerlings (about 2 cups)
3½ cups (1 pound/453 grams) kosher salt
¼ cup (21.7 grams) fennel seeds
¼ cup (15.2 grams) coriander seeds
2 (2.2 grams) star anise
10 (1.6 grams) green cardamom pods, shelled and seeds reserved
½ orange, preferably a blood orange
¼ large grapefruit
½ lemon
3 large egg whites
Grapeseed or canola oil (if sautéing the potatoes)
Rosemary leaves
Extra virgin olive oil for finishing (optional)
Crunchy sea salt (optional)

Wash and dry the potatoes. Put the salt in a large bowl. Put a piece of parchment paper on the work surface.

Combine the fennel, coriander, star anise, and cardamom seeds in a medium heavy frying pan, set it over medium heat, and swirl the pan, flipping or stirring the spices occasionally so they toast evenly, until fragrant, 2 to 3 minutes. Pour onto the parchment paper and let cool.

Lift the edges of the parchment and pour half the spices into a spice grinder. Coarsely grind them and add to the bowl of salt. Repeat with the remaining spices and mix to combine all the ingredients.

Using a Microplane, grate the zest from the orange, grapefruit, and lemon. You should have about 1 generous tablespoon (12.5 grams) total. Mix it into the salt mixture.

Preheat the oven to 400°F.

Beat the egg whites until they are just beginning to hold a shape, and stir them into the salt mixture.

Line a 9-inch square baking dish with parchment paper. Form a 1-inch-thick bed of salt in the baking dish and arrange the potatoes on it in a single layer. Cover with the remaining salt, to completely encase the potatoes.

Roast for 30 minutes for 1-inch potatoes, or 35 minutes for 2-inch potatoes, or until they are tender. Remove from the oven and let rest for 10 minutes.

You can break away the salt crust with your hand or hit it with a wooden spoon to crack it. Remove the potatoes and brush off any excess salt clinging to them.

There are two ways to serve the potatoes: *For thin, chip-like potatoes* (see photograph, page 299), put the potatoes between pieces of parchment paper lightly brushed with oil and press a meat pounder against them to flatten. Heat a generous film of oil in a nonstick skillet over medium-high heat and sauté the potatoes on both sides to brown, about 2½ minutes per side. Drain on paper towels. Add some rosemary leaves to the oil and fry and crisp them for about 30 seconds. Arrange the potatoes on a plate and sprinkle with crunchy sea salt and the rosemary. *Or serve the potatoes whole,* in a bowl, tossed with fresh rosemary leaves and drizzled with olive oil.

SERVES 6

BARLEY
BALSAMIC CRANBERRIES

I always wonder why people overlook barley as a grain-based side dish. It's flavorful and has that appealingly chewy texture that works so well with meat and poultry.

This is my take on the Moroccan breakfast porridge *herbel,* which is made by cooking barley with milk and cinnamon, and then adding butter and honey or sugar. I wanted to do a savory version, so I make it with lamb sauce and add Parmesan, but the sugar, Riesling, and cranberries are there to recall the sweetness of the original. It works as a light entrée with Chicory Salad (page 158) or, if you like, a bit of shredded duck confit (see page 246). Or make it with Chicken Jus (page 366) instead of the lamb sauce and serve it with grilled or roasted chicken.

Sometimes rinsing barley doesn't completely clean it. I recommend first soaking it in water, as directed below, to make sure any traces of grit and starch are completely removed.

2½ cups (500 grams) barley
¼ cup (60 grams) Riesling
¼ cup (50 grams) granulated sugar
One 1½-inch piece (1.6 grams) cinnamon stick
1½ teaspoons (4.5 grams) kosher salt, plus more to taste
¼ cup (53 grams) grapeseed or canola oil
¾ cup (101 grams) diced red onion

2 cups (470 grams) heavy cream
¾ cup (207 grams) Lamb Sauce (page 370)
1 cup (140 grams) Balsamic Cranberries (page 359)
1 to 2 tablespoons (15 to 30 grams) fresh lemon juice
¾ cup (114 grams) freshly grated Parmigiano-Reggiano or Grana
1½ tablespoons (5 grams) minced chives

Put the barley in a large bowl with enough cold water to cover. Soak for 2 minutes, drain, and repeat.

Put the barley, 6 cups (1.4 kilograms) water, the wine, sugar, cinnamon, and salt in a large saucepan, bring to a simmer, and cook for about 10 minutes, or until the barley is tender but not mushy. Drain.

Heat the oil in a large saucepan over medium heat. Add the onions and cook gently for 5 to 7 minutes, until they are tender and slightly caramelized. Add the barley and stir to combine. Pour in the cream, stir, and cook over medium-high heat for about 3 minutes to reduce the cream and coat the barley. Stir in the lamb sauce and cranberries. Simmer for 6 to 8 minutes, stirring often, to reduce and thicken the liquid enough to coat the barley.

Fold in 1 tablespoon (15 grams) lemon juice, about three-quarters of the cheese, and the chives. Season to taste with salt and additional lemon juice if needed. Top the barley with the remaining cheese.

SERVES 6

PARSNIP RISOTTO

If you've got a juicer, give this a try. In a typical vegetable risotto, the vegetables are added toward the end. Here I juice the parsnips and use their "milk" as the main cooking liquid. The rice gets completely infused with the essence of parsnip, and because parsnips are white, people are often mystified by what they're tasting, even though they love the rich, sweet-starchy flavor. I like sneakily converting new parsnip fans that way.

The important thing here is to buy very good, fresh farmers' market parsnips in season (fall or winter). They will have much more juice and flavor than standard-issue supermarket ones.

The same technique also works well with other flavorful root vegetables, like celery root or beets, as well as corn, peas, and asparagus. I serve an asparagus risotto made with white asparagus juice, with shaved green asparagus on top. Because the risotto stays white, as it does with the parsnips, people can never figure out how those few shavings of green asparagus could give the rice so much flavor! Serve this as a main course, on the side with guinea hens, or as a base for sliced panseared duck breasts.

2 pounds (907 grams) parsnips
Vegetable Stock (page 364) or water as needed
¼ cup (53 grams) grapeseed or canola oil
1½ cups (202 grams) diced (¼-inch) onions
1½ cups (300 grams) Arborio rice
Kosher salt
2 tablespoons (6 grams) chopped chives

Peel the parsnips and cut off the ends. Juice the parsnips, and strain the juice through a fine-mesh strainer into a spouted measuring cup. You will need 4 to 4½ cups (472 to 531 grams) liquid to cook the risotto. If you have less, add stock or water.

Heat the oil in a large saucepan over medium heat. Add the onions and cook for 10 minutes, or until tender and translucent. Stir in the rice and a generous pinch of salt and cook for 5 minutes, stirring often to toast the grains.

Add 1 cup (118 grams) of the parsnip juice and simmer, stirring often, for about 5 minutes, or until the liquid has evaporated. Add another cup of juice, and then repeat the process, until you are left with about 1 cup (118 grams) of juice. Taste the rice; if it is not tender, add more juice ½ cup (59 grams) at a time, cooking until the rice is tender. You may not need all the juice. The total cooking time will be about 25 to 30 minutes.

Add salt to taste, spoon into a serving bowl, and top with the chives.

SERVES 6

STEAMED EGG NOODLES

You'll be pleasantly surprised when you try steaming egg noodles, vermicelli, or other fine pasta in a couscoussier or steamer. It comes out remarkably light, springy, and fluffy, like couscous. This is a version of *seffaa* (pronounced *"s'fuh"*), a dish often served in Morocco as a holiday treat: steamed broken-up noodles sprinkled with cinnamon, sugar, and nuts. It's sometimes mounded with a layer of saffron-braised chicken hidden in the middle, in which case it's called *seffaa medfouna* (*medfouna* means "buried"), but you'll also find it served on its own as part of a festive breakfast spread.

For more flavor, layer in some plumped raisins or dried apricots, Balsamic Cranberries (page 359), or sliced Spiced Prunes (page 360) along with the almonds. Or top the mounded noodles with the caramelized onion filling from *Rghaif* (page 129). You can also make this dish, as people often do in Morocco, using couscous instead of noodles.

½ cup (77 grams) skin-on whole almonds
1 pound (453 grams) fine egg noodles
2 tablespoons (27 grams) extra virgin olive oil
2 cups (468 grams) warm water (about 110°F)
1½ teaspoons (4.5 grams) kosher salt
2 tablespoons (14 grams) powdered sugar
½ teaspoon (1.3 grams) ground cinnamon
4 tablespoons (2 ounces/57 grams) unsalted butter,
    at room temperature

Preheat the oven to 350°F.

Toast the almonds in the oven for about 10 minutes, or until they are golden brown (break one open to check). Let cool.

Put the almonds in a small food processor or spice grinder and pulse to a coarse powder. Set aside.

Fill the bottom of a couscoussier half-full with water and bring to a simmer. Toss the egg noodles with the olive oil, put in the top of the couscoussier, and set over the simmering water (without the lid) to steam for 30 minutes.

Meanwhile, combine the 2 cups water and the salt in a spouted liquid measuring cup, stirring to dissolve the salt.

Carefully remove the top from the couscoussier, being careful not to burn yourself with the steam. Put the noodles in a large bowl, add ¼ cup (58.5 grams) of the salted water, and toss with a pair of tongs. Some of the water will settle in the bottom of the bowl, so keep tossing until all of the water has been absorbed.

Add more water to the bottom of the couscoussier to bring it back to the original level and return to a simmer. Clean the top of the couscoussier, add the noodles, set over the boiling water, and steam for another 20 minutes.

Carefully remove the top and toss the noodles as before, this time incorporating ½ cup (117 grams) of the salted water. Steam for another 20 minutes.

Repeat once more with another ½ cup (117 grams) of water, then steam for 10 minutes. Taste the noodles. They won't have the same texture as traditionally cooked pasta, but they should be al dente. If they taste at all raw, continue to steam, tasting every 5 minutes, and adding additional salt water only if the noodles begin to dry out, until cooked.

Meanwhile, combine the powdered sugar and cinnamon.

Toss the noodles with the butter. Put half the noodles on a serving tray. Sift half the sugar mixture over the top, and spoon on half of the ground almonds. Top with the remaining noodles, sugar mixture, and almonds.

SERVES 6 TO 8

COUSCOUS
PRUNES
TOASTED ALMONDS

When I was growing up, this couscous, with a glass of cold milk, was one of my favorite snacks in the morning or midafternoon. The cinnamon and prunes make it particularly good with any kind of lamb— shanks, chops, roasted lamb or *Merguez* (page 270)— as well as with a simply cooked steak.

1 cup (130 grams) blanched whole almonds
6 cups (870 grams) Classic Steamed Couscous
   (page 62), still hot
¾ cup (180 grams) Spiced Prunes (page 360),
   pitted and cut into ¼-inch dice
5 tablespoons (60 grams) Clarified Butter (page 375)
6 tablespoons (90 grams) fresh lemon juice
6 tablespoons (18 grams) chopped chives
½ teaspoon (1.3 grams) ground cinnamon
Kosher salt

Preheat the oven to 350°F.

Toast the almonds in the oven for 10 minutes, or until they are golden brown (break one open to check). Let cool.

Combine the almonds and all the remaining ingredients except the salt in a large bowl. Season to taste with salt.

SERVES 6

COUSCOUS
MEYER LEMON
PARSLEY

It's not traditional, but I love couscous with butter, parsley, finely diced preserved lemons, and a bit of lemon juice. This is another version of that idea, for when you don't have preserved lemons on hand. You start with a technique similar to making candied lemon peel, simmering it in sugar and lemon juice, and then make a sweet, tangy vinaigrette from the lemon syrup.

7 Meyer or regular lemons
⅔ cup (154 grams) water
3½ tablespoons (43.8 grams) granulated sugar
6 tablespoons (80 grams) extra virgin olive oil
6 cups (870 grams) Classic Steamed Couscous
   (page 62), still hot
1½ teaspoons (7 grams) finely chopped flat-leaf parsley
Kosher salt

Using a vegetable peeler, cut away the peel and part of the pith of the lemons in strips about ⅛ inch thick. Cut the peel into ⅛-inch dice; you need a scant 1 cup (100 grams). Juice enough of the lemons to make 6 tablespoons (150 grams) juice.

Combine the lemon peel, lemon juice, water, and sugar in a small saucepan and bring to a simmer. Cook for 5 to 6 minutes, or until the lemon peel is tender. Drain the peel in a strainer set over a small bowl; set the peel aside.

Whisk 3 tablespoons (40 grams) of the olive oil into the syrup and let cool to room temperature.

Stir the reserved peel and about 1 cup (230 grams) of the vinaigrette into the couscous, along with the parsley and remaining 3 tablespoons (40 grams) olive oil. Season to taste with salt and additional vinaigrette.

SERVES 6

the sweet spot

I have never been someone who believes that a good meal is not complete without dessert. Growing up, I loved sweet stuff like any kid, but I didn't associate it with the end of a meal, because that's not the way it is in Morocco—especially back then. We'd finish eating lunch and have a bowl of fresh fruit with tea. If there were guests, the bowl would turn into a platter, the types of fruit would multiply, and dried fruit and nuts would be arranged on top like gemstones on a crown. But humble or fancy, it wasn't dessert.

The sweets came later in the afternoon, with the rounds of tea and the visiting friends and relatives. These were mostly variations on a theme: almonds, honey, dates, and some kind of flaky dough. There would be fried *warqa* pastries, like almond-filled *briwat* triangles, or a similar filling rolled in a *warqa* coil to make the "snake" pastry, *m'hansha*, as well as *chebakiya* (fried sesame cookies) and dates stuffed with almond paste. And that's the basic DNA of Moroccan sweets, which, after all, come out of the tradition of village food, limited ovens, and making something special out of everyday ingredients.

SESAME PARFAIT

I'm using the term *parfait* here (and in the recipe on page 330) in the classic French sense of the word—a frozen cream, as opposed to a layered dessert. This one is infused with sesame seeds and enriched with tahini for even more sesame depth. It's an easy make-ahead dessert—a no-churn alternative to homemade ice cream that's dense and golden from egg yolks, with a flavor that reminds me a bit of halvah. You can make it as individual servings, as directed here, or freeze the whole batch in a container and serve it with an ice cream scoop.

1 cup (130 grams) sesame seeds
About 2 cups (470 grams) heavy cream
⅓ cup plus 1½ teaspoons (85 grams) cold water
⅜ teaspoon (1.2 grams) powdered gelatin
½ cup plus 1 tablespoon (113 grams) granulated sugar
1 large egg
5 large egg yolks
1 tablespoon (15 grams) tahini

6 Sesame Tuiles (page 341)

Preheat the oven to 350°F.

Toast the sesame seeds in the oven for 6 to 8 minutes, or until they are light golden. Set aside.

Put 2 cups (470 grams) cream in a small saucepan and bring to a simmer over medium-high heat. Remove the pan from the heat and add the toasted seeds. Let steep for 1 hour to infuse the sesame flavor.

Fill a large bowl with ice water and set a smaller bowl inside. Strain the cream through a fine-mesh strainer into a spouted measuring cup. You will need 1½ cups (118 grams). If there is less, add additional cream. Pour into the bowl set over the ice water and chill until cold.

Put 1½ teaspoons (7 grams) of the water in a small bowl and sprinkle the gelatin over the top. Agitate the bowl slightly to dampen all the gelatin. Once the gelatin solidifies, remove it from the bowl and cut into ¼-inch pieces.

Whisk the sesame cream mixture in the bowl of a stand mixer fitted with the whisk attachment at medium-high speed for about 2 minutes. When the whisk is lifted the cream should hold a light ribbon that falls back into the bowl. Transfer to a bowl and refrigerate. Wash the bowl and whisk.

Put the remaining ⅓ cup (78 grams) water in a small saucepan and sprinkle the sugar evenly over the top (this will help the sugar dissolve evenly). Heat over medium-high heat for about about 7 minutes, or until the temperature is 240°F.

Meanwhile, put the egg and yolks in the mixer bowl and place on the mixer fitted with the whisk. When the syrup has reached 220°F, turn the mixer speed to medium and mix until the egg and yolks are blended and thickened. With the mixer running, add the diced gelatin to the egg mixture.

Turn the mixer speed to medium-low and pour the syrup very slowly down the side of the bowl. Increase the speed to medium-high and whisk for about 8 minutes, or until the bottom of the bowl is cool to the touch.

Reduce the mixer speed to low, add the tahini, and mix for about 1 minute to combine. Remove the mixer bowl and fold half of the sesame cream into the yolk mixture, then fold in the remaining sesame cream.

Spoon about ½ cup (44 grams) of the cream into each serving bowl. Freeze uncovered (to prevent condensation) for about 2 hours, or until set, then cover with plastic wrap and freeze. (The parfaits can be kept frozen for up to 1 week.)

Serve with the sesame tuiles on the side.

SERVES 12

YOGURT MOUSSE
WALNUT NOUGATINE
RASPBERRIES

Inspired by the classic Mediterranean combination of yogurt, honey, and figs, this mousse is made without eggs, so it's quite light and refreshing. You can accompany it with the nougatine, nuts, berries, and honey, as indicated here, or just serve it simply, with nothing more than a drizzle of honey, a dusting of cinnamon, and some fresh figs.

yogurt mousse
¼ cup plus 3 tablespoons (102 grams) cold water
1 teaspoon (3.2 grams) powdered gelatin
6 tablespoons (87 grams) heavy cream
1 cup (238 grams) whole-milk Greek yogurt
¼ cup (28 grams) powdered sugar

(MAKES 2 CUPS/421 GRAMS)

½ cup (69 grams) raspberries
½ recipe (87.5 grams) Candied Walnuts (page 345)
¼ cup (38 grams) Walnut Crumble (page 342)
Thinly julienned zest of 1 navel orange
Blackberry honey, preferably from Marshall Farms
Ground cinnamon for dusting
6 irregular pieces (4 grams each) Walnut Nougatine
   (page 342)

FOR THE MOUSSE: Put 1 tablespoon (15 grams) of the water in a small bowl and sprinkle the gelatin over the top. Agitate the bowl slightly to dampen all the gelatin. Once the gelatin solidifies, remove it from the bowl and cut into ¼-inch pieces. Put the pieces in a small bowl.

Put the remaining 6 tablespoons (87 grams) water in a small saucepan and heat over medium-high heat for about 1½ minutes, or until it just begins to simmer. Pour it over the gelatin and whisk to dissolve the gelatin. Let cool for about 5 minutes, or until just warm to the touch.

Meanwhile, put the cream in the bowl of a stand mixer fitted with the whisk attachment, and whisk for about 2 minutes, or until the cream has thickened but does not yet hold a shape. Transfer it to a medium bowl and refrigerate.

Wash the mixer bowl and whisk. Put the yogurt in the bowl. Sift the powdered sugar through a fine-mesh strainer over the yogurt. Place the bowl and whisk on the mixer and whisk on low speed to blend the sugar and yogurt, then pour in the warm gelatin mixture and whisk to combine. Scrape down the sides of the bowl, then increase the speed to medium-high and whisk for about 7 minutes, or until the mixture has thickened and you see the trail of the whisk as it whips. Lift the whisk; the mixture will not hold a shape but it should be very thick.

Fold half the yogurt mousse into the whipped cream, then fold in the remaining half. Pour into 6 cups or serving bowls and refrigerate until firm, about 2 hours, or up to 1 day.

TO SERVE: Arrange the raspberries, candied walnuts, and crumble on top of the mousse. Garnish with the zest, a drizzle of honey, a light dusting of cinnamon, and the nougatine.

SERVES 6

THINK LIKE A PASTRY CHEF: Before making the mousse, line a quarter-sheet pan with parchment paper, spread the mousse mixture on it, and refrigerate until set. Cut Walnut Nougatine (page 342) into 1½-by-3-inch rectangles and layer with the mousse (see photograph, page 327). Garnish as above.

FIG LEAF ICE CREAM

Figs come in two seasons, and between them, the trees are covered with leaves, which I often find for sale at the farmers' market. The French idea of making ice cream with peach leaves is something that's become quite popular, so we thought we'd give fig leaf ice cream a try. The leaves contribute a kind of grassy, herby flavor, but, to my amazement, they also add an unmistakable hint of fig.

This is a natural with nuts, particularly walnuts. Serve it with Walnut Brittle, Nougatine, or Crumble (page 342), or Candied Nuts (page 345).

3 medium fresh fig leaves
¾ cup (150 grams) granulated sugar
8 large egg yolks
1 cup plus 2 tablespoons (282 grams) whole milk
1½ cups plus 2 tablespoons (382 grams) very cold heavy cream
5 tablespoons (34 grams) very cold crème fraîche
Pinch of kosher salt

Fill a large bowl with ice water. Put a medium bowl with a fine-mesh strainer in the ice water.

Wash the fig leaves and dry them thoroughly. Cut out and discard the ribs and coarsely chop the leaves. You will need ⅓ cup (7.5 grams).

Combine the fig leaves and sugar in a food processor and blend until the leaves are finely chopped. The pieces of leaves will not become powdered.

Whisk the egg yolks together in a medium bowl.

Combine the sugar mixture and milk in a medium saucepan and bring to just below a simmer over medium heat. Remove it from the heat and, whisking constantly, pour the hot milk mixture into the egg mixture, whisking until combined. Return it to the pan, put it over medium-low heat, and whisk constantly for about 2 minutes, until steam begins to rise from the surface, the bubbles in the center of the pan begin to lessen, and the custard has thickened enough to coat the back of a spoon.

Strain the custard into the bowl in the ice water. Whisk in the cream, crème fraîche, and salt. Cool the custard to room temperature, then transfer to a storage container and refrigerate for at least 2 hours, or, preferably, overnight.

Pour the ice cream base into an ice cream maker and spin it according to the manufacturer's instructions. The finished ice cream will have a soft texture. If desired, transfer to a freezer container and freeze for a firmer ice cream.

MAKES ABOUT 5 CUPS (950 GRAMS)

CHOCOLATE GINGERSNAPS

This is a dual-purpose recipe. Make it with half an egg, and you'll get a dough you can roll out to make flat, crisp cookies. (Freezing the rolled-out dough briefly helps keep their shapes precise.) Or use a whole egg to make plump, soft drop cookies. For either version, because the dough is so dark, it's not easy to tell when they're done by looking at them. The best way to judge this is the smell of chocolate filling the air. The tops will also just begin to crack slightly.

1½ cups (197 grams) all-purpose flour
6 tablespoons (33 grams) unsweetened cocoa powder, preferably Cacao Barry Extra Brute
½ teaspoon (2.3 grams) baking powder
1 tablespoon (6.2 grams) ground ginger
1½ teaspoons (4 grams) ground cinnamon
¼ teaspoon (0.5 gram) freshly ground black pepper
⅛ teaspoon (0.3 gram) ground cloves
Pinch of kosher salt
12 tablespoons (6 ounces/170 grams) unsalted butter, at room temperature
¾ cup (144 grams) packed light brown sugar
2 tablespoons (41 grams) unsulfured blackstrap molasses
½ or 1 whole large egg (see the headnote)
1 tablespoon (18 grams) grated fresh ginger
½ teaspoon (1 gram) grated lemon zest
Turbinado or large crystal sugar for sprinkling or rolling

Combine the flour, cocoa, baking powder, ground ginger, cinnamon, pepper, cloves, and salt.

Put the butter, brown sugar, and molasses in the bowl of a stand mixer fitted with the paddle and beat on medium speed for about 1 minute, or until smooth. Scrape the sides and bottom of the bowl. Beat for another 5 minutes, until fluffy.

Scrape the bowl again, add the half or whole egg, fresh ginger, and zest, and mix on medium-low speed for about 1 minute, until combined. Mix in about one-third of the dry mixture until combined, then mix in the remaining dry mixture. Remove the bowl and use a spatula to give the dough a final mix, incorporating any dry ingredients that may have settled in the bottom of the bowl.

Remove the dough from the bowl, shape it into a block, wrap in plastic wrap, and refrigerate for at least 2 hours, or, preferably, overnight. (The dough can be frozen for up to 1 month; thaw in the refrigerator.)

FOR THE HALF-EGG VERSION: Cut the dough into thirds and put one piece on a Silpat or a piece of parchment sprayed lightly with nonstick cooking spray. Refrigerate the other pieces while you work with the first. Roll the dough to a ¹⁄₁₆-inch-thick sheet. Repeat with a second piece of dough on a second Silpat. (This recipe makes a lot of cookies; if you'd like, the third piece can be frozen to use at a later date.)

Trim the edges (leave the trimming in place) and score the dough into 2½-by-1¼-inch rectangles, or into other shapes, if you prefer. Carefully slide the Silpats or parchment onto baking sheets and freeze for 30 minutes to firm the dough. (If you don't have space in your freezer, you can bake the cookies now, but you will need to cut through them again after they have baked.)

Position the oven racks in the upper and lower thirds of the oven and preheat to 325°F.

Take the cookies out of the freezer and carefully remove the trimmings. If necessary, rearrange the rectangles on the baking sheets to leave some space between the cookies. (The trimmings can be baked, cooled, and crumbled to use as a topping for ice cream, or they can be pushed back together, refrigerated until firm, and rolled out for more cookies.) Sprinkle the tops of the cookies with turbinado sugar and bake for about 12 minutes, until the tops are slightly cracked, rotating the pans after 6 minutes. Cool on racks.

FOR THE WHOLE-EGG VERSION: Position the oven racks in the upper and lower thirds of the oven and preheat the oven to 300°F. Line two baking sheets with Silpats, or parchment paper sprayed lightly with nonstick cooking spray.

Divide the dough into scant 1-tablespoon (15-gram) portions, shape each portion into a ball, roll the balls in the turbinado sugar, arrange them about 2 inches apart on the prepared pans, and press the tops slightly. Bake for about 12 minutes, until the tops are slightly cracked, rotating the pans after 6 minutes. Cool on racks.

MAKES 6 DOZEN 2½-BY-1¾-INCH RECTANGLES OR 3 DOZEN DROP COOKIES

THINK LIKE A PASTRY CHEF: The half-egg version is perfect for making ice cream sandwiches, or just for serving with a scoop of ice cream. Vanilla and white chocolate ice cream would both be good choices. You can add chunks of chocolate to the whole-egg version, if you like.

TWO TUILES
HAZELNUT
SESAME

Lacy, buttery tuiles are a good way to add crunch and toasty flavor to a dessert while still keeping it delicate and light. If you've never made them, I'd suggest starting with the Sesame Tuiles, which are a bit easier to shape. The trick is to work with them while they're just cool enough to handle but still hot enough to be flexible. It takes a little practice, but both recipes give you plenty of batter, so you can feel free to experiment.

HAZELNUT TUILES

¾ cup plus 2 tablespoons (87 grams) hazelnut
    meal/flour
¼ cup (25 grams) almond meal/flour
2 tablespoons (16 grams) all-purpose flour
Pinch of kosher salt
8 tablespoons (4 ounces/113 grams) unsalted butter
1 cup plus 2 tablespoons (225 grams) granulated sugar
¼ cup (63 grams) whole milk
⅛ teaspoon (0.5 gram) pure vanilla extract

Combine the hazelnut meal, almond meal, flour, and salt in a bowl.

Put the butter, sugar, and milk in a medium saucepan and heat over medium-low heat, stirring to combine as the butter starts to melt. When the butter is about half melted, stir in the dry ingredients and continue to stir until the butter is completely melted and the mixture is combined. Stir in the vanilla.

Pour the batter into a bowl or storage container and let cool to room temperature, then refrigerate for at least 2 hours, or, preferably, overnight.

Preheat the oven to 300°F.

For flat tuiles, position the racks in the upper and lower thirds of the oven. If you are shaping the tuiles, it is best to bake one baking sheet at a time, on the center oven rack. Line two baking sheets with Silpats.

Using 1 teaspoon (6 grams) for each tuile, spoon 6 small mounds of cold batter onto a Silpat, leaving generous space between them. Using your fingertips or a small offset spatula, spread the batter into 2-inch rounds.

Bake for 10 to 12 minutes, or until golden brown. Tuiles that will be left flat can cool on the Silpats. If you are shaping the tuiles, let cool for about 2 minutes, or until they are firm enough to lift with a small offset spatula. Drape them over a rolling pin or dowel for a curved shape, and let cool. If the tuiles harden too much to shape them, return them to the oven for about 30 seconds to soften.

The tuiles are best eaten the day they are made. Store in an airtight container.

MAKES 8 DOZEN TUILES

SESAME TUILES

5 tablespoons (47 grams) sesame seeds, plus about
  1 tablespoon (9 grams) for sprinkling
½ cup plus 2 tablespoons (125 grams) granulated
  sugar
¼ cup (33 grams) all-purpose flour
¼ cup (63 grams) fresh orange juice
½ teaspoon (3 grams) fresh lemon juice
1½ teaspoons (8 grams) tahini
2 tablespoons (1 ounce/28 grams) unsalted butter,
  melted and cooled to warm
Kosher salt for sprinkling

Pulse the sesame seeds in a spice grinder until ground
and fluffy, similar to the texture of flour.

Combine the ground sesame seeds, sugar, and
flour in a medium bowl. Whisk in the orange and lemon
juice, followed by the tahini and butter. Refrigerate
for at least 2 hours, or, preferably, overnight.

Preheat the oven to 350°F.

For flat tuiles, line two baking sheets with
Silpats and position the racks in the upper and lower
third of the oven. If you are shaping the tuiles, it is
best to bake one baking sheet at a time, on the center
oven rack.

Using 1½ teaspoons (9 grams) for each tuile,
spoon 4 small mounds of cold batter onto a Silpat,
leaving generous space between them. Using a small
offset spatula, spread the batter into strips about
2½ by 6 inches long. Sprinkle with the sesame seeds
and salt.

Bake for 6 to 8 minutes, or until golden. Tuiles
that will be left flat can cool on the Silpats. If you are
shaping the tuiles, let cool for about 2 minutes, or
until they are firm enough to lift with a small offset
spatula. Twist the tuiles into a shape you like or drape
them over a rolling pin or dowel for a curved shape.
If the tuiles harden too much to shape them, return
them to the oven for about 30 seconds to soften.

The tuiles are best eaten the day they are made.
Store in an airtight container.

MAKES ABOUT 2½ DOZEN TUILES

WALNUT BRITTLE CRUMBLE AND NOUGATINE

Nougatine is a cool thing. It's basically nuts encased in caramel, and you can turn that mixture into anything from a brittle to tuile-thin nougatine or a crumble. In this version, the caramel stays quite crisp and won't get soggy when you layer it napoleon-style (see photo, page 327), or use it to garnish a moist dessert. The flavor is also very clean, making it extra-versatile for layering with other ingredients.

1 cup (100 grams) walnuts
2 tablespoons (50 grams) liquid glucose
¾ cup (150 grams) granulated sugar
Kosher salt

Preheat the oven to 325°F. Line a baking sheet with a Silpat.

Spread the walnuts on a baking sheet and toast in the oven for 5 to 7 minutes. Remove from the oven and let the nuts sit in a warm spot (the nuts should be warm when you add them to the caramel) while you prepare the caramel.

Put the glucose and ¼ cup (50 grams) of the sugar in a medium saucepan and cook over medium-high heat, stirring occasionally at first to melt the sugar, for 5 to 6 minutes, until the caramel is a very pale amber; the mixture will be foamy, so stir it to check the color.

Add about half of the remaining sugar, return to the heat, and stir constantly for about 1½ minutes, or until the sugar has dissolved. Add the remaining sugar and stir for about 3 minutes, until it is the color of peanut butter (medium amber). Stir in the nuts and remove the pan from the heat. Stir in a generous pinch of salt.

Spread the brittle on the prepared pan in as thin a layer as possible, and cool to room temperature. The brittle can be broken into pieces and stored in an airtight container, or you can continue to make the nougatine and crumble.

FOR THE CRUMBLE AND NOUGATINE: Preheat the oven to 350°F. Line a baking sheet with a Silpat.

Remove the brittle from the baking sheet and coarsely chop it. Working in batches, put the brittle in the food processor and process it to the texture of coarse sand. You will have about 2 cups (260 grams).

Spread half of the "sand" on the baking sheet; reserve the rest to use as a crumble (or to make a second batch of nougatine). Put the baking sheet in the oven for about 5 minutes, or until the brittle has melted and is a rich golden brown.

Carefully slide the Silpat off the baking sheet. Put a piece of parchment paper over the top of the nougatine and roll over the parchment with a rolling pin until the nougatine is paper-thin. Flip the nougatine over, peel off the Silpat, and move the nougatine, on the parchment paper, back to the baking sheet. The mixture can be cooled and then broken into irregular shapes; if you'd rather cut it into shapes with a knife, return the nougatine to the oven for 1 minute to soften before cutting. If the nougatine hardens too much as you cut it, return it to the oven for about 30 seconds to soften. Let cool.

Carefully remove the pieces using a small offset spatula, and store in an airtight container for up to 1 week.

**MAKES ABOUT 9 OUNCES (260 GRAMS) BRITTLE
OR 1 CUP (130 GRAMS) CRUMBLE AND
ABOUT 4½ OUNCES (130 GRAMS) NOUGATINE**

THINK LIKE A PASTRY CHEF: When you make homemade granola, mix in some of the crumble during the last few minutes of baking.

tea and me

I go through a love-hate thing every time I go to Morocco. It's about the tea. The minute I get to wherever I'm staying, tea gets made. And through the fog of jet lag, I'll take a first sip without paying much attention to it, and suddenly experience a kind of shock reaction as I think, "Oh, man. Painfully sweet." I can't help it. I'm not used to eating or drinking anything with that much sugar in it anymore. But I'll politely finish the glass—and the second or third one that's invariably offered.

The next day, I'll sometimes try to be out and about in the afternoon to avoid teatime altogether, but it never works. Sooner or later, I'm offered tea by a smiling friend or relative. Sometimes I'll say, "Yes, please, and can you make it without sugar?" This evokes a variety of expressions, ranging from perplexed to pitying, and then a special pot is made for me with *half* the usual amount of sugar. That's as far as "without sugar" will get you.

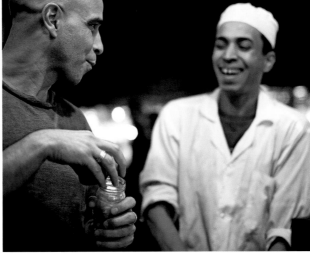

By day three, I find myself getting used to the tea. And by day four, I'm back. I can't stop drinking it. I start craving the buzz of the sugar and caffeine, the "tea sweat," and the amped-up feeling of connection with everyone gathered around the pot. I end up loving the stuff. That's my version of the Moroccan tea ritual.

When I was growing up, the ritual was more traditional. As soon as the lunch dishes were cleared, Grandpa would make tea. That might sound odd, since Moroccan men don't generally do much in the way of food preparation or serving. But tea is more of a ceremonial thing, and it's the duty—the privilege, really—of the head of the household, whether that's a man or a woman.

As everyone leaned back on the banquettes around the table or the ledge along the wall of the courtyard, someone would drag a small pro-pane tank over to wherever we were, and then they'd bring out two round trays. One had two metal teapots on it, ringed with small tea glasses. The other held a box of gunpowder tea, a heap of fresh mint and some other herbs, and blocks of sugar half the size of my hand.

First Grandpa would set one of the pots, filled with water, to boil on the burner. Then he'd pour some tea leaves into the other pot and add a bit of boiling water. This would be swished around to make the leaves bloom and rinse them. He'd pour the liquid into a glass and study it. If it was cloudy, he'd rinse the tea again once or twice. Then he'd fill the pot with boiling water and put it directly on the fire to boil for a few minutes.

When the tea was quite dark and strong, he'd add a huge amount of sugar—I'm talking about a cup of sugar for a one-quart pot of tea. Then he'd add a big handful of mint sprigs to the pot, gently tamping them

basics

CHERRY-RASPBERRY JAM

2 cups (468 grams) water
2 cups (400 grams) granulated sugar
3 cups (480 grams) dried tart cherries
1 cup (138 grams) fresh raspberries
2½ teaspoons (15 grams) grated fresh ginger
1 teaspoon (5 grams) fresh lemon juice
About 2 teaspoons (11 grams) balsamic vinegar
    (optional)

Pour 1 cup (234 grams) of the water into a large saucepan and sprinkle the sugar evenly over it (this will help the sugar dissolve more evenly). Put over medium heat and cook, swirling the pan occasionally, until the sugar has dissolved and the caramel is a rich amber, 20 to 25 minutes.

Working carefully, as the caramel will bubble up, remove the pan from the heat and slowly add the remaining 1 cup (234 grams) water. Return the pan to the heat if necessary to melt any sugar that has crystallized. Add the cherries and let them soften in the caramel at room temperature for 1 hour.

Using a slotted spoon, transfer the cherries to a food processor, and process until smooth (discard the caramel). Add the raspberries, ginger, and lemon juice and process again until smooth. Strain through a fine-mesh strainer into a bowl and season to taste with the balsamic vinegar, if using.

Store in an airtight container in the refrigerator for up to 1 week.

MAKES ABOUT 1½ CUPS (445 GRAMS)

CARROT JAM

This sweet, spicy carrot jam makes more than you'll need for Beef Cheeks (page 274), but it will keep in the refrigerator for up to 2 weeks, and it's one of those things that's worth making in quantity if you're making it at all. You can also serve it, as they do in Morocco, as a pre-meal "seven salad" appetizer, sprinkled with sesame seeds, or use it as an accompaniment for other hearty braised meats. In addition, you can blend it, strain it, and serve it as a sauce with steak, lamb chops, or grilled fish. And I've even browned some ground beef, simmered it briefly in the jam, and piled it on a bun.

5 (18 grams) flat-leaf parsley sprigs
3 (3 grams) thyme sprigs
1½ teaspoons (1.9 grams) coriander seeds
½ teaspoon (1.2 grams) cumin seeds
One 1½-inch piece (1.7 grams) cinnamon stick
2 (1.2 grams) chiles de árbol
3 (0.4 gram) allspice berries
4 (0.3 gram) cloves
1 (0.2 gram) bay leaf
¼ cup (53 grams) grapeseed or canola oil
3 cups (404 grams) diced (¼-inch) onions
¼ cup (37 grams) finely chopped garlic
½ cup (116 grams) Riesling
3½ cups (508 grams) diced (¼-inch) carrots
1½ cups (195 grams) diced (¼-inch) celery hearts
About 2 cups (510 grams) carrot juice
One 28-ounce (793-gram) can San Marzano tomatoes
½ cup (117 grams) Vegetable Stock (page 364)
1½ tablespoons (20 grams) sherry vinegar
2 tablespoons (27 grams) extra virgin olive oil
1 teaspoon (3 grams) kosher salt, or to taste
1 teaspoon (2.4 grams) Marash pepper
1 tablespoon (15 grams) fresh lemon juice, or to taste

Wrap the parsley, thyme, coriander, cumin, cinnamon stick, chiles, allspice, cloves, and bay leaf in a piece of cheesecloth and tie to make a sachet. Set aside.

Heat the canola oil in a small stockpot over medium heat. Add the onions and garlic and cook for 45 minutes, or until the onions are a rich golden brown, stirring often and reducing the heat as needed.

Pour in the Riesling and scrape the browned bits from the bottom of the pot to deglaze. Bring to a simmer and cook for about 8 minutes, or until the wine has evaporated. Add the carrots and celery and cook for 8 to 10 minutes, or until they begin to soften. Add enough carrot juice to cover the ingredients and simmer for about 20 minutes, or until the reduced liquid comes about halfway up the carrots.

Meanwhile, set a fine-mesh strainer over a bowl and squeeze the tomatoes over the strainer to remove the seeds. Discard the seeds and reserve the juices. Coarsely chop the tomatoes and add to the juice.

Add the tomatoes, with their juices, and the sachet to the pot, bring to a simmer over medium heat, and cook for about 25 minutes, stirring often, until the liquid has reduced by half.

Add the vegetable stock and return the liquid to a simmer. Cover with a parchment lid (see page 379), brush with water to keep the edges from curling up, and cover with the lid. Simmer over medium-low to low heat, stirring occasionally, for about 5 hours; check the jam more frequently after 4 hours, because it may begin to stick to the bottom of the pot. Cook until the jam is very thick, and there is no liquid remaining in the pot.

Remove from the heat and discard the sachet. Stir in the vinegar, olive oil, salt, Marash, and lemon juice. Season to taste with additional salt and/or lemon juice if necessary. Place the pot over medium heat to "fry" the mixture for about 5 minutes, or until the oil begins to separate from the jam. Remove from the heat and let cool to room temperature, then refrigerate. (The jam can be refrigerated for up to 2 weeks; reheat it in the microwave or in a saucepan over a burner, with a little more water added to keep it from sticking.)

MAKES 4 CUPS (1 KILOGRAM)

BALSAMIC CRANBERRIES

I use these with grains like the Barley on page 300, and they make a nice sweet addition to chicory salads too. When you're serving duck, they're a great way to add sweetness to the plate.

1 cup (140 grams) dried cranberries
2 cups (508 grams) balsamic vinegar
1 cup (200 grams) granulated sugar

Put the cranberries in a bowl.

Put the vinegar and sugar in a saucepan and bring to a simmer, stirring to dissolve the sugar. Pour over the cranberries (the cranberries should be covered by the vinegar) and let cool to room temperature.

Let stand in an airtight container at room temperature for at least 1 week before using. The cranberries can be stored at room temperature for up to 6 months.

MAKES ABOUT 1½ CUPS (255 GRAMS)

SPICED PRUNES

I use Moyer prunes here for their flavor, texture, and deep, rich color. Unlike French prunes, which are often pitted, Moyers are usually sold with the pits, and it's important to use prunes with pits here, so that the brine doesn't get inside the prune and make it mushy. The pits also add an almondy sweetness.

4 cups (630 grams) unpitted Moyer or other prunes
1 cup (234 grams) water
¾ cup (175 grams) champagne vinegar
¾ cup (150 grams) granulated sugar
2 tablespoons (27 grams) brandy
One 3-inch (3.3 grams) cinnamon stick
¾ teaspoon (2.3 grams) Tellicherry peppercorns
3 (0.4 gram) allspice berries
1 (0.2 gram) bay leaf

Put the prunes in a medium bowl.

Combine all the remaining ingredients in a saucepan and bring to a boil over medium-high heat, stirring to dissolve the sugar. Pour over the prunes and let cool to room temperature.

Let stand in an airtight container at room temperature for at least a week before using. The prunes can be stored at room temperature for up to 6 months.

MAKES 4 CUPS (1.7 KILOGRAMS)

GARLIC CONFIT
GARLIC PUREE

3 cups (450 grams) garlic cloves
About 2½ cups (530 grams) extra virgin olive oil, plus additional for storing

Put the garlic cloves in a small saucepan and add enough olive oil to cover them. Bring the oil to a simmer over medium heat and cook, stirring occasionally, for about 20 minutes, or until the garlic is soft and golden brown. At this point *you have garlic confit,* which can be stored in its oil for up to 3 weeks in the refrigerator.

To make garlic puree, use a skimmer or slotted spoon to remove the garlic from the oil, and pass it through a fine-mesh strainer or *tamis.*

Put the puree in an airtight container, smooth the top, and cover with a thin layer of fresh olive oil. The puree can be refrigerated, covered, for up to 3 weeks.

MAKES ABOUT 1 CUP (313 GRAMS)

RED WINE VINAIGRETTE

½ shallot, thinly sliced
1 garlic clove, thinly sliced
1 tablespoon (9 grams) kosher salt
½ teaspoon (2.1 grams) granulated sugar
¼ cup (60 grams) red wine vinegar
1 cup (212 grams) extra virgin olive oil

Put the shallot, garlic, salt, sugar, and vinegar in a
plastic squeeze bottle or a jar. Shake and let sit at
room temperature for 15 minutes to dissolve the
salt and sugar.

Add the oil and shake to combine. If the vinaigrette
is in a jar, strain out the shallots and garlic before
serving. The vinaigrette should be used the day it is
made.

MAKES 1¼ CUPS (210 GRAMS)

PICKLED GREEN STRAWBERRIES

6 to 8 medium green strawberries with stems
    (½ cup/60 grams)
½ cup plus 3 tablespoons (161 grams) water
3½ tablespoons (50.5 grams) apple cider vinegar
3 tablespoons (37.5 grams) granulated sugar
2½ teaspoons (7.5 grams) kosher salt
1 thyme sprig

Cut the strawberries in half or into quarters, and put
in a small bowl.

Combine the water, vinegar, sugar, salt, and
thyme in a small saucepan and bring to a simmer,
stirring to dissolve the sugar and salt. Pour over the
strawberries. Let stand at room temperature for
15 minutes, or until cool.

The berries can be kept refrigerated in their
pickling liquid, covered, for up to 2 days.

MAKES ABOUT ½ CUP (75 GRAMS)

SWEET PICKLING LIQUID
3 PICKLED VEGETABLES

This pickling liquid also works well with carrots, cucumbers, and other vegetables.

cauliflower
2 cups (192 grams) cauliflower florets
2 cups (465 grams) water
½ cup (72 grams) kosher salt

turnips
1¾ cups (210 grams) baby turnips or 5 small turnips
　(0.5 ounce/14 grams each)

fennel
2 small fennel bulbs

pickling liquid
2 tablespoons (8.5 grams) coriander seeds
1 tablespoon (6 grams) fennel seeds
1 teaspoon (3 grams) cumin seeds
1 tablespoon (11 grams) yellow mustard seeds
1 tablespoon (11 grams) brown mustard seeds
2 cups (466 grams) champagne vinegar
1 cup (234 grams) water
½ cup (100 grams) granulated sugar
8 garlic cloves, smashed
8 (1.8 grams) bay leaves
2 tablespoons (28 grams) kosher salt

FOR THE CAULIFLOWER: Put the cauliflower in a medium bowl or storage container.

Combine the water and salt in a medium saucepan and heat, stirring to dissolve the salt. Let cool completely.

Pour the salted water over the cauliflower and let sit at room temperature for 4 hours.

The cauliflower will taste salty at this point. Drain it and rinse under cold water to remove some of the salt. Pack the cauliflower into a pint canning jar.

FOR THE TURNIPS: If using baby turnips, trim the stems to ¼ inch. For small turnips, cut away both ends and the tough peel with a paring knife, then cut the turnips into ½-inch-thick wedges. Pack the turnips into another pint canning jar.

FOR THE FENNEL: Cut off the fennel fronds. Trim the bottoms and cut the fennel bulbs into ½-inch-thick wedges. Stand the wedges into a third pint canning jar.

FOR THE PICKLING LIQUID: Combine the coriander, fennel, and cumin in a medium frying pan and heat over medium heat, swirling the pan and flipping or stirring the spices occasionally to make sure they toast evenly, until fragrant, 2 to 3 minutes. Pour them into a medium saucepan.

Put the mustard seeds in the frying pan over medium heat, cover with a lid, and toast until the seeds begin to pop, about 2 minutes. Toast for 30 seconds more, then add to the saucepan.

Add the remaining ingredients, bring to a simmer, and simmer for 15 minutes. Remove from the heat and let sit at room temperature for 45 minutes to infuse the flavors.

Strain 1 cup (240 grams) of the liquid into a small bowl and refrigerate until cold.

Strain the remaining liquid into a clean saucepan. Heat, but do not boil.

Pour the hot liquid over the turnips and fennel. Pour the cold liquid over the cauliflower. Refrigerate the pickled vegetables for at least 2 days before using. They can be refrigerated for up to 4 weeks.

**MAKES 3 CUPS (700 GRAMS) PICKLING LIQUID,
ENOUGH TO PICKLE 6 CUPS VEGETABLES**

PICKLED PEARL ONIONS

If your pearl onions are large, trim off the outer layers and reserve them for another use. You can separate the onions into layers to pickle them, as described below, or cut very small pearl onions in half. This recipe also works well with 1½ cups (159 grams) of thinly sliced red onions.

1 cup (200 grams) granulated sugar

1 cup (233 grams) champagne vinegar

1 cup (234 grams) water

Two 3-inch (6.6 grams) cinnamon sticks

1 teaspoon (3 grams) pink peppercorns

One 2-inch piece (2.8 grams) licorice root

2 (2.16 grams) star anise

12 (1.9 grams) green cardamom pods, lightly crushed with the side of a chef's knife

24 (1.5 grams) Tellicherry peppercorns

2 (1.5 grams) black cardamom pods, lightly crushed with the side of a chef's knife

2 (1.2 grams) chiles de árbol

½ teaspoon (0.8 gram) roughly crumbled whole mace

10 (0.7 gram) cloves

2 (0.3 gram) bay leaves

10 ounces (283 grams) red pearl onions, not peeled

Combine all the ingredients except the pearl onions in a medium saucepan and bring to a simmer over medium heat, stirring to dissolve the sugar. Remove from the heat and let sit at room temperature for 30 minutes to infuse the flavors.

Meanwhile, bring a large saucepan of water to a boil. Fill a medium bowl with ice water.

Blanch the onions in the boiling water for 20 seconds (this will make it easier to peel them), and immediately transfer to the ice water to chill. Drain and peel the onions and cut them in half through the root end. Remove the outer layers and put them in a medium bowl. Discard the center pieces of onion attached to the root end.

Bring the pickling liquid back to a boil, and strain over the onions. Rest a small plate on the onions to keep them submerged, cover the bowl tightly with plastic wrap, and let sit at room temperature until cool.

Refrigerate the onions for at least 1 day before using. They can be refrigerated for up to 4 weeks.

MAKES ABOUT 1½ CUPS (215 GRAMS)

MUSHROOM STOCK

5 pounds (2.26 kilograms) button mushrooms (about 9 quarts)

12 quarts (11.16 kilograms) cold water

Wash the mushrooms and put them in a large stockpot. Add the water and bring to a simmer, skimming off any foam that forms on the surface. Simmer for 1 hour.

Strain the stock through a fine-mesh strainer into a large pot. Bring to a simmer and cook for 1 to 1½ hours, or until the stock has reduced to 5 quarts (4.6 kilograms). Let cool to room temperature.

Refrigerate the stock in an airtight container for up to 3 days, or freeze for up to 3 months.

MAKES 5 QUARTS (4.6 KILOGRAMS)

VEGETABLE STOCK

5 quarts (4.65 kilograms) cold water

2 pounds (907 grams) carrots (about 8 large), peeled
 and cut into 2-inch pieces

2 pounds (907 grams) fennel bulbs (about 2 large),
 fronds removed, bulbs quartered

1 pound (453 grams) zucchini (about 3 medium),
 cut into 1-inch pieces

12 ounces (340 grams) onion (2 to 3 medium), halved

12 ounces (340 grams) celery (about 6 ribs), cut into
 2-inch lengths

8 ounces (226 grams) leek (about 1 large; white and
 light green parts only), cut into 2-inch pieces and
 rinsed thoroughly

12 (42 grams) flat-leaf parsley sprigs

8 garlic cloves, lightly crushed

1 tablespoon (9 grams) Tellicherry peppercorns

6 (6 grams) thyme sprigs

3 (0.45 gram) bay leaves

Combine all the ingredients in a 10- to 12-quart
stockpot and bring to a simmer over medium-high
heat. Simmer for 1½ hours. Remove from the heat
and allow the stock to sit and steep for 45 minutes.

Line a chinois or large fine-mesh strainer with
4 layers of dampened cheesecloth and set over a large
storage container or bowl. Strain the stock, and cool
to room temperature.

Refrigerate the stock, covered, for up to 2 days,
or freeze for up to 2 months.

MAKES ABOUT 2½ QUARTS (2.35 KILOGRAMS)

CLAM STOCK

Make this stock when you feel like eating clams,
because, as a by-product, you will have a cup of really
tasty, if somewhat overcooked, clams.

5 pounds (2.26 kilograms) littleneck clams

1¼ cups (290 grams) Riesling

1¼ cups (292.5 grams) water

4 (4 grams) thyme sprigs

2 garlic cloves, smashed

Scrub the clams, rinse them several times in cold
water, and soak in a large bowl of cold water for
30 minutes.

Put the wine, water, thyme, and garlic in a
saucepan or wide sauté pan large enough to hold the
clams and bring to a boil. Lift the clams from the
water, leaving any dirt in the bottom of the bowl, and
add them to the pot. Cover with a lid and simmer for
about 5 minutes, or until all the clams have opened.
Remove the clams and strain the stock through a
fine-mesh strainer into a bowl. Let the stock sit to
allow any grit to settle to the bottom of the bowl.

Meanwhile, remove the clams from the shells
and reserve for another use.

Transfer the stock to a storage container, leaving
the grit in the bowl. Refrigerate for up to 1 day, or
freeze for up to 2 months.

MAKES 1 QUART (1.11 KILOGRAMS)

CHICKEN STOCK

Using chicken feet will add a lot of viscosity to the stock, which is especially important if you're using the stock to make the jus and sauce. But if you're using the stock for other purposes, or you can't get chicken feet, add 2 pounds (907 grams) of chicken bones in their place.

Canola oil

8 pounds (7.48 kilograms) chicken backs, necks, and bones

8 quarts (7.48 kilograms) cold water

2 pounds (907 grams) chicken feet

2 pounds (907 grams) carrots (about 8 large), peeled

2 celery stalks

1 large onion

4 garlic cloves

8 (8 grams) thyme sprigs

2 (0.3 gram) bay leaves

2 teaspoons (6 grams) Tellicherry peppercorns

FOR CHICKEN STOCK THAT WILL BE USED TO MAKE CHICKEN JUS OR CHICKEN SAUCE: Put a large roasting pan in the oven and preheat the oven to 475°F.

Remove the pan from the oven and coat with a film of oil. Add all of the bones (but not the feet; browning the feet would remove too much gelatin from them). Drizzle more oil over the bones and roast for about 20 minutes, until browned. Turn the bones over and roast for about 20 minutes longer to brown the second side. Transfer the bones to a 16- to 20-quart stockpot.

Position the roasting pan over two burners and turn the heat to medium-high. Add 4 cups (930 grams) of the water to the pan and deglaze, scraping the browned bits from the bottom of the pan. Strain the deglazing liquid through a fine-mesh strainer into the stockpot. Add the chicken feet to the pot and cover with the remaining 7 quarts (6.5 kilograms) water. It is all right if some of the chicken feet are not completely submerged.

FOR ALL-PURPOSE CHICKEN STOCK (THIS WILL ALSO BE USED FOR CHICKEN BOUILLON): Put the bones and feet in a 16- to 20-quart stockpot and cover with the water.

FOR EITHER STOCK: How you cook the stock can make the difference between a clean, clear stock and a cloudy stock, so take your time, and never stir the liquid. Cover the bones and liquid with a parchment lid (see page 379), and brush it with water to keep the edges from curling up. Bring to a simmer over medium heat (high heat would bring the temperature up too quickly). Putting the pot on one side of the burner will move the impurities to one side, making them easier to skim.

Meanwhile, line a strainer with a double layer of dampened cheesecloth and set over a bowl near the stove. You may have used a skimmer in the past to remove the impurities that rise to the surface, but I use a ladle or spoon and inevitably take a bit of the stock with them to be certain I get them all. I ladle the liquid into the strainer, and then return the strained liquid in the bowl to the stockpot.

Rinse the ladle or spoon and the cheesecloth between uses to avoid returning impurities to the pot. Simmer the stock, skimming often, for 2 hours. From time to time, use a pair of tongs to gently move the bones, checking that none are sticking to the bottom of the pot.

Add the remaining ingredients to the pot. Add just enough water to keep the vegetables covered and simmer for 2 hours. Taste the stock; it should have a rich chicken flavor, but remember that no salt has been added. If it seems weak, simmer for an additional 30 minutes to 1 hour.

CONTINUED

MOROCCAN SAUCE

⅛ teaspoon (0.1 gram) saffron threads
1 tablespoon plus 1 teaspoon (5.1 grams) coriander
    seeds
1 teaspoon (2.5 grams) cumin seeds
½ teaspoon (1.5 grams) Tellicherry peppercorns
3½ quarts (3.28 kilograms) Chicken Stock (page 365)
1⅓ cups (150 grams) thinly sliced shallots
One 1½-inch piece (22.5 grams) fresh ginger, peeled
    and sliced
One 1½-inch piece (7 grams) fresh turmeric, peeled
    and coarsely chopped
2 teaspoons (8 grams) diced (⅛-inch) preserved lemon
    rind (see page 45)

Put the saffron in a spoon (toasting the saffron this way will toast it more evenly and it will be less likely to burn), hold 4 to 5 inches above a medium-low flame, and toast until fragrant, about 1 minute. Set the saffron aside.

Combine the coriander, cumin, and peppercorns in a medium frying pan and heat over medium heat, swirling the pan and flipping or stirring the spices occasionally so they toast evenly, until fragrant, 2 to 3 minutes. Pour the spices into a small stockpot.

Add the chicken stock, shallots, ginger, turmeric, and saffron to the pot and bring to a simmer over medium heat. Cook for 3½ to 4 hours, until the sauce has reduced to ¾ cup (190 grams). As the stock reduces to a sauce, it is important to strain it into a smaller saucepan each time a ring develops around the sides of the pot. Strain into a storage container or bowl and stir in the preserved lemon.

Let cool to room temperature, then refrigerate for up to 5 days, or freeze for up to 3 months.

MAKES ABOUT ¾ CUP (188 GRAMS)

DUCK STOCK

Canola oil
4 pounds (1.81 kilograms) duck carcasses, ideally with
    the wings attached, cut into 5- to 6-inch pieces
2 pounds (907 grams) duck legs (about 4)
3½ quarts (3.25 kilograms) water
2 pounds (907 grams) chicken feet
12 ounces (340 grams) carrots (about 3), peeled
12 ounces (340 grams) leeks (about 2; white and light
    green parts only), cut into rounds and thoroughly
    rinsed
12 ounces (340 grams) onion (2 to 3 medium), cut
    lengthwise in half
½ bunch (2 ounces/56 grams) flat-leaf parsley
1 small head garlic, cut in half through the equator
½ (0.16 gram) bay leaf
1 teaspoon (3 grams) Tellicherry peppercorns
4 (0.3 gram) cloves
2 Burnt Onions (page 372)

Put a large roasting pan in the oven and preheat the oven to 475°F.

Remove the pan from the oven and coat with a film of oil. Add all the bones, drizzle oil on top of the bones, and roast for about 20 minutes, until browned. Turn the bones over and return to the oven for about 20 minutes longer to brown the second side. Transfer the bones to a 10- to 12-quart stockpot.

Meanwhile, heat a film of oil in a large nonstick frying pan over medium heat. Add the duck legs skin side down and brown for 8 to 10 minutes, spooning off any excess fat as it renders and adjusting the heat as necessary. Turn and brown on the second side for 8 to 10 minutes. Transfer to the stockpot.

Position the roasting pan over two burners and turn the heat to medium-high. Add 4 cups (930 grams) of the water to the pan and deglaze, scraping up the browned bits from the bottom of the pan. Strain the deglazing liquid through a fine-mesh strainer into the stockpot. Add the chicken feet to the pot and cover with the remaining 2½ quarts (2.34 kilograms) water. It is all right if some of the feet are not completely submerged in the water.

How you cook the stock can make the difference between a clean, clear stock and a cloudy stock, so take your time, and never stir the liquid. Cover the bones and liquid with a parchment lid (see page 379) and brush it with water to keep the edges from curling up. Bring to a simmer over medium heat (high heat would bring the temperature up too quickly). Putting the pot on one side of the burner will move the impurities to one side, making them easier to skim out.

Meanwhile, line a strainer with a double layer of dampened cheesecloth and set over a bowl near the stove. You may have used a skimmer in the past to remove the impurities that rise to the surface, but I use a ladle or spoon and inevitably take a bit of the stock with them to be certain I get them all. I ladle the liquid into the strainer, and then return the strained liquid in the bowl to the stockpot.

Rinse the ladle or spoon and the cheesecloth between uses to avoid returning impurities to the pot. From time to time, use a pair of tongs to gently move the bones, checking that none are sticking to the bottom of the pot. Simmer the stock, skimming often, for 1 hour.

Add the remaining ingredients to the pot. Add just enough water to keep the vegetables covered and simmer for 2 hours. Taste the stock; it should have a rich duck flavor, but remember that no salt has been added. If it seems weak, simmer for an additional 30 minutes to 1 hour.

Line a chinois or large fine-mesh strainer with a double layer of dampened cheesecloth and set it over a large storage container or bowl. Using a large ladle, ladle the stock from the pot into the strainer, disturbing the bones as little as possible, to avoid clouding the stock. Tilt the pot as necessary to get the liquid at the bottom. Then discard the bones and vegetables.

To store the stock, let cool to room temperature, then refrigerate for up to 3 days, or freeze for up to 3 months.

MAKES ABOUT 2 QUARTS (1.8 KILOGRAMS)

DUCK SAUCE

8 cups (1.8 kilograms) Duck Stock (page 368)

Put the duck stock in a large saucepan and bring to a simmer over medium heat. Cook for 3½ to 4 hours, until the stock is reduced to a generous ¾ cup (180 grams). As the stock reduces, it is important to strain it into a smaller saucepan every time a ring develops around the sides of the pan. Strain into a storage container or bowl.

Let cool to room temperature, then refrigerate for up to 5 days, or freeze for up to 3 months.

MAKES ABOUT ¾ CUP (180 GRAMS)

LAMB STOCK

Canola oil
11 pounds (4.98 kilograms) lamb neck bones
6 quarts (5.58 kilograms) water
1 calves' foot (3 pounds/1.36 kilograms)
1½ pounds (680 grams) carrots (about 6), peeled
1½ pounds (680 grams) leeks (about 4 medium; white and light green parts only), cut into rounds and thoroughly rinsed
1½ pounds (680 grams) onions (about 2 large), cut lengthwise in half

CONTINUED

1 bunch (4 ounces/113 grams) flat-leaf parsley
2 small heads garlic, cut in half through the equator
1 tablespoon (3.8 grams) coriander seeds
1 teaspoon (3 grams) Tellicherry peppercorns
10 (1 gram) juniper berries
2 (0.6 gram) bay leaves
4 Burnt Onions (page 372)

Put a large roasting pan in the oven and preheat the oven to 475°F.

Remove the pan from the oven and coat with a film of oil. Add the lamb bones, drizzle more oil on the top of the bones, and roast for 25 to 30 minutes, until browned. Turn the bones over and roast for 25 to 30 minutes longer to brown the second side. Transfer the bones to a 16- to 20-quart stockpot.

Position the roasting pan over two burners and turn the heat to medium-high. Add 4 cups (930 grams) of the water to the pan and deglaze, scraping the browned bits from the bottom of the pan. Strain the deglazing liquid through a fine-mesh strainer into the stockpot. Add the calves' foot and cover with the remaining 5 quarts (4.65 kilograms) water.

How you cook the stock can make the difference between a clean, clear stock and a cloudy stock, so take your time, and never stir the liquid. Cover the bones and liquid with a parchment lid (see page 379) and, brush it with water to keep the edges from curling up. Bring to a simmer over medium heat (high heat would bring the temperature up too quickly). Putting the pot to one side of the burner will move the impurities to one side, making them easier to skim.

Meanwhile, line a strainer with a double layer of dampened cheesecloth and set over a bowl near the stove. You may have used a skimmer in the past to remove any impurities that rise to the surface, but I use a ladle or spoon and inevitably take a bit of the stock with them to be certain I get them all. I ladle the liquid into the strainer, and then return the strained liquid in the bowl to the stockpot.

Rinse the ladle or spoon and the cheesecloth between uses to avoid returning any impurities to the pot. From time to time, use a pair of tongs to gently move the bones, checking that none are sticking to the bottom of the pot. Simmer the stock, skimming often, for 1 hour.

Add the remaining ingredients to the pot. Add just enough water to keep the vegetables covered and simmer for 3 hours. Taste the stock; it should have a rich lamb flavor, but remember that no salt has been added. If it seems weak, simmer for an additional 30 minutes to 1 hour.

Line a chinois or large fine-mesh strainer with a dampened double layer of cheesecloth and place it over a large storage container or bowl. Using a large ladle, ladle the stock from the pot into the strainer, disturbing the bones as little as possible, to avoid clouding the stock. Tilt the pot as necessary to get the liquid in the bottom. Then discard the bones and vegetables.

Let cool to room temperature, then refrigerate for up to 3 days, or freeze for up to 3 months.

MAKES ABOUT 2½ QUARTS (2.35 KILOGRAMS)

LAMB SAUCE

Lamb Stock (page 369)

Put the lamb stock in a small stockpot or large saucepan and bring to a simmer over medium heat. Cook for 3½ to 4 hours, until the stock has reduced to ¾ cup (207 grams). As the stock reduces to a sauce, it is important to strain it into a smaller saucepan each time a ring develops around the sides of the pot. Strain into a storage container or bowl.

Let cool to room temperature, then refrigerate for up to 5 days, or freeze for up to 3 months.

MAKES ABOUT ¾ CUP (207 GRAMS)

RED WINE GASTRIQUE LAMB SAUCE

6 tablespoons (38 grams) minced shallots
½ cup (117 grams) champagne vinegar
¼ cup (59 grams) water
¼ cup (50 grams) granulated sugar
⅔ cup (143 grams) red wine, preferably Pinot Noir
3 tablespoons plus 2 teaspoons (55 grams) red wine vinegar
1 tablespoon (25 grams) liquid glucose
Lamb Sauce (page 370)
Kosher salt

Put the shallots in a medium bowl.

Combine the vinegar, water, and sugar in a small saucepan and heat over medium heat, stirring to dissolve the sugar. Pour over the shallots and let sit at room temperature for 30 minutes to "pickle" the shallots. Strain the shallots, reserving the liquid.

Put the wine in a small saucepan, bring to a simmer over medium heat, and simmer for 6 to 8 minutes, until it has reduced by half. Add the red wine vinegar, glucose, and shallots and simmer for about 15 minutes, or until reduced to 6 tablespoons (100 grams). Remove from the heat and stir in the lamb sauce, then strain through a fine-mesh strainer into a storage container or bowl. Season to taste with the reserved vinegar mixture and salt.

Let cool to room temperature, then refrigerate for up to 5 days, or freeze for up to 3 months.

MAKES ABOUT 1 CUP (250 GRAMS)

BEEF STOCK

Canola oil
5½ pounds (2.49 kilograms) beef short ribs, cut flanken-style
5½ pounds (2.49 kilograms) oxtails
6 quarts (5.58 kilograms) water
1 calves' foot (3 pounds/1.36 kilograms)
1½ pounds (680 grams) carrots (about 6), peeled
1½ pounds (680 grams) leeks (about 4 medium; white and light green parts only), cut into rounds and thoroughly rinsed
1½ pounds (680 grams) onions (about 2 medium), cut lengthwise in half
1 bunch (4 ounces/113 grams) flat-leaf parsley
2 small heads garlic, cut in half through the equator
1 tablespoon (3.8 grams) coriander seeds
1 teaspoon (3 grams) Tellicherry peppercorns
1 teaspoon (2.5 grams) cumin seeds
2 (0.6 gram) bay leaves
4 Burnt Onions (page 372)

Put two large roasting pans in the oven and preheat the oven to 475°F for 15 minutes. (If you don't have two roasting pans, you can brown one of the meats in a large pan on the stovetop.)

Remove the pans from the oven and coat each one with a film of oil. Add the short ribs to one pan and the oxtails to the other, drizzle more oil on top of them, and roast for 25 to 30 minutes, until browned. Turn the pieces over and roast for another 25 to 30 minutes to brown the second side. Transfer the short ribs and oxtails to a 16- to 20-quart stockpot.

Place one roasting pan over two burners and turn the heat to medium-high. Add 4 cups (930 grams) of the water to the pan and deglaze, scraping up the browned bits from the bottom of the pan. Strain the deglazing liquid through a fine-mesh strainer into the stockpot. Repeat with the second pan. Add the calves' foot to the pot and cover with the remaining 4 quarts (3.72 kilograms) water.

How you cook the stock can make the difference between a clean, clear stock and a cloudy stock, so take your time, and never stir the liquid. Cover the meat and liquid with a parchment lid (see page 379) and brush it with water to keep the edges from curling up. Bring to a simmer over medium heat (high heat would bring the temperature up too quickly). Putting the pot on one side of the burner will move the impurities to one side, making them easier to skim.

Meanwhile, line a strainer with a double layer of dampened cheesecloth and set over a bowl near the stove. You may have used a skimmer in the past to remove any impurities that rise to the surface, but I use a ladle or spoon and inevitably take a bit of the stock with them to be certain I get them all. I ladle the liquid into the strainer, and then return the strained liquid in the bowl to the stockpot. Rinse the ladle or spoon and the cheesecloth between uses to avoid returning any of the impurities to the pot. From time to time, use a pair of tongs to gently move the bones, checking that none are sticking to the bottom of the pot. Simmer the stock, skimming often, for 1 hour.

Add the remaining ingredients to the pot. Add just enough water to keep the vegetables covered and simmer for 3 hours. Taste the stock; it should have a rich beef flavor, but remember that no salt has been added. If it seems weak, simmer for an additional 30 minutes to 1 hour.

Line a chinois or large fine-mesh strainer with a double layer of dampened cheesecloth and place it over a large storage container or bowl. Using a large ladle, ladle the stock from the pot through the strainer, disturbing the bones as little as possible, to avoid clouding the stock. Tilt the pot as necessary to get the liquid in the bottom. Then discard the meats and vegetables.

Let cool to room temperature, then refrigerate for up to 3 days, or freeze for up to 3 months.

MAKES ABOUT 2 QUARTS (2.2 KILOGRAMS)

BURNT ONIONS FOR STOCK

Medium onions (10 ounces/283 grams each), peeled, ends trimmed flat, and cut in half through the equator

Heat a large dry cast-iron skillet for 5 minutes over high heat. Reduce the heat to medium-high, arrange the onions cut side down in the pan, and cook for 12 to 15 minutes, until blackened and burnt on the bottom. Turn over and cook for about 7 minutes, until the second side is burnt as well. Remove from the heat.

CHICKEN OR DUCK CRACKLINGS

People often make cracklings by slowly cooking poultry skin in a skillet until it's crisp. My two-step method involves a bit more effort, but it's worth it. I roast the skins pressed between two sheet pans to flatten them and render as much fat as possible, and then I cut them into strips and fry them. Made this way, they are extra crisp and light, unlike cracklings made in a skillet, which can be chewy and greasy. Chicken skin is something that you can easily ask the butcher for. Duck skin, on the other hand, is harder to find, but you can order it online through Sonoma County Poultry. The chicken and duck cracklings can be used interchangeably. We use the skin in Fava Beans and Ramps (page 152) and in other dishes.

1 pound (453 grams) chicken skin or 2 pounds (907 grams) duck skin, preferably from the back and neck
Grapeseed or canola oil for deep-frying

FOR CHICKEN CRACKLINGS: Preheat the oven to 250°F and line a rimmed baking sheet with a Silpat.

Turn the skin fat side up and cut away any clumps of fat, then scrape away any remaining fat. You may remove as much as 8 ounces (226 grams) fat from the skin. Rinse the skin thoroughly and dry well on paper towels. Spread the skin on the baking sheet, and top with a second Silpat and another baking sheet to weight it down.

Put in the oven and cook for 1 hour. Remove the pan from the oven and lower the oven temperature to 225°F.

Carefully remove the top baking sheet and Silpat and pour off the rendered fat. Replace the Silpat and pan and return to the oven for another 15 minutes or so. The skin is done when all the fat appears to have rendered but the skin has not browned or crisped. Remove from the oven and let cool completely.

FOR DUCK CRACKLINGS: Preheat the oven to 350°F and line a rimmed baking sheet with a Silpat.

Turn the skin fat side up and cut away any clumps of fat, then scrape away any remaining fat. You may remove as much as 1½ pounds (680 grams) fat from the skin. Rinse the skin thoroughly and dry well on paper towels. Spread the skin on the baking sheet. Top with a second Silpat and another baking sheet to weight it down.

Put in the oven and cook for 45 minutes. Remove the pan from the oven. Carefully remove the top baking sheet and Silpat and pour off the rendered fat. The edges of the skin will be slightly crusty, but the middle will still be supple. Replace the Silpat and pan

and return to the oven for another 15 minutes, or until all the fat has rendered.

Remove from the oven and let the skin cool completely.

TO FRY THE CHICKEN OR DUCK SKIN: Pour 2 inches of oil into a small stockpot fitted with a thermometer and heat to to 375°F.

Cut the skin into eighteen ¾- to 1-inch-wide strips. Add the strips to the hot oil in batches, without crowding the pot, and fry until golden brown and crisp, 3 to 4 minutes for the chicken, 8 to 10 minutes for the duck. Drain on paper towels. The cracklings will keep at room temperature for up to a day.

MAKES EIGHTEEN ¾- TO 1-INCH-WIDE STRIPS

FRESH BUTTER WITH FLEUR DE SEL

If you have access to great organic cream, you can make your own butter to use in cooking, at the table, or for making Aged Butter (page 374). The yield may vary slightly depending on the quality of the cream.

3 cups (705 grams) heavy cream, preferably organic
1 teaspoon (3.6 grams) fleur de sel, or to taste

Put the cream in the bowl of a stand mixer fitted with a whisk. Turn the speed to medium-low and whisk for about 10 minutes. The cream will whip to peaks and then begin to break down. At that point, wrap a large piece of plastic wrap around the machine, covering the whisk and bowl, to keep the liquid from splashing out as it separates from the butter. Increase the speed to medium and continue to whisk for about 5 minutes, or until the butter has collected around the beater.

Fill a large bowl with ice water. Remove the butter from the liquid and submerge it in the ice water to harden enough so you can roll it. (Reserve the liquid—i.e., buttermilk—for Fresh Cheese, page 113, if desired.)

Put a piece of parchment paper on the work surface and place the butter on it. With a rolling pin, roll the butter into a ¼-inch-thick layer. Press a clean kitchen towel over the top. Line a baking sheet with parchment. Flip the butter over onto the baking sheet and remove the top piece of parchment paper. Cover the butter with another towel and a clean piece of parchment paper. Refrigerate overnight, to allow any excess liquid to drain.

Remove the butter from the pan, break it up, and put it in a bowl. Let soften enough so you can mold it.

Using a fork, mash the butter with the salt. Put a piece of parchment paper on the work surface. Put the butter toward the bottom edge of the parchment and shape into a log. Roll the butter up in the parchment, squeezing the ends as you roll to eliminate any air spaces. Twist the ends to seal.

The butter can be refrigerated for up to 1 month.

MAKES ABOUT 12 OUNCES (340 GRAMS) BUTTER

AGED BUTTER

Aged butter *(smen)* is a traditional Moroccan cooking ingredient that adds a mildly cheesy richness to dishes. Here are two versions I like. The first is seasoned with oregano in the way that the herb *za'atar* would traditionally be used. It's best when aged for at least a month. The second, made with blue cheese, is ready to use right away.

MAKES ABOUT 8 OUNCES (227 GRAMS)

OREGANO WATER–AGED BUTTER

1 tablespoon (2.2 grams) dried oregano
½ cup (117 grams) water
½ pound (227 grams) unsalted butter, at room temperature
1 tablespoon (9 grams) kosher salt

Combine the oregano and water in a small saucepan and bring to a boil. Remove from the heat and let sit for 30 minutes to infuse the flavor of the oregano.

Strain the water through a fine-mesh strainer into a spouted liquid measuring cup. (You will not need all the water but it is difficult to make less.) Combine the butter, 2 tablespoons (30 grams) of the oregano water, and the salt in a large bowl and blend well.

Spoon the butter into a clean canning jar and keep in a cool, dark spot for at least 1 day, or for up to 6 months. Once opened, the butter should be stored in the refrigerator.

BLUE CHEESE–AGED BUTTER

½ pound (227 grams) unsalted butter, at room temperature
1½ teaspoons (7 grams) blue cheese, preferably Cashel, at room temperature
½ teaspoon (1.5 grams) kosher salt

Combine the butter, blue cheese, and salt in a large bowl and blend well.

Place a piece of parchment paper on the work surface. Put the butter toward the bottom edge of the paper and shape into a log. Roll the butter up in the parchment, squeezing the ends as you roll to eliminate any air spaces. Twist the ends to seal.

The butter can be refrigerated for up to 3 months.

CLARIFIED BUTTER

At least ½ pound (227 grams) unsalted butter

Melt the butter in the top of a double boiler. Skim off the foam that rises to the top. If time allows, refrigerate the butter to solidify it, which will separate the clarified butter from the liquid; then make 2 holes in the top of the butter, and drain off the liquid. Or, if you need the butter immediately, strain it through a fine-mesh strainer lined with cheesecloth. Discard any white milky liquid remaining in the bottom of the pan.

Store the butter in an airtight container in the refrigerator for up to 2 months.

SHALLOT OIL

¾ cup (159 grams) canola oil
1¼ cups (131 grams) coarsely chopped shallots

Put the oil and shallots in a small saucepan and set over medium-low heat. If you have a diffuser, place it under the saucepan to help maintain a gentle heat. After about 2 minutes, you should see some bubbles. Adjust the heat as needed to maintain a very gentle simmer and simmer for 1½ hours, or until the oil is very fragrant and flavorful.

Strain the oil through a fine-mesh strainer lined with a coffee filter, or with 6 layers of cheesecloth, into an airtight container. Store in the refrigerator for up to 2 weeks.

MAKES ½ CUP (108 GRAMS)

POACHED EGGS

When you poach eggs, it's always best to use a large pot of water, which makes it easy to keep the water temperature constant. These can be made just before serving or held in ice water and reheated in simmering water for about a minute when you're ready to serve them.

2 tablespoons (29 grams) distilled white vinegar
Large eggs, at room temperature

Bring a large pot of water to a simmer over medium-high heat. Add the vinegar. Adjust the heat to keep the water at a very gentle simmer.

If you are planning to hold the eggs, fill a large bowl with ice water.

Poach no more than 3 eggs at a time. Break each egg into a ramekin. With a large spoon, swirl the water, creating a vortex in the center, then add the eggs one right after the other to the center of the vortex. The swirling water will help the egg whites wrap around the yolks. Keep the water at just below a simmer, and cook to set the whites, about 2½ minutes. With a slotted spoon, remove the eggs from the water, blot them with a paper towel, and put them on a plate if using immediately. Or slide into the ice water if holding them. (The poached eggs can be refrigerated in the water for up to 3 hours.)

To reheat the chilled eggs, transfer them to a plate and bring them to room temperature. Just before serving, put them in a bowl, cover with the hottest-possible tap water, and let stand for 1 minute. Blot the eggs dry on a paper towel before serving.

5½-MINUTE EGGS

It's important to use an accurate digital timer to cook these eggs just right. The eggs will be done in 5½ minutes to 5 minutes 45 seconds, depending on their exact size. I recommend first cooking a single egg for 5 minutes and 30 seconds as a test. The white should just be set and the yolk runny. If your test egg is undercooked, cook the rest for a little longer. And make a few extra in case you have trouble peeling them. The vinegar won't flavor the eggs but will make them easier to peel.

2 tablespoons (29 grams) distilled white vinegar
Large eggs, at room temperature

Fill a large bowl with ice water. Bring a large saucepan of salted water to a simmer and add the vinegar. Add the eggs (up to 6 at a time) and reduce the heat to a bare simmer. There should be small bubbles coming up around the eggs. Cook for 5½ minutes. Remove the eggs with a slotted spoon and put in the ice water to cool completely.

Carefully peel the eggs. To reheat the eggs, bring them to room temperature. Just before serving, place them in a bowl and cover with the hottest-possible tap water for 1 minute.

The eggs can be served as is, or with the yolk exposed. To expose the yolk, trim the pointed end slightly so the egg can stand on end, and trim enough of the rounded end to expose the yolk.

THREE SAVORY GRANOLAS

To add crunch and flavor to soups, salads, and texturally challenged dishes, I like to sprinkle on homemade savory granolas. They're best stored in airtight containers with a piece of paper towel on top to absorb any moisture (which would make the granola chewy). Store them for up to 3 days at room temperature, refrigerate for up to 2 weeks, or freeze for up to 2 months.

5-SPICE OAT GRANOLA

1 tablespoon (0.5 ounce/14 grams) unsalted butter
2 tablespoons (25 grams) granulated sugar
½ cup (90 grams) steel-cut oats
¼ cup (33 grams) pine nuts
¾ teaspoon (1.7 grams) 5-spice powder
Kosher salt

Preheat the oven to 250°F. Line a baking sheet with a Silpat.

Melt the butter in a medium saucepan over medium heat. Add the sugar and swirl the pan for about 2 minutes, or until the sugar has melted and the mixture is beginning to foam. Add the oats and pine nuts and stir for about 2 minutes to coat them with the sugar. When they begin to pop, remove them from the heat and stir in the 5-spice powder and a generous pinch of salt.

Spread the oats and nuts in an even layer on the Silpat. Bake for about 30 minutes, tossing the oats and nuts every 10 minutes, until they are evenly browned. Remove from the oven and cool completely.

Crush the oats and nuts lightly with a mortar and pestle, or spread them between two pieces of parchment paper and crush them with a rolling pin. Season to taste with salt. Serve with quail or chicken livers.

MAKES ABOUT 1 CUP (155 GRAMS)

VADOUVAN-SHALLOT-SUNFLOWER GRANOLA

½ cup (70 grams) unsalted sunflower seeds
Grapeseed or canola oil
¼ cup (38 grams) very thinly sliced shallots (preferably on a Japanese mandoline)
Kosher salt
1 tablespoon (0.5 ounce/14 grams) unsalted butter
2 tablespoons (25 grams) granulated sugar
2 tablespoons (13.5 grams) *Vadouvan* (page 34)

Put the sunflower seeds in a small frying pan and heat over medium-low heat, swirling the pan and flipping or stirring the seeds so they toast evenly, until fragrant, about 2 minutes. Remove from the pan and set aside.

Pour 1 inch of oil into a large saucepan fitted with a thermometer and heat to 230°F. Add the shallots and fry for 8 to 10 minutes, until a rich golden brown. Drain on paper towels and sprinkle with salt. Fluff the shallots with your fingers as they cool to prevent them from sticking together.

Preheat the oven to 250°F. Line a baking sheet with a Silpat.

Melt the butter in a medium saucepan over medium heat. Add the sugar and swirl the pan for about 2 minutes, or until the sugar has melted and the mixture is beginning to foam. Add the sunflower seeds and stir for about 2 minutes to coat them with the sugar. When they begin to pop, remove them from the heat.

Spread the seeds in an even layer on the Silpat. Bake for about 30 minutes, tossing the seeds every 10 minutes, until they are evenly browned. Remove from the oven and let cool completely.

Crush the seeds lightly with a mortar and pestle, or spread them between two pieces of parchment paper and crush them with a rolling pin. Put them in a medium bowl. Crush the *vadouvan* in the mortar and pestle, or break it up by hand (it will not crush with the rolling pin), and add to the sunflower seeds. Roughly chop the fried shallots. Add to the sunflower seeds and toss to combine. Add salt to taste. Serve as a garnish with Carrot Soup (page 180).

MAKES ABOUT 1 CUP (120 GRAMS)

Z'HUG–PUMPKIN SEED GRANOLA

1 tablespoon (0.5 ounce/14 grams) unsalted butter
1 tablespoon (12.5 grams) granulated sugar
½ cup plus 2 tablespoons (90 grams) raw pumpkin seeds
1 teaspoon (2.7 grams) *Z'hug* (page 38)
Kosher salt

Preheat the oven to 250°F. Line a baking sheet with a Silpat.

Melt the butter in a medium saucepan over medium heat. Add the sugar and swirl the pan for about 2 minutes, or until the sugar has melted and the mixture is beginning to foam. Stir in the pumpkin seeds and stir for about 2 minutes to coat them with the sugar. When they begin to pop, remove them from the heat and stir in the *z'hug* and a generous pinch of salt.

Spread the seeds in an even layer on the Silpat. Bake for about 30 minutes, tossing the seeds every 10 minutes until they are evenly browned. Remove from the oven and let cool completely.

Crush the seeds lightly with a mortar and pestle, or spread them between two pieces of parchment paper and crush them with a rolling pin. Season to taste with salt. Serve as a garnish for Sunchoke Puree (page 184).

MAKES ABOUT ¾ CUP (115 GRAMS)

BREAD CRUMBS

3 cups (144 grams) ½-inch cubes crustless white bread
or (192 grams) ½-inch cubes crustless brioche

FOR FRESH BREAD CRUMBS: Put the bread in a food
processor and pulse to crumbs. The crumbs can be
stored in an airtight container in the refrigerator for
up to 3 days or frozen for up to 1 month.

FOR DRIED BREAD CRUMBS: Preheat the oven to 350°F.
Put the bread in a food processor and pulse to
crumbs. Spread the crumbs on a baking sheet and
toast in the oven for about 5 minutes. Turn the
crumbs and toast another 7 to 9 minutes, or until
golden brown. The crumbs can be stored in an airtight
container at room temperature for up 3 months.

MAKES 2½ CUPS (144 GRAMS) FRESH OR
1½ CUPS (64 GRAMS) DRY WHITE BREAD CRUMBS
OR 2½ CUPS (192 GRAMS) FRESH OR
1½ CUPS (168 GRAMS) DRY BRIOCHE CRUMBS

COOKING BEANS

8 ounces (226 grams) dried butter beans, navy beans,
or chickpeas
1 large carrot, peeled and quartered lengthwise
1 celery stalk, cut into 2-inch pieces
1 garlic clove
2 tablespoons (24 grams) brown sugar
1 tablespoon (9 grams) kosher salt

Put the beans in a large container and pour enough
cold water over them to cover by 2 inches. Let soak
overnight at room temperature.

Discard any beans that have floated to the top of
the water. (These are beans that are too "tight" to
allow the water to be absorbed and will end up being
tough after cooking.) Drain the beans and put them in
a large heavy pot, such as an enameled cast-iron
Dutch oven. Add the carrot, celery, garlic, and brown
sugar, then add enough cold water to cover the beans
by 1½ inches. Put the pot over medium-high heat and
bring the water to a simmer. Cook the beans at a
simmer until tender, 45 minutes to 1 hour for navy
beans and chickpeas, 1 hour to 1 hour and 15 minutes
for butter beans. They should be tender but not falling
apart. Remove the beans from the heat, add the salt,
and let the beans cool in the liquid for at least 30
minutes to allow the salt to flavor them.

The beans can be refrigerated for up to 3 days in
their liquid.

MAKES ABOUT 3 CUPS (720 GRAMS)
BUTTER BEANS,
(695 GRAMS) NAVY BEANS,
OR (635 GRAMS) CHICKPEAS

SIMPLE SYRUP

½ cup (100 grams) granulated sugar
½ cup (117 grams) water

Combine the sugar and water in a small saucepan and
bring to a simmer over medium heat, stirring to
dissolve the sugar. Remove from the heat and let cool
to room temperature.

Store in the refrigerator for up to 2 weeks.

MAKES ABOUT 1 CUP (265 GRAMS)

PARCHMENT LIDS

A parchment lid floats directly on the surface of soups, stocks, and braises as they cook, helping to seal in flavor and keeping any ingredients that rise to the surface of the liquid from drying out. It's generally not a replacement for the pot's lid but is used in combination with it.

Cut a square of parchment larger than the diameter of the pot to be covered. Fold two opposite corners together to form a triangle, then fold this triangle in half into a smaller triangle; it will have two short sides and one long side. Position the triangle so that one of the short sides faces you. Fold this bottom edge up, making a narrow triangle, and crease it, maintaining the point of the triangle, as if you were making a paper airplane. Repeat another 4 or more times until you have a very slender triangle.

   Turn the pot bottom up and align the tip of the triangle with the center of the pot, mark the edge of the pot with your thumb, and cut the excess off the triangle, trimming to make a gentle curve. Cut about ¼ inch off the tip. Unfold the triangle. You will have a circle the size of your pot, with a steam hole in the center.

SHAPING QUENELLES

Use a soupspoon the size of the quenelle that you want to shape; one with a pointed tip is ideal. The ice cream, or whatever you are shaping, shouldn't be either rock hard or too soft. Have a container of very hot water nearby. Dip the spoon in the water to heat it and dry it with a towel. Holding it at a 30-degree angle, dip the bottom edge of the spoon into the ice cream so that the ice cream reaches from the tip of the spoon to the bottom of the handle. Drag the spoon toward you so the ice cream curls onto itself and fills the bowl of the spoon. Continue to shape the quenelle by rotating the scoop of ice cream inside the spoon against the side of the container. If the quenelle doesn't shape properly, dip the spoon in the water again, dry it, and reshape the scoop of ice cream.